UNDER-CONSUMPTION THEORIES

A History and Critical Analysis

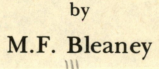

by

M.F. Bleaney

1976
INTERNATIONAL PUBLISHERS
New York

Library of Congress Cataloging in Publication Data

Bleaney, Michael Francis
　　Underconsumption theories.

　　Bibliography.
　　Includes index.
　　1. Business cycles.　2. Consumption (Economics)
3. Economics—History.　I. Title.
HB3721.B55　　　330.1　　　76–26935
ISBN 0–7178–0476–3

© M. F. Bleaney

Produced by computer-controlled phototypesetting,
using OCR input techniques, and printed offset by
UNWIN BROTHERS LIMITED
The Gresham Press, Old Woking, Surrey.

PREFACE AND ACKNOWLEDGEMENTS

This book is intended as a Marxist analysis of underconsumption theories. It is at once a history and a critique—for underconsumption theories are by no means dead. Their influence may still be discerned in the economic programmes put forward by political parties and trade unions, and in articles and books on the general tendencies of capitalism.

No final conclusion as to the correctness of underconsumption theories is reached, for too little theoretical work of the necessary quality has been carried out to justify such a conclusion. But the weight of the theoretical evidence would seem to be against them. Much of their attractiveness in the end stems from the links which they maintain with the dominant ideology of capitalist society and the restricted extent of the theoretical break required to arrive at an underconsumptionist position. This, in conjunction with certain obviously appealing conclusions which emerge from them, has sufficed to ensure their continuing reproduction in the working-class movement.

Not all of the authors discussed here are in fact underconsumptionist — Karl Marx and Rosa Luxemburg, in particular, are not — but all of them have been accused of being so at one time or another. Two main strands of underconsumptionism are identified, whose main propositions are somewhat different. One strand — the Malthusian heritage — emphasises the absolute level of saving, while the other — stemming from Sismondi — emphasises the distribution of income *per se* as the cause of crises. One interesting question is why, in the general glut debate of the early nineteenth century, all those who argued for the possibility of a general glut should have been underconsumptionists. An explanation of this, in terms of the classical conception of investment and the relationship between Adam Smith and the Physiocrats, is given in Chapter Five.

3

4

This book is a revised and extended version of a Ph.D. thesis written for the University of Cambridge over the period 1971 to 1974. I should like to thank the Social Science Research Council, my parents and Clare College for financing my studies during this period.

It would be impossible to do credit to all the discussions I have had which have helped me to develop the ideas presented here. However, I should particularly like to mention the names of Maurice Dobb, Brenda Kirsch and Ronald Meek, who have read and criticised earlier drafts of the work. Above all, I owe a great debt to Bob Rowthorn, the supervisor of the research, whose continuous encouragement and incisive criticism have been invaluable. But any mistakes that remain are entirely my own responsibility.

February 1976   M.F.B.

CONTENTS

One of the most dangerous by-products of a period of depression is the crop of false economic theories which win popular credence and gain political support. . . .

As in all previous depressions the commonest explanation which is offered to the mass of thinking people is some form of the underconsumption theory. In the last two years this theory has grown like a forest of mushrooms about us. It claims far more adherents than any other theory, and the voices of those who believe in it drown all other counsel in the ears of democratic peoples. Trade Unionists and employers alike, and even the authority of the Church itself are enlisted to support the demand that the purchasing power of the people shall be reinforced.

E.F.M.Durbin, 1934.

1

WHAT IS UNDERCONSUMPTIONISM?

THE DEFINITION OF 'UNDERCONSUMPTION THEORIES'

Underconsumption theories have a long history — and a long history of influence in the working-class movement — but in spite of this no general study of them has yet appeared. This book is intended to fill that gap.

Orthodox economists have generally dismissed underconsumption theories with contempt, and in orthodox histories of economic theory underconsumptionist writers, with the exception of Malthus, rarely receive more than a passing reference — if indeed they are mentioned at all. This might perhaps be explained by their proneness to elementary mistakes, but by itself that does not seem a sufficient explanation: if we think for instance of the way writers in the Marxist tradition and indeed Marx himself have been left out of consideration, it seems clear that in this case the block has been applied even before the question of technical errors has arisen. Marxist writers have been ignored because of their basic premises and the implications of their line of approach, and nowadays even many non-Marxists are prepared to admit that ideological factors have underlain the silence about Marxism in academic circles. It seems essential, then, to examine the possible ideological reasons why underconsumption theories might have been ignored by the mainstream of Western economic thought.

In this connection, two things are immediately apparent. Firstly, underconsumption theories, even in their tamest versions, have always retained a slant of criticism of capitalist production. This slant exists independently of the ideology of the individual writer, since it arises out of one of the general features of underconsumption theories: their tendency to imply that ultimately capitalism cannot guarantee continuous full employment and rising living standards and is liable sooner or later to slip down into prolonged stagnation. Potentially, therefore, underconsumption theories have always been grist to the mill of popular anti-capitalist movements, and it should be added that in many variants they imply support for a strong and militant trade-union movement, a characteristic which threatens to undermine all the carefully constructed arguments, so common today, about the need for sacrifice and desertion of "the militants" at times of crisis. Therefore, without raising at this stage the question of the scientificity of underconsumption theories, it is clear that their ideological power, inserted into contemporary political struggles, is essentially at the service of the working class.

Secondly, underconsumption theories, being explicit criticisms of the dominant schools of thought of their time, were bound to be treated as a negative development by those who saw in the increased sophistication and elaboration of these tendencies the growth of a truly scientific economics. It is still true, in spite of the crisis at present being experienced by bourgeois economics, that marginalism remains the only general theory which it has to put forward in opposition to Marxism, and that the dominant tendency is to treat the history of economic thought since Adam Smith as a struggle first of all to produce a consistent marginalist theory and then to develop it. Since underconsumptionism, like Marxism, contributed nothing to this process, it is regarded as legitimate for histories of economic thought to ignore it.

These would seem to be the two main factors behind the lack of interest shown by orthodox economists in underconsumption theories and their history. It is not so clear, however, why no general Marxist study of underconsumptionism has yet appeared. In part, probably, this reflects the penetration of underconsumptionism into Marxist economic writing itself. Because, as will be shown below, many Marxist writers have absorbed elements of underconsumptionism into their own work, it has been difficult for Marxists to arrive at an adequate definition of underconsumptionism and to carry through a thorough analysis of it. For instance, passages in Marx definitely tend in an underconsumptionist direction, and the whole theory of the immiserisation of the proletariat has obvious underconsumptionist implications. Thus, although in general (although not entirely) the Marxist tradition has been hostile to underconsumptionism, it has had difficulty in settling accounts with it.

DEFINITIONS

The phrase 'underconsumptionism' is quite current in the literature on the history of economic thought, of all shades, but actual definitions of it are virtually absent. I propose to use the following definition, which accords as closely as can be expected with the general use of the term:

An underconsumption theory is a theory of the capitalist economy which contains both of the following two elements:

1) the idea that a state of depression is not just a phase of the industrial cycle or the result of a temporary conjunction of circumstances but is the state towards which the economy naturally tends in the absence of offsetting factors;

2) the idea that this is the result of a persistent tendency towards insufficiency of demand for *consumption* goods.

Both elements are necessary. It is quite possible to have a stagnationist theory of the capitalist economy which does not single out lack of demand for consumption goods as the cause — Steindl's *Maturity and Stagnation in American Capitalism*, for example, deduces a tendency to stagnation by developing a theory of the investment behaviour of firms in response to such factors as the rate of profit, degree of capacity utilisation, and the degree to which investment can be financed from internal funds. Equally, to isolate demand for consumer goods as the primary factor in the movement of the economy would merely be a theory of the trade cycle that identified consumption as the leading force. It would not be an *underconsumption theory* unless combined with the idea that slumps and crises are the manifestations of inherent difficulties in capitalist production, whereas booms are periods in which the difficulties are temporarily overcome. This is obviously a different theory from one which sees economic fluctuations *in general* as inherent in a capitalist economy, since it is an 'asymmetrical' theory in which slumps represent the 'normal' state (unless offsetting factors intervene).

A brief review of the existing literature is perhaps in order here. I have already mentioned that no general study of underconsumption theories has existed up till now, but there do exist certain 'partial' studies of relevance. Of these, the earliest and also the most interesting is the second part of Rosa Luxemburg's *Accumulation of Capital* (1913), which discusses in

succession the ideas of Sismondi, Malthus, Rodbertus, Vorontsov, Nikolai-on and one or two others, each receiving a chapter
to himself. Luxemburg's purpose, however, is not to give a
review of the development of underconsumption theories in the
nineteenth century — indeed she doesn't even use the phrase
'underconsumption theory' — but to assess how far each of
these writers, in tackling the problem of effective demand, has
progressed towards the correct diagnosis of the problem which
she identifies in capitalist production: the problem of accumulation. As I shall argue in Chapter Nine, this is a different question
from that of underconsumptionism. Because Luxemburg's
discussion is so much dominated by her own problem, her
treatment of these earlier authors is often very limited in scope,
focussing on only one or two aspects of their work, and although
it contains much useful material, ultimately it does not serve as a
history of underconsumption theories.

The nearest attempt at, at least, a partial history of underconsumption theories is E.E.Nemmers's *Hobson and Underconsumption,* of which the first chapter discusses 'earlier underconsumptionists', although the book is basically a study of Hobson. But
Nemmers makes a number of mistakes. Firstly, he includes
Marx as an underconsumptionist; secondly, he makes a distinction between "two broad paths of development" of the theory:
the 'real' and the 'monetary' theory.[1] In my opinion this is not a
useful distinction. Thirdly, he gives no coherent definition of
underconsumptionism but only lists a number of 'elements'
present in Sismondi and "recurring in the writings of most 'real'
underconsumptionists".[2] These elements (seven of them) are a
disparate collection of observations which together add up to
nothing in particular since they have little connection with one
another. The consequences of this quickly reveal themselves:

> (Lord Lauderdale) is not a true underconsumptionist in the
> same sense as Sismondi, Rodbertus or Hobson. Three
> elements are missing from his thinking: there is no objection
> to capital directing production on a basis of short-run profits
> rather than needs of consumers, no criticism of competition
> as leading to overproduction, and no emphasis on welfare
> considerations as such.[3]

Since Nemmers has not troubled to establish a definition of
underconsumptionism, we are left in the dark as to why the

absence of these three elements makes Lauderdale a marginal figure. Moreover, none of the points listed includes the vital thing: the focus on the demand for consumption goods. This list is the nearest that Nemmers comes to a definition of underconsumption theories, but it is so inadequate that although his book is as close as any to the task in hand very little can be gleaned from it.

Durbin's book, *Purchasing Power and Trade Depression* (1934), is not a historical study but a polemic against the versions of underconsumption theory current at the time (Hobson, Foster and Catchings, Major Douglas). He identifies their central thesis as the statement that in advanced capitalist societies there is a deficiency of purchasing power, of consumers' income, so that all products cannot be bought at profitable prices.[4] This seems to me too narrow a definition, even for the restricted range of authors that Durbin is considering. It would be incorrect, for instance, to describe the deficiency of purchasing power as the centre of Hobson's argument; what Hobson points out is the *unequal distribution* of that purchasing power, in such a way that not enough of it is *actually* spent. Its polemical intent and narrow historical focus restrict the scope of this book considerably from our point of view.

Haberler devotes a chapter to underconsumption theories as part of a general study of the trade cycle.[5] But his aim is to see what interesting ideas can be picked up from them, and used in conjunction with other theories of the cycle, as he himself states,[6] and he devotes most of the chapter to analysing and discussing underconsumptionist ideas on the mechanism of various stages of the cycle (e.g. Section Three: Insufficiency of Consumers' Demand versus Shortage of Capital as the Cause of the Collapse of the Boom). While it is quite legitimate for Haberler to do this, it must be recognised that, as has already been said, underconsumption theory is not a theory of the trade cycle in this sense but a theory of depression as revealing certain deep contradictions in the capitalist economy, and to approach a study of underconsumption theories in this way is bound to obscure some of their distinctive features.

Haberler says:

It is true that all underconsumption theories are concerned with the alleged insufficiency either of money incomes or of expenditure on consumers' goods out of those incomes; but the variations between the different theories are very great.[7]

This definition is essentially correct, since the major point, the stress on the demand for consumption goods, is covered. Haberler is quite right also in not including Keynes's *General Theory* as an underconsumptionist work, since Keynes is concerned with aggregate demand from all sources, and not just consumption demand (Nemmers describes Keynes as "in a broad sense and in essence" marking the culmination of 'monetary' underconsumptionism, which seems to me to be a quite wrong assessment of the situation).

In his massive history of economic thought, Schumpeter suggests that underconsumption theories can be classified into three types:

1) the over-saving type: "stagnation ensues when people save and invest to such an extent as 'to leave no motive to a further increase of production' owing to the incident fall in prices and profits";

2) the non-spending type "that emphasises disturbances which arise from savings decisions *not* offset by decisions to invest";

3) the mass poverty type that "attributes gluts to the inability of labour, owing to low wages, to 'buy its own product' ".[8]

In my opinion the distinction between the first and the third (broadly the Malthusian and the Sismondian traditions) is definitely helpful and I shall refer to it again. The second category, though, falls outside the range of underconsumption theories since it relates to the deviation of planned saving from planned investment, and therefore brings in not only the level of consumption but also the question of the expansion of production envisaged. Thus the problem here is not primarily *within* the consumption goods industry itself. Schumpeter says on the question of definitions:

In a sense, of course, underconsumption can always be described as overproduction. Accordingly, von Bergmann labelled Malthus's theory a 'motivated overproduction theory'. It seems more conducive to clear distinctions to avoid the latter phrase whenever an author locates the seat of the trouble with the behaviour of consumers, even if the result is also some sort of overproduction — just as, for the same reason, we have adopted a strict definition of the phrase Disproportionality.[9]

This seems to be in agreement with the definition suggested above.

SOME THEORETICAL ISSUES

Some remarks should be made here about the theoretical problems of the study of the history of economic theory, or of theory of any kind. Not all writers on the subject are sufficiently aware of the significance of these issues, and although those who set out to write general treatises on the history of economic thought usually give some space in the introductory chapter to these questions, authors writing about more specialist topics are inclined to plunge ahead without giving them sufficient attention. A good example of this is the book by M.Paglin on *Malthus and Lauderdale*, discussed below, which is based entirely on an implicit thesis — which is not directly discussed or set out explicitly — that these two authors can be seen as the basis of an anti-Ricardian school of theory. The author has arrived at this position as a result of a specific theory as to how to interpret the theoretical disputes of the early nineteenth century, but he does not feel the necessity to examine thoroughly his own theoretical assumptions or to face the issues in the book itself. This creates problems for readers, who find it more difficult to evaluate the work, and serves only to obscure the real sources of differences of interpretation. This manner of proceeding, which is extremely common in the West, is a reflection of the view that theory is superfluous in the study of ideas and that all that is required is to get down to reading the books.

I do not intend here to examine the ways in which the history of economic thought has been interpreted by different writers at different times, or to trace the anti-theoretical prejudice to is epistemological roots. Both of these could be the subjects of major studies in themselves. Instead it seems best to set out for the benefit of the reader the most important positions which underlie the interpretation which is presented here. Hopefully these brief comments, in conjunction with the practical use of these principles in the interpretation of the history of underconsumption theories, will help to show the relevance of theory in this field as well as to demonstrate the usefulness of the particular approach chosen in this book. The problems encountered by Nemmers, simply because he has not bothered to clarify what he means by the term 'underconsumption theory', should be a warning to everyone.

In this study I have concentrated on conceptual developments, on the principle that the concepts employed are the basic elements of any theoretical system. Thus I have laid emphasis particularly on the development from the simple idea of expenditure, which prevails throughout most of the eighteenth century up to and including the Physiocrats, to the separate ideas of consumption and investment as two different branches of expenditure. This development is central to the history of underconsumption theories as I have defined them, because without it there is no possibility of separating consumption demand from general aggregate demand. Similarly, in looking at over-saving types of underconsumption theory, I have paid close attention to whether they accept the usual nineteenth-century idea that savings are at all times automatically invested, or whether they ever consider the possibility of a deviation of planned saving from planned investment (other than by hoarding). This enables us to work out whether they have made any progress towards Keynes, and, indeed, whether they strictly qualify as underconsumptionist at all. The basic assumption here is that Keynesian theory is possible only on the basis of Keynesian conceptual advances. Thus I have not paid much attention here to practical recommendations of the writers concerned, in order to concentrate on the basic theoretical ideas in their work.

But it should be emphasised that concepts cannot be used at will in any combination, as if they were completely independent one from another. The 'box of tools' analogy which is sometimes used is wrong in so far as it implies that the student can build up a conceptual system as if there were no links or taboos between concepts or groups of concepts. Concepts always form part of a theoretical system, and the complex of concepts around which such a system is built has a coherence and unity of its own, by virtue of the way in which the concepts interact with and complement one another. The history of theory cannot therefore be based simply on the history of individual concepts in isolation, since their meaning and application is likely to be crucially modified by the theoretical system in which they are used.

The argument which is developed in Chapter Five is based on the idea that Adam Smith's conceptions represented a far-reaching transformation of economic theory as compared with the Physiocrats which can only be understood as a fundamental shift in theoretical outlook. As a result of this shift, new concepts were developed, while some Physiocratic concepts were rendered redundant. For instance the Physiocratic conception of productivity and sterility of various sectors of the economy, rooted as it was in a particular view of the economic role of agriculture, could not be meaningfully imported into *The Wealth of Nations,* in which *all* economic activity, in whatever sector, is basically treated as equivalent — so it fell out of use. However Adam Smith was not completely consistent in his break with Physiocracy, and it is argued in Chapter Five that this was a significant factor in the development of underconsumption theories in the early nineteenth century. The underlying theory here is that Physiocracy represented one consistent theoretical system, while in essence *The Wealth of Nations* is founded on an entirely different one.

This implies a definite interpretation of the role of ideology in economic theory. Ideology is often seen as merely a distortion of science, like a cloud passing before the eyes of the observer which obscures his vision. But in reality ideology enters into the concepts which form the very basis of a theoretical system, and a clash of rival theoretical systems represents the sharpest form of ideological cleavage. A classic example of this is that of marginalism and Marxism, which are each based on an entirely different set of concepts, behind which one can see a world-view reflecting the interests of the major classes in capitalist society.

Underconsumptionism does not constitute a theoretical system. As I have defined it, it might rather be described as a thesis about the nature of a capitalist economy, its long-term tendencies and the role of consumption within it. Its validity as a subject of investigation lies in its being a particular theory of this aspect of capitalism. How it combines with other aspects of theory can only be established by examination of specific examples, although its likely connection with radical social movements has already been noted. It is perhaps worth saying, however, that one of the conclusions of this study is that underconsumption theories are associated with a view of production as an activity which is, or ought to be, related to the satisfaction of human needs, and that this is what frequently underlies the special emphasis placed on consumer demand.

Of course, not all those who wished to make a critical analysis of capitalist production had to have resort to underconsumptionist ideas, and it is one of the objects of this study to show that two of these people who have sometimes been labelled underconsumptionist, Marx and Rosa Luxemburg, do not in fact fall within this category. Indeed, Marx's reproduction schemes provide a much more powerful basis for a critique of Malthus and Sismondi that any of the arguments of their contemporary opponents.

A notable characteristic of underconsumption theories is that although they are never accepted in respectable circles, all the same they never go away, and the periodic theoretically coherent expressions of them appear like eruptions of a volcano: they bring to the surface something which has existed all the time underneath. This is all the more remarkable because so many of the expressions of them are guilty of what are really quite fundamental and easily detectable errors; and yet they persist. In the Conclusion I shall come back to this point and try to provide an explanation for it; but it is something to be kept in mind throughout the study since it is important to try to understand how people come to have an underconsumption theory and how they justify it.

It is contended here that underconsumption theories could not be said to exist before 1800, their starting date being defined by the timing of the development, already mentioned, from the idea of expenditure in general to that of consumption and investment as two distinguishable types of expenditure. It is Smith's *Wealth of Nations* which first makes the distinction clearly,* but as is well known economic theory experienced something of a lull for a quarter of a century after this, and it is really only with Lauderdale's book (1804) that underconsumption theories can be said to make their appearance.

From the very start, underconsumption theories are mixed up in the debate about the possibility of a general glut, entirely monopolising one side of it, so that their character as explana-

*For a further discussion of this see Chapter 2.

tions of capitalist crises appears from the very first. One might get the idea from this that in fact underconsumption theories are only conceivable as theories of capitalist crisis, and because these could not be said to exist in the eighteenth century in anything like their later nineteenth century form, this is a sufficient reason for judging them to have grown up around 1800. This idea would however be mistaken; these theories focussed on crises because these seemed to be the obvious manifestations of the problems which they identified. Even in the eighteenth century, without these crises, it would have been quite possible to produce a theory which made the rate of development of the economy dependent on high and rising consumption, and which also identified a tendency for consumption to be insufficient, so that growth was held back. Such a theory would have fulfilled the basic criterion for an underconsumption theory, and even a theory which said nothing about the tendencies of consumption, but still stressed its overriding importance, could be seen as an important point of departure for later theories, and should be mentioned as a forerunner. However, no forerunner of this type existed, because of the failure to distinguish between consumption and investment expenditure.

There undoubtedly did exist many writers in the seventeenth and eighteenth centuries who do not take the same view of parsimony as Smith. Pierre de Boisguilbert is a prominent one who was very emphatic that it was the level of consumption (*la consommation*) which determined production, and that the most important thing in a State was to maintain and increase the level of consumption.[10] But, as Nagels and other writers have noted, Boisguilbert's concept of 'consommation' is equivalent to what we would now call aggregate demand.[11] We could also cite the example of Mandeville, a case made famous by Keynes. *The Fable of the Bees* is shot through with the idea that if rich people save all their money instead of having a good time with it, many others will starve. And there are others:

Though complaints of under-consumption were a very subsidiary aspect of mercantilist thought, Professor Heckscher quotes a number of examples of what he calls "the deep-rooted belief in the utility of luxury and the evil of thrift. Thrift, in fact, was regarded as the cause of unemployment, and for two reasons; in the first place, because real income was believed to diminish by the amount of money which did not enter into exchange, and secondly, because saving was believed to withdraw money from circulation.[12]

Furniss, also, quotes a number of writers, such as Bishop Berkeley and Nicholas Barbon, who invoke the 'liberality of the rich' in order to stimulate the manufactures of a nation,[13] but these people definitely seem to be thinking of the stimulation of demand in general in opposition to simple hoarding. There are also examples of writers who, contrary to the general eighteenth century view, preached the importance of the labouring class on the basis of the demand that they constituted,[14] but this was never raised from a casual idea into a significant theoretical statement. Indeed much of it simply reflected the hope of seeing higher food prices on the part of the landed interest.

So really, before Adam Smith, no idea of separating consumption from investment as different categories of aggregate demand existed. To my mind, this is definitely connected with the recognition in Smith of the capitalist as controller of the economy, and not the landlord, and the decisive rejection of feudal conceptions. For in examining the circulation of capital and the revenue of the capitalist, it is impossible not to recognise that he has a continuous choice as to whether to consume his profit or to advance it as additional capital, and in a capitalist economy it is the accumulation of capital that is the motor of development. The landlord, however, is not in the same position, and it is important only that he should stimulate the economy as best he can, indirectly. If demand is important then the most important thing for him to do is to spend his money. So here the distinction between the two ways of spending money is not of the same significance. This split is very clearly reflected in Physiocracy, as we shall see in the next Chapter. Quesnay sees the landowning class as the guardian of the fortunes of the economy, and demands that it should spend half its money on agriculture. But he makes no real distinction between investment and consumption. When, however, he looks at the tenant farmer, the capitalist who actually controls agricultural production, he inevitably makes the distinction, because it is inherent in capitalist production.

NOTES

1 E.E.Nemmers, *Hobson and Underconsumption*, p.1.
2 ibid, p.7.
3 ibid, pp.7–8.
4 E.F.M.Durbin, *Purchasing Power and Trade Depression*, p.20.
5 G.Haberler, *Prosperity and Depression*, Ch 5.
6 ibid, p.119.
7 ibid, p.119.
8 J.Schumpeter, *A History of Economic Analysis*, p.740.
9 ibid, p.740.
10 See the essays in Institut National d'Etudes Démographiques, *Pierre de Boisguilbert*, Vol 1.
11 J.Nagels, *Genèse, contenu et prolongements de la notion de reproduction du capital selon Karl Marx, Boisguillebert, Quesnay, Leontiev*, p.45.
12 J.M.Keynes, *The General Theory of Employment, Interest and Money*, p.358.
13 E.S.Furniss, *The Position of the Labourer in a System of Economic Nationalism*, pp.57–8.
14 ibid, pp.140–2.

2

THE EARLY BRITISH UNDERCONSUMPTIONISTS

INTRODUCTORY

In the late eighteenth century economic thought was dominated by two sets of ideas: those of the Physiocrats and those of Adam Smith. It is argued here that neither of them could be said to be underconsumptionist, but it is important to say something about their views on consumption and saving in order to establish the background against which the first underconsumption theories developed.

Adam Smith's views are best summarised by the following passage:

Capitals are increased by parsimony, and diminished by prodigality and misconduct.
Whatever a person saves from his revenue he adds to his capital, and either employs it himself in maintaining an additional number of productive hands, or enables some other person to do so, by lending it to him for an interest, that is for a share of the profits. As the capital of an individual can be increased only by what he saves from his annual revenue or his annual gains, so the capital of a society, which is the same as that of all the individuals who compose it, can be increased only in the same manner. . . .
What is annually saved is as regularly consumed as what is annually spent; and nearly in the same time too; but it is consumed by a different set of people. That portion of his revenue which a rich man annually spends is in most cases consumed by idle guests and menial servants, who leave nothing behind them in return for their consumption. That portion which he annually saves, as for the sake of profit it is immediately employed as capital, is consumed in the same manner, and nearly in the same time too, but by a different

set of people, by labourers, manufacturers, and artificers, who reproduce with a profit the value of their annual consumption.[1]

There are two important points to be noted.

Firstly, Adam Smith does not mean by parsimony saving in the modern sense (i.e. simply abstention from consumption) but saving and investment of those savings. It is assumed that the savings are invested somewhere, either by the saver himself or by someone else to whom the money is lent. This is the implication of the statement that "whatever a person saves from his revenue he adds to his capital, and either employs it himself in maintaining an additional number of productive hands, or enables some other person to do so, by lending it to him for an interest". Smith was of course aware that the money could be hoarded in a chest, but to his mind it was so illogical to forego the interest on it in this way that hoarding could be discounted as a serious real phenomenon. Therefore, when Smith talks of saving, he is also talking of investment. This point is of great significance because if it is not clearly grasped, some of the early British underconsumptionist writers can be seriously misunderstood; Smith's way of thinking about these questions remained current throughout the general glut debates. 'Parsimony' or 'accumulation' to writers at this time meant saving that was met by an exactly equivalent level of investment.

Secondly, Adam Smith is not worried that savings could ever be excessive, or could result in a deficiency of aggregate demand. He says: "what is annually saved is as regularly consumed as what is annually spent". In the later disputes, this is one of the crucial points at issue, and one of the main points of attack of the British underconsumptionists. It would appear to align Smith with Mill and Ricardo, who denied that any general overproduction was possible or that saving could ever be excessive, and claimed that phenomena which appeared to support such a theory merely represented a temporary disproportionality of supply to demand of the various commodities. The debate did not open up until thirty years after *The Wealth of Nations* was written, and so Adam Smith was far from being a participant; but his remarks lay the foundations of the arguments of one side, and it is he who is the target of the first broadside from Lauderdale and Spence.

The Physiocrats were a more important intellectual influence on British economic thought at this time than has generally been acknowledged. Although only one or two minor writers (including William Spence — of whom more below) adopted their system in its entirety, the essentially Physiocratic idea of the unique character of agriculture, to which even Adam Smith was susceptible, was very much more widespread. R.L.Meek has shown very clearly how the early British underconsumptionists were influenced by, and made use of, Physiocratic arguments in their defence of the consumption of landowners, the Church and other 'unproductive consumers'.[2] It would be a mistake, however, to deduce from this that Physiocracy contains elements of underconsumptionist thinking; it is only after the arrival of the conceptual developments introduced by Adam Smith that it can provide the material for underconsumptionist ideas.

This can be shown by an analysis of the *Tableau Economique,* which encapsulates the main features of Physiocratic theory. In the Physiocratic view agriculture alone produces wealth, because it alone produces a 'net product' over and above the annual advances for the purchase of raw materials and the subsistence of the labourers. Manufacturing is regarded as a sterile activity, unproductive of wealth, because it generates no surplus in the form of rent. The fortunes of the nation depend upon where the receivers of the net product (the landowners) spend their money. If they spend it on manufacturing (sterile expenditure), no extra wealth is generated. The Physiocrats did not take the view that all sterile expenditure was harmful, but they insisted that it should be limited so that the needs of agriculture could be provided for. In his commentary on the *Tableau,* Quesnay, the leading figure of the Physiocratic school, states:

> In the state of prosperity of a Kingdom whose territory was fully cultivated by the best possible methods, where trade was as free and unobstructed as possible, and where consequently the revenue of the proprietors could not be further increased, the proprietors would be able to spend one half of their revenue in making purchases from the sterile classes. But if the territory were not completely cultivated and improved, if roads were lacking, if there were rivers to be made navigable and canals to be constructed for the transport of products, the proprietors ought to economise on their

expenditure with the sterile class, in order to undertake the expenditure necessary to increase their revenue and their enjoyments to the maximum possible. Until they had reached this point, their superfluous expenditure with the sterile class would be luxury expenditure (*luxe*), detrimental to their opulence and to the nation's prosperity.[3]

There are obvious complications here. For example, although investment in roads, canals and river improvements may be very beneficial to agricultural producers, the demand for commodities created by this expenditure is likely to be in the manufacturing sector. The point to be noticed, however, is that Quesnay uses the term 'expenditure' to cover consumption and investment expenditure indiscriminately: he makes no distinction between them. The issue is simply whether or not the expenditure is beneficial to agriculture.

But underconsumptionist arguments always presuppose this distinction between consumption and investment expenditure. The theme of the early British underconsumptionists, for example, is the need for a correct balance between them, and the prevention of accumulation from getting out of hand. Without this distinction, there is nothing specifically underconsumptionist about a general emphasis on aggregate demand. Quesnay, like Adam Smith, is quite aware of the possibility of hoarding, and the fact that it would interrupt the smooth circulation depicted in the *Tableau*. He states as one of the assumptions underlying it the matching of the formation of hoards by those "which come back into circulation".[4] But the concepts of 'expenditure' and 'hoarding' are already familiar from earlier writing, and it is only with Adam Smith that the further distinction is made within the 'expenditure' category.

It is of course quite true that the British underconsumptionists could use the Physiocratic emphasis on expenditure as a support for their case, because their opponents were so adamant that it was irrelevant. But this should not delude us into thinking that the Physiocrats were in any sense forerunners of underconsumptionism.

LORD LAUDERDALE

We have seen that neither of the two major schools of

economic thought of the late eighteenth century — Physiocracy and *The Wealth of Nations* — could be described as underconsumptionist, or as planting the seeds of a later underconsumptionism. In fact the first writer who could legitimately be called underconsumptionist is the Earl of Lauderdale, whose *An Inquiry into the Nature and Origin of Public Wealth* was published in 1804.

Lauderdale takes *The Wealth of Nations* as his point of departure, but he has grave doubts about it. He attacks Smith's theory of value, arguing instead for what might be called a 'demand and supply' theory; and he utterly rejects the idea that individual thrift is the road to national prosperity. He concentrates on the theory of value because he thinks that Smith's mistaken ideas about thrift ultimately stem from there. In particular, he feels that the analogy between the increase of private and of national wealth derives from incorrect ideas about value.

Lauderdale attacks the conception of exchangeable value as the basis of wealth,[5] arguing that wealth should be understood to consist of "all that man desires, as useful or delightful to him", and that since the value of a thing is affected not only by its desirability but also by its scarcity (i.e. its cost of production), value can never be synonymous with wealth.[6] In other words, wealth is a sum of use values and, since exchange values are not exclusively determined by use values, wealth cannot be equated either with exchange value or with the riches of the individuals of a nation. Smith is led into an erroneous conception of wealth by his theory of value, which emphasises cost of production above everything else. Lauderdale vigorously attacks any idea of a standard measure of value, on the basis that all things are constantly varying in value in response to the forces of demand and supply.[7]

Lauderdale is making the mistake here of confusing his own with Smith's use of the word 'value'. What Lauderdale means by 'value', Smith refers to as 'market price', and when Lauderdale talks about an individual's wealth being measured by the exchangeable value of his possessions, meaning their marketable value, he is using 'value' in a sense quite different from that of Adam Smith. Smith's conception of accumulation of capital as the road to national prosperity, which is Lauderdale's ultimate target, is in any case independent of his particular theory of value. There does not therefore exist the close connection between Smith's ideas on value and his ideas on thrift that Lauderdale imagines.

The significance of Lauderdale's attack on the analogy between private and national riches becomes clearer as we progress through his book. Some key points come out in his discussion of the sources of wealth. He says:

> Land, labour and capital are indeed the only sources to which the origin of any part of our wealth has ever been ascribed. But while some have eagerly contended, that land is the sole source of opulence, and that whatever is acquired by labour or capital is derived from the landholder, others have discovered equal anxiety to attribute the origin and increase of our wealth to commerce and manufacture; that is, to the operations of labour and capital.[8]

Compare this with what he has to say about parsimony:

> Popular prejudice, which has ever regarded the sum-total of individual riches to be synonymous with public wealth, and which has conceived every means of increasing the riches of individuals to be a means of increasing public wealth, has pointed out parsimony or accumulation by a man's depriving himself of the objects of desire, to which his fortune entitles him, (the usual means of increasing private fortune), as the most active means of increasing public wealth. When we reflect that this abstinence from expenditure, and consequent accumulation, neither tends to increase the produce of land, to augment the exertions of labour, nor to perform a portion of labour that must otherwise be executed by the hand of man; it seems that we might be entitled at once to pronounce, that accumulation may be a method of transferring wealth from A, B and C, to D; but that it cannot be a method of increasing public wealth, because wealth can alone be increased by the same means by which it is produced.[9]

One very interesting point about these passages is the fact that they already contain the germs of the marginalist conception of production: there exist certain 'factors of production' — land, labour, capital — each of which can be conceived of as making a separate contribution to output, and is rewarded accordingly. This parallels certain other moves in the same direction in

Lauderdale's book: particularly his equation of value with market price. These aspects of Lauderdale's work are symptomatic of developing tendencies in economic theory at this time.

The question posed by this last passage is: why does it appear to Lauderdale that there is no connection between accumulation and the increase of capital? This is undoubtedly what is implied here, for otherwise it could not be argued that accumulation does not perform "any portion of labour that must otherwise be executed by the hand of man". Hence accumulation is only a device for Mr.D to get rich at the expense of his neighbours.

But what does the term accumulation mean, if it does not mean accumulation of capital? This is obviously what Adam Smith means by it. Lauderdale appears to think that it means only the accumulation of money by an individual, and in the phrase "abstinence from expenditure, and consequent accumulation" it seems as though accumulation in his mind is synonymous with the act of saving, and nothing else. We have already seen that this is not Adam Smith's conception. Is Lauderdale denying the connection between the saving of money and the accumulation of capital? Let us follow the argument further.

Lauderdale now passes to a more detailed investigation; but he decides that the problem should be attacked by considering the effects of accumulation in "a simple state of society" in which agriculture is the chief form of activity, and in which the question is transformed into one of at what point the devotion of resources to investment ceases to be beneficial to the community as a whole. This results, as we shall see, in the reduction of the problem to a purely technological one relating to the marginal productivity of capital, which is very different from the question of accumulation with which we started.

In this "simple state of society" property divides itself into three branches: the land, stock reserved for consumption, and capital in the shape of animals and machinery used in production. This capital is beneficial in so far as it allows the same level of production to be attained with a smaller quantity of immediate human labour, so that if a man does not have enough machinery and animals, society can only benefit if he makes the effort to procure them. But this is not true to an unlimited extent:

If, on the other hand, however, he is already in possession of as much capital, as, in the existing state of his knowledge, he can use for the purpose of supplanting labour in cultivating the quantity of land he possesses, it can neither be advantageous to himself nor to the public that he should abridge his consumption of food, clothing, and the other objects of his desire, for the purpose of accumulating a much greater quantity of capital . . . than can by possibility be employed in supplanting labour. The extension of his lands, or the invention of new means of supplanting labour, would justify a desire for increasing his capital; but, otherwise, accumulation, by deprivation of expenditure, must be detrimental to himself as well as to the public.[10]

It is disadvantageous to the farmer, because he finds himself with more tools and animals than he can usefully employ on his land. It is disadvantageous to the public, because it diverts resources into the production of superfluous objects. But in the example chosen, it is the scarcity of land on any one farm that sets a natural limit to the accumulation of capital (in a given state of technical knowledge); in other words, it is a purely agricultural example which cannot readily be extended to industry, where factories could be multiplied almost indefinitely before this problem becomes serious. The attempt to argue for an absolute limit to the level of investment which is socially useful at any one time is therefore inadequate. Furthermore, it has no connection with Lauderdale's previous statements about parsimony, which presumed nothing about the possibility of increasing the productive powers of the community but claimed only that individual thrift had nothing to do with these increases.

But now, suddenly, monetary questions are reintroduced when Lauderdale returns to his previous discussions on value in an attempt to marshal some more arguments. Since the value of a commodity depends only on the proportion between the demand for it and the supply of it,[11] changes in value must be the result of changes in either demand or supply. The precise estimation of the relation between these variables requires the concepts of elasticity of demand and elasticity of supply, which presuppose also the notion of schedules of demand and supply. Lauderdale did not possess these concepts, and nor did his predecessors, so his discussion takes the form of a tracing of the effects on the value of one commodity and then on other commodities of, respectively, a rise and a fall in supply, and a rise and a fall in demand for one commodity (sugar). But he follows the adjustments through only on the demand side (the allocation of consumers' expenditure), and ignores the supply side (the distribution of productive resources).

He produces the following spurious argument: suppose the demand for sugar is doubled, with unchanged supply. Then the price will rise (Lauderdale assumes that the supply of all commodities remains the same, so that the same quantity of sugar is bought at a higher price). Consumers can only pay this price by paying less for other commodities. Lauderdale claims, without any proof, that the resulting fall in value of other commodities is greater than the rise in value of sugar. So the total value of all produce has fallen as a result of the shift in demand.[12]

Lauderdale now takes this a step further and says: suppose demand for wine, mustard and meat is reduced not in order to buy more sugar, but in order to finance some investment. Now we have a fall in the total expenditure on consumption goods, together with an accumulation of capital which will soon be found to be excessive, so that the demand for ploughs and other 'instruments of agriculture' which has temporarily increased will dwindle away as farmers find these things piling up in their sheds, and the value of these commodities too will fall. So the result of this accumulation will be a general fall in value.

> Thus a diminution of value must be produced, not only in the articles for which parsimony occasions an abstraction of demand, but even in the article for which it creates a demand; and public wealth must severely feel the effects of the discouragement by this means given to the production of both. The public must, therefore, suffer by this love of accumulation, if pushed beyond its due bounds;-1. By the creation of a quantity of capital more than is requisite;-and, 2. By abstracting a portion of encouragement to future reproduction.[13]

The cornerstone of the argument once again is the idea of a technical limit to the quantity of capital that can be usefully employed. This is the reason for the eventual fall in the value of capital goods. But there is another factor mentioned which indicates a line of thinking we shall meet again, more prominently, in Malthus: the abstraction of "a portion of encouragement to future reproduction"; in other words, the reduction in demand. Why is there a reduction in demand? Lauderdale himself recognises that the reduced demand for consumption goods is replaced by increased demand for capital goods. The reason must be that it is not all demand which is relevant to "the encouragement of future reproduction", but only *demand for consumption goods*. This reveals itself on the very next page:

> By abstracting a portion of encouragement to future reproduction, a diminution must be occasioned in the wealth to be produced; for, as long as the nature of men remains unchanged, the knowledge of what has been consumed, and of the degree of avidity displayed in the market for the different articles of consumption, must imperiously regulate the nature of what is subsequently produced. This, indeed, may be assumed as a proposition universally admitted; inasmuch as even those who hold deprivation of expenditure, and consequent accumulation, to be a mode of increasing wealth, acknowledge (with unaccountable inconsistency) that the whole quantity of industry annually employed to bring any commodity to market, suits itself to the effectual demand.[14]

Here we have a repetition of the idea that accumulation represents deprivation of expenditure coupled with a statement that the effective demand for the various articles of consumption is the determining factor in the quantity produced. In other words, somehow the demand for capital goods is irrelevant to the question. But we have seen from the previous passage that Lauderdale recognises that accumulation implies increased demand for these commodities.

This contradiction is never resolved by Lauderdale himself. When, a few pages later, he discusses the problem of the National Debt, he just reproduces the same ambiguities. Suppose, he says, the government spends £15m. on warfare, or some other consumption goods, and raises the money in taxes. Then there will be no mischief apart from that caused by the sudden shift in demand. But if it raises this £15m, for the purpose of repaying the National Debt, things will be altogether different:

> In this, as in the former case, there would have ensued all the mischief occasioned by abstracting a portion of demand . . . from the commodities which the subjects of accumulation were accustomed to acquire with this part of their revenue; but, in this case, there would unfortunately have existed no extraordinary expenditure, to counteract the full effects of this enforced parsimony; for it would have been difficult to persuade the proprietors of stock, from whom such extensive purchases would have been made by the Commissioners of the Sinking Fund, all at once to spend, as revenue, that which habit had taught them to regard as capital.[15]

In other words, there will be a diminution of effective demand to the extent that the owners of the National Debt save more of their new cash than the people who were the subjects of the increased taxation would have. Here the possibility of money being spent *as capital*, of the holders of the National Debt investing more as a result of being paid off, is not raised. It is impossible to know whether Lauderdale does not mention it because he thinks this would not be "genuine" expenditure, or because he thinks it inconceivable that a rise in investment should coincide with a fall in demand for consumption goods, or because he thinks a rise in investment is unlikely for some completely different reason.

Lauderdale himself is very confused, but it is clear that underlying at least some of his arguments is the idea that the level of demand for consumption goods is what is important to stimulate the growth of the economy, and that the level of investment is in some sense dependent on the demand for consumption goods. Since this idea is more or less implied by our definition of underconsumption theories, we shall meet it again in later writings. As to his attempts to justify the idea that there can be too much saving, he seems to have managed to combine at least three different arguments:

1) That accumulation of capital cannot increase the productive powers of the community, and can therefore only be a means of transferring wealth from one individual to another.

2) That whether accumulation of capital increases the productive powers of the community or not, it represents a

subtraction from present aggregate demand and is therefore dangerous. This is the substance of his ideas on the National Debt.

3) That although accumulation of capital does increase the productive powers of the community, there nevertheless exists a physical limit to the quantity of capital that can be usefully employed in society at any one time, either because of the limitations of technical knowledge or for some other reason, and therefore accumulation becomes socially useless (and also, by his theory of value, economically depressing) beyond a certain point. Lauderdale does not state anywhere that these represent three different opinions on the subject, and it is probable that he did not notice the contradictions.

Of these arguments, only the second is a truly underconsumptionist one.

By way of conclusion, we can say that Lauderdale opens the debate on the question of the possibility of overproduction, which takes the form (in Britain at least) of discussing whether there can be excessive saving. He is not a consistent underconsumptionist, but he does put forward in a not very clear way the idea that the crucial problem is that investment involves the reduction of present consumption expenditure, and this is a consistent theme of the early British underconsumptionists, from Spence and Malthus to Chalmers and Patrick Plough.

WILLIAM SPENCE

The next work to be considered is the pamphlet *Britain Independent of Commerce* by William Spence. The main intention of this work, which was first published in 1808, four years after Lauderdale's book, is to undermine the common assumption that foreign trade was one of the pillars of Britain's prosperity and could not be appreciably reduced without great loss to the nation. At the time, incidentally, this was a highly topical subject, since it was written during Napoleon's attempted economic blockade of the British Isles, and it was chiefly the reactions to this blockade in the British press that prompted Spence to write his pamphlet.

The pamphlet could hardly have been more different from Lauderdale's contribution. While Lauderdale's intention was to disprove certain theses of Adam Smith's, it is clear that he accepts the fundamental premises of Smith's work, that is, the division of the total revenue into the wages of labour, the profits of stock and the rent of land, corresponding to the class divisions of workers, capitalists and landlords, which distinguish him from previous economic writings. William Spence, by contrast, takes the Physiocratic system as his basis for analysis. In his introductory remarks he divides "the political economists who have investigated the sources of wealth" into two great classes: on the one side, the "mercantile sect" comprising the vast majority, who contend that manufactures are by far the greatest, if not the only source of wealth, and have pressed for (and often got) monopolies, restrictions and bounties on their behalf; and on the other side, the "agricultural sect", or the Physiocrats and their followers, who maintain agriculture to be the only source of wealth. Manufacturing creates no additional wealth, and in foreign trade it is only the profits of the exporter, but not of the importer, that add to national wealth. According to this division, a writer must be either a Mercantilist or a Physiocrat, and in Spence's opinion it is the "agricultural sect" who are right (Adam Smith is classed as an agriculturalist). Manufacturing, he says, changes the form of the objects it works up, but the value added to these objects is no greater than the value of the necessities consumed by workers during that time, and no new value has been created by their labour. If by chance the manufacturer should charge the landowners who buy his products a price that will give him more in revenue than he paid out in wages, then this does not represent any wealth created in manufacturing, but merely the profit of the manufacturer made at the expense of the landowner.

This is a familiar Physiocratic idea, leading logically to the Physiocratic division of the population into proprietors of the land, productive classes and sterile classes. But Spence shows definite traces of influence by Adam Smith. He does not conclude in the same decisive way as the Physiocrats that agriculture is the primary branch of economic activity, for which the expenditure of the landowners on manufactures is to be sacrificed whenever necessary. He argues that, in Europe at least, the main cause of the prosperity in agriculture has been the growth of manufacturing, and that "in Britain, agriculture has thriven only in consequence of the influence of manufactures; and the increase of this influence is requisite to its further extension".[16] It is not quite clear, however, how this assertion combines with the logic of the Physiocratic system which Spence otherwise accepts.

Spence divides society into four basic classes: landowners, cultivators of the soil, manufacturers, and unproductive classes who comprise the remainder of the population. The revenue of the last two classes, who were lumped together by the Physiocrats as "the sterile class", is drawn from that of the landed proprietors; the wealth of the nation is created in agriculture, and those employed in non-agricultural occupations are necessarily dependent on the expenditure of the landowners for their livelihood. Spence draws the following conclusions from this:

> It is a condition, then, essential to the creation of national wealth, in societies constituted like those of Europe, that the class of land proprietors, expend the greater part of their revenue which they derive from the soil. They are the agents, through whose hands the revenue of society passes, but in order that wealth and prosperity should accrue to the community, it is absolutely necessary that they should spend this revenue. So long as they perform this duty, everything goes on in its proper train.[17]

Here we have a different emphasis from that of the Physiocrats. While they were concerned that landowners should properly distribute their expenditure between agriculture and manufacturing, Spence is worried about whether they spend their money at all. Consider what happens if they fail in this respect:

> Let us make the supposition, that fifty of our great landowners, each deriving £20,000 a year from his estates, which they had been accustomed to spend, were to be convinced, by the arguments of Dr.Smith, that the practice of parsimony is the more effectual way of accumulating national riches: Let us suppose, that, patriotically induced by this reflection, they resolved not to spend, but to save, the £1m which their revenue amounted to. Is it not self-evident, that all those members of the manufacturing and unproductive classes who had, directly or indirectly, been accustomed to draw the revenue destined for their subsistence, from the expenditure of this sum, would have their power of consum-

ing the produce of the earth diminished, by the whole of this
£1m?[18]

It is quite clear from this argument that Spence imagines
parsimony to be equivalent to a simple abstraction of demand,
like an act of hoarding. As for Adam Smith's arguments, he
expressly repudiates the view that money lent at interest will still
be "employed in circulation" and give employment to labourers,
and maintains that saving reduces the level of effective demand,
and hence the number of profitable outlets for capital, at the
same time that it increases the quantity of capital in existence.[19]
Naturally this leads to an entirely different conclusion as to the
economic role of the landowners. While Smith had maintained
that the labour of menial servants was unproductive because it
added to the value of nothing, and rich men, if they wanted to
increase the wealth of the country, should not dissipate their
fortunes on good living but should accumulate them as capital to
be used as a fund for the employment of productive labourers,
Spence advocates precisely the opposite:

> It is clear, then, that expenditure, not parsimony, is the
> province of the class of land proprietors, and, that it is on the
> due performance of this duty, by the class in question, that
> the production of national wealth depends. And not only
> does the production of national wealth depend upon the
> expenditure of the class of land proprietors, but, for the due
> increase of this wealth, and for the constantly progressive
> maintenance of the prosperity of the community, it is
> absolutely requisite, that this class should go on progressively
> increasing its expenditure.[20]

So it is the demand provided by the landowning class that is
the propelling power behind the increase of national wealth.
Landowners do not merely appropriate to themselves through
rent a portion of wealth that is produced by others; they
determine through the disposition of their money the fortunes
of the country.

Spence's pamphlet provoked a reply from James Mill (a
pamphlet entitled *Commerce Defended*), which really marks the
transition of the general glut question — as it later became
known — from being the object of isolated contributions to the
field of an active debate. Mill attacks Spence for his Physiocratic

assumptions. Although he has no quarrel with his praise of land as a source of wealth — he says that "of all species of labour, that which is bestowed upon the soil, is in general rewarded by the most abundant product"[21] and notes that the soil for the most part manages not only to pay the wages of labour and the profits of stock, but the rent of land as well — he cannot accept that it is the *only* source of wealth.

The difference is profound. Spence says manufacturing is not a source of wealth; Mill says it is [22]. Similarly on commerce: Spence says the export trade is productive of national wealth, since the profits come out of the pockets of foreign consumers, while the import trade is unproductive, since the profits are made at the expense of home consumers (the consumers being landowners, who thus suffer a reduction in their net product. On a world scale, of course, neither importing nor exporting would be productive). Mill on the other hand regards all trade as a source of wealth insofar as it produces a profit.

These are very basic differences. It is in the chapter on 'Consumption' that Mill raises his disagreements with Spence's ideas on parsimony. He identifies his basic mistake as the inaccurate and ambiguous use of the word 'consumption'. According to Mill, Spence fails to distinguish between consumption proper, the final removal of the goods from production and circulation for the satisfaction of human needs, and productive consumption, the re-employment of these goods as a part of capital laid out, as wages, raw materials or whatever.

> We perceive, therefore, that there are two species of consumption; which are so far from being the same, that the one is more properly the very reverse of the other. The one is an absolute destruction of property, and is consumption properly so called; the other is a consumption for the sake of reproduction, and might perhaps with more propriety be called employment than consumption.[23]

In other words, Spence does not distinguish consumption from investment, but uses the term consumption to cover them both. This was the Physiocratic practice (although they used the term expenditure), but Spence's argument requires a rigorous distinction. Mill continues:

The whole annual produce of every country is distributed into two great parts; that which is destined to be employed for the purpose of reproduction, and that which is destined to be consumed. That part which is destined to serve for reproduction naturally appears again next year, with profit. This reproduction, with the profit, is naturally the whole produce of the country for that year.[24]

So, Mill concludes, if Spence means by consumption what Mill means by unproductive consumption, then his doctrine that the interests of the country are best promoted by the greatest consumption is the very reverse of the truth.

Spence, of course, would argue that Mill has avoided the whole question of effective demand. Mill's answer is that shifting money from unproductive to productive consumption in no way reduces effective demand.

That part (of annual produce) which is destined for future profit, is just as completely consumed as that which is destined for immediate gratification.[25]

And these two parts make up the whole of the annual produce. Having disposed of Spence's arguments, Mill gets down to elaborating his own position:

No proposition however in political economy seems to be more certain than this which I am going to announce, how paradoxical soever it may at first sight appear . . . If a nation's power of purchasing is exactly measured by its annual produce, as it undoubtedly is; the more you increase the annual produce, the more by that very act you extend the national market, the power of purchasing and the actual purchases of the nation. Whatever be the additional quantity of goods therefore which is at any time created in any country, an additional power of purchasing, exactly equivalent, is at the same instant created; so that a nation can never be naturally overstocked either with capital or with commodities; as the very operation of capital makes a vent for its produce.[26]

If a nation's purchasing power is exactly measured by its annual produce, and as Mill, like Spence, has dismissed hoarding as insignificant, (though theoretically possible), there can never be a general glut. This proposition is what has generally become known as "Say's Law".

This formulation goes some way beyond Adam Smith, who did little more than to point out that savings which were invested did not reduce the demand for labour and commodities, in stating bluntly that there is no possibility of overproduction of either capital or commodities, because the purchasing power and the total production of a nation always balance each other exactly. Smith never openly says this, although it would be correct to say that his arguments definitely tend in this direction.

In reply to Mill, Spence produced a further tract entitled *Agriculture the Source of Wealth of Great Britain*. He claims that Mill has misunderstood him on two points:

1) Just because he supports the basic axioms of the Physiocrats, it is not true to say that he wants to reduce the share of total labour in Britain today that is employed in industry.

2) Likewise with commerce, just because he claims that in general commerce is not productive of wealth, this does not mean that he recommends a reduction in foreign trade.

He also objects to Mill's assertion that if he starts from Physiocratic axioms he should accept the whole of their system and their practical conclusions and not just part of them. The general tenor of the early pages of the essay is that Mill is boxing largely with a shadow opponent and that the difference between them is not half as great as Mill would like to make out. He says that "there is no essential difference between our doctrines as to the grand sources of national wealth" and that he and Mill differ only "in some subordinate theoretical points."[27] Spence's idea that the theoretical points of difference between Mill and himself — to which the rest of the pamphlet is devoted — are of only minor significance is a consequence of his simple division of economic theorists into two great schools, the agriculturalists and mercantilists; since both the Physiocrats and Adam Smith (and Spence and Mill) are agriculturalists, they are agreed on the major points at issue and their disagreements matter relatively little. This reconciliatory position finds its counterpart in the concessions to Smith introduced by Spence in his own reworking of Physiocracy.

The pages he spends on a reply to Mill's chapter on 'Consumption' show how great is the theoretical gulf between the two men. James Mill thinks primarily in terms of consumption and investment, unproductive and productive consumption. Spence, on the other hand, thinks primarily in terms of expenditure in different branches of production, agriculture and manufacturing. One is a follower of Adam Smith, the other of the Physiocrats. But in addition, Spence does not accept investment as expenditure in the same sense as consumption: this is what makes him an underconsumptionist, where Quesnay was not. So when Mill says that in the interests of the community the landowners should employ their incomes as capital and not spend them as revenue, to Spence this is "stark nonsense". Suppose, he says, that they lay out this new capital in agriculture. Then "all the manufacturers and idlers, which comprise 5/6 of the community, must become cultivators, or they must starve"[28] because the revenue off which they formerly lived has been removed. But it is ridiculous to suppose that landowners would employ their revenue in feeding 12 million people to do the work which may be performed by 2 million.

It is not clear what the argument is here. Is he saying that it would be madness on the part of landowners to invest so much in their land at one time (in which case he would appear to be harking back to Lauderdale's idea of a physical limit to the amount of capital that can be profitably employed in agriculture in a given state of technical knowledge)? Or is he saying that the demand for agricultural products is more or less fixed and this branch of production could not absorb many more labourers? We have no way of knowing.

Then he turns to the case where the landlords lend all their saved £50m to a manufacturer.

> Does (Mr Mill) really suppose that employment could be found for fifty millions of additional capital, at the moment when those who are to employ it have lost customers for their articles to the same amount? Was there ever a project conceived by man more extravagant than this?[29]

This is a basic idea which we shall meet again in the underconsumptionist writings of this period: that increased investment implies reduced demand, and since it also implies increased supply, the result must be overproduction. Spence does not advocate this absolutely, in the sense of saying that any investment at all must lead to overproduction, for he cannot deny the necessity of investment to an increase in prosperity. His position is that farmers and master-manufacturers should provide the funds for investment out of their own profits, and not borrow from the landowners, which would imply a reduction in landowners' consumption.[30] This again reveals the Physiocratic basis of Spence's position, for instead of looking at the total volume of demand for consumption goods, from whatever source, he makes a fetish out of the demand provided by landowners.

Spence does not really understand the arguments which Mill puts in opposition to this. He correctly conceives the long paragraph beginning on p.81 of *Commerce Defended* (of which a section was quoted above) to mean this:

> There can never be a superabundance of capital; because if one part of it be employed in producing commodities of one description, and another, commodities of another description, the one may be exchanged for the other, and thus the market will never be overstocked.[31]

Spence would completely agree if this means that there will be no superabundance of capital if new capital is laid out in agriculture in proportion as it is laid out in manufactures. But if it means that capital may be employed ad infinitum in producing manufactures, with no addition to agricultural capital, then he thinks it absurd. All this increase in capital necessarily implies an increase in labour employed; but where is the extra food for these extra workers going to come from if no more capital is laid out in agriculture?

> Here again Mr. Mill has lost sight of the important truth, that the great use of manufactures is to enable those who possess no share of the soil to obtain their daily bread from those who have monopolised it, by presenting them with some attractive object in exchange for its produce.[32]

This is indeed the central issue. Spence has missed the main point that Mill is making, that an increase in investment, in whatever branch of production, in no way affects the adequacy of the total purchasing power to the total output at normal prices, because he focusses always on the surplus of food produced in agriculture that is available for the consumption of other sections of the community.

The controversy between Spence and Mill is a very dislocated debate, in the sense that each of them is operating with an entirely different set of distinctions, which are regarded by the other as useless or irrelevant. Nevertheless it represents an important step in the development of the general glut question, as can be seen when we reflect on what had gone before. Up till 1808 there had been a few short, indicative remarks in *The Wealth of Nations,* and a book by Lauderdale aimed to sink the idea that parsimony was the source of wealth, but which was argued in a confused and not very consistent fashion. Spence takes up the same refrain as Lauderdale, although from a different point of view. To him the important question is what the landowners do with their money, a concern which derives from the essentially Physiocratic framework of his thought, although where the Physiocrats were concerned only that landowners should spend their money and not hoard it, and that they should distribute it correctly between agriculture and manufacturing, Spence is worried not so much about this — since he regards the growth of manufacturing as necessary to the stimulation of agriculture — as about whether they consume their incomes or invest them (or lend them to someone else to invest). This Physiocratic residue of "fetishism of landowner-ship" is quite specific to Spence in the history of underconsump-tion theories,[33] but the more general and enduring aspect of his theories is the idea that investment simultaneously increases supply and reduces demand, which is really the core idea of the over-saving type of underconsumption theory. Lauderdale had hinted at this approach without stating it clearly. Spence sets it out in an especially bold form which finds its reflection throughout the remainder of nineteenth century British under-consumptionism.

MALTHUS

A question which must arise at some point is: how deep is the unity amongst the early British underconsumptionists? How much do they really have in common? Since Malthus is undoubtedly the outstanding figure in the crowd, and since later writers have generally been regarded — more or less accurately — as pale imitations of him, the immediate form in which this question comes up is usually that of to what extent Lauderdale and Spence can be seen as forerunners of Malthus. It is obvious that they precede him in questioning the dogma of the impossibility of general overproduction. But do the resemblances go further than that?

This question is inextricably mixed up with the problem of what, if anything, can be pinpointed as the essence of Ricardian economics; for if Lauderdale or Spence is to be seen as a forerunner of Malthus in a wider theoretical sense than merely the general glut debate, then such an argument must centre around the ideas expressed in Malthus's *Principles*, which was explicitly conceived as an answer to Ricardo. Spence would clearly not qualify as a forerunner in this sense, for he goes back to before Adam Smith and bases himself on Physiocracy, whereas Malthus is a Smithian through and through. As Schumpeter remarks, there is nothing in Malthus which cannot be found in Smith, except his remarks on general overproduction. Lauderdale, however, is a more likely candidate. In this respect the publication of a book entitled *Malthus and Lauderdale — the anti-Ricardian tradition*, by Morton Paglin, is extremely interesting, for it openly puts forward the idea that Lauderdale must be seen as a forerunner of Malthus and an opponent of Ricardianism on a wide theoretical front. The interest of this book is that it opens up the extremely complex question of how this period of economic thought is to be understood and interpreted — a difficult problem which is far from being solved by historians of theory — but the defect of it is that it assumes an answer to this question without an explicit discussion of the issues. Its underlying thesis is that there is a deep theoretical chasm between Ricardo and Malthus, and that since on some major theoretical issues Lauderdale was on the side of Malthus, therefore he can justifiably be regarded as a forerunner of Malthus. On the other hand, if, as has been remarked by many people, Ricardo and Malthus can be seen as representing opposite sides of Adam Smith, how could these ideas coexist in Adam Smith when there was such a theoretical gulf between them? This crucial question is the key to the Ricardo-Malthus debate, and some of the difficulties in answering it can be judged by the variety of ideas put forward as to the distinguishing feature of Ricardo's system.

It is not my intention here to enter into this debate, which is only incidental to the question of underconsumption theories. But at the same time, it is true that Paglin is led into definite errors by the position which he takes. In discussing the question of aggregate demand, he looks at Lauderdale and Malthus at length, but he makes no mention at all of Spence (of course here it could be argued that he only set out to look at Lauderdale and Malthus, but the question then is whether it is valid to do that). In actual fact, however, as should be clear from our previous discussions of Lauderdale and Spence, Spence's contribution is extremely important. Lauderdale attacked the idea that parsimony is the source of national wealth, and he must be accorded the priority of this, but he did so from a very unclear and not necessarily underconsumptionist position. Spence is the first person to state explicitly and clearly what is really the central tenet of the Malthusian type of underconsumption theory, that accumulation reduces aggregate demand relative to aggregate supply. This is the important theoretical point, beside which the fact that it is wrapped up in a Physiocratic framework is not important. From the simple point of view of the development of underconsumption theories, Spence's contribution is in fact an important step between Lauderdale and Malthus, which cannot be omitted.

It is a basic theme of this study that the problem of underconsumption theories at this time can be discussed separately, in relative isolation from, say, problems of the theory of value. Only relative isolation because, although there does not seem to be any necessary logical correlation or unique correspondence between a given position on value and a given position on "Say's Law", certain individuals may use the theory of value to justify their position on gluts. This is definitely true of Lauderdale, and, in a more subtle way, of Malthus. This is a position which would probably be admitted by Paglin, but which is actually implicitly denied by his procedure. For in his comparison of Malthus and Lauderdale the two major items are the theory of value and the question of aggregate demand. Now it is undoubtedly true that on these two issues each of these authors can be starkly contrasted to Ricardo, but this is a negative definition of their unity. By itself it does not justify picking out these two authors from a collection of others and setting them up together by themselves as the centre of anti-Ricardianism. It might be justified, if Malthus's work could be identified as a consistent piece of theoretical construction which stood as a coherent alternative to the Ricardian system; in this case it would have some meaning to look for the evolution of the elements of this construct in previous writings. Actually, however, this is not the case, and this is admitted even by Paglin himself. As many writers have noted, a study of Malthus's work does not reveal a consistent theoretical framework.*

Malthus is the most famous of the British underconsumptionists of this time, and also the most difficult to assess. Some people have gone so far as to see in him a forerunner of Keynes, while others emphatically reject such claims. In this study, I tend very much towards the latter view, but I recognise the specific contribution made by him in probing some of the inadequacies in the "Say's Law" formulation. I start by looking at his early

---

*In fact the points at issue here come down to the question of the interpretation of this period of political economy in its totality. It is my opinion that no simple description can be given of it, that it can by no means be represented as a struggle between two camps, and that it would be much more accurate to picture it as a period of extreme turbulence, like a sea in which there are many cross-currents, no one of which is strong enough to impose its will on the others. Only in this way can it be explained that while clear-cut issues can be identified — the theory of value, of rent, of aggregate demand — it is difficult to trace direct theoretical connections between them and individual writers may be on 'one' side on one issue and on the 'other' side on another. It is only with the increasing predominance of marginalism that a coherent theoretical system becomes widely accepted. It seems to me that the "two camps" idea results mainly from an overconcentration on Britain, for in Britain the effect of the sharp social conflict over the Corn Laws, because it was an issue of economic policy, was to bring political differences into the centre of theoretical debates by splitting economists into two camps on this one issue. The intensity of these conflicts, combined with the publication of Ricardo's and Malthus's works which implied directly opposite conclusions on this problem and displayed very profound theoretical disagreements, has tended to generate the idea that here we have a struggle between two major theoretical traditions, even though a study of other writers of the same period does not really justify it. The disputes over policy have tended to be confused with deeper theoretical issues.

Even Paglin, who starts with the idea of the fundamental opposition of Lauderdale and Malthus to Ricardo, is obliged to admit that Malthus's work (and Lauderdale's so much the more) has none of the theoretical coherence of Ricardo's, and the fact is that it is essentially a politically-inspired critique whose main arguments cannot be traced back to a consistent alternative theoretical framework, so that it would be entirely wrong to treat Lauderdale's and Malthus's ideas on parsimony as a reflection of very profound theoretical differences.

correspondence with Ricardo, in which he takes a clear but hardly tenable point of view, the errors of which are indicated by Ricardo in his replies, and move on to the *Principles*, the exact interpretation of which is rather more difficult.

Malthus and Ricardo had corresponded on the question of accumulation and effective demand as early as 1814. In one letter Malthus had said:

> Effectual demand consists of two elements the *power* and the *will* to purchase. The power to purchase may perhaps be represented correctly by the produce of the country whether small or great; but the will to purchase will always be the greatest, the smaller is the produce compared with the population, and the more scantily the wants of society are supplied. . . . In short I by no means think that the power to purchase necessarily involves a proportionate will to purchase, and I cannot agree with Mr. Mill in an ingenious position which he lays down in answer to Mr. Spence, that in reference to a nation, supply can never exceed demand. A nation must certainly have the power of purchasing all that it produces, but I can easily conceive it not to have the will: and if we were to grow next year half as much corn again as usual, a great part of it would be wasted, and the same would be true if commodities of all kinds were increased one half. It would be impossible that they should yield the expense of production.[34]

This comment arose out of a discussion on the cause of high profits and high interest rates carried on in an exchange of letters over the previous two or three months.

Malthus is saying here that he does not agree with James Mill's proposition, which implies that a superabundance of commodities is impossible. Mill fails to distinguish between the power and the will to purchase, and although the nation's purchasing power may (perhaps) be equal to its total produce, this does not resolve the question of whether the will to purchase is there. Malthus illustrates this using the example of corn: if the output of it is increased by 50 per cent in one year, much of it would be wasted because the demand does not exist. The same is true for an increase of commodities of all kinds.

Ricardo does not accept this argument. Although he has no quarrel with the distinction between the power and the will to purchase, he thinks that if the power is there, the will will be there too:

> For the desire of accumulation will occasion demand just as effectually as a desire to consume, it will only change the objects on which the demand will exercise itself. If you think that with an increase of capital men will become indifferent both to consumption and accumulation, then you are correct in opposing Mr. Mill's idea, that in reference to a nation, supply can never exceed demand, — but does not an increase in capital beget an increased inclination for luxuries of all description?[35]

Ricardo puts his finger on the flaw in Malthus's argument when he points out the illegitimacy of his direct transition from the example of corn to that of all commodities. For while a very sudden increase in the production of any one commodity will very likely result in wastage, the real question is whether, if men find their *incomes* suddenly increased by 50 per cent, they will still spend them all. In Ricardo's view, they will, because "the wants and tastes of mankind" are unlimited.[36]

In his reply, Malthus says that he cannot by any means agree with Ricardo that "the desire of accumulation will occasion demand just as effectually as a desire to consume" and that "consumption and accumulation equally promote demand". His reasons are interesting. In his previous letter he had already said:

> When capital is abundant it is not easy to find new objects sufficiently in demand. When capital is scarce nothing is more easy. In a country abundant in capital the value of the whole produce cannot increase with rapidity from the insufficiency of demand. In a country with little comparative capital the value of the yearly produce may very rapidly increase from the greatness of demand.[37]

In other words when a country is highly developed it is difficult to find outlets for profitable investment, whereas in less developed countries it is comparatively easy. This is the kind of statement which sounds plausible on the basis of the chapter on 'Profits' in *The Wealth of Nations,* but its implications must be closely looked at. What it amounts to is an assertion that the accumulation of capital is generally subordinate to effective demand. Investment can be carried on only if the demand is already there for it. This is a very different approach from that of James Mill. These impressions are confirmed when Malthus says that the real question is not whether a man would like to spend half as much again,

> but whether you can furnish to persons of the same incomes a great additional quantity of commodities without lowering their price so much compared with the price of production as to destroy the effective demand for such a supply and consequently to check its continuance to some extent.[38]

This treats the increase in production as a new swarm of products coming onto the market to face consumers whose situation remains unchanged. But these products have to be produced, and in their production incomes are generated, so that we have not only an increased supply but also an increased demand. This is the basis of Mill's argument, and of Ricardo's reply to Malthus's letter.

Malthus's fundamental mistake throughout this exchange is that he can conceive the general movement of the whole economy only by a simple analogy with the production of one single commodity. This is the only meaning that can be attributed to the passage just quoted. Of course, if we look at just one branch of production expanding fast (as in the corn example), it is likely that supply will outstrip demand at a given price and the price will fall. What is in question here, however, is merely a disproportion between the distribution of demand and supply before the forces of competition have had time to correct the situation. But obviously, considering the economy as a whole in the hypothetical case of "balanced growth", all sectors can expand without experiencing a lack of demand. This is clearly recognised by Ricardo, who rightly shifts the debate from the expansion of one branch of production (corn) to the increase of real incomes of consumers.

Malthus's arguments in the correspondence have some affinity to what Lauderdale had said ten years earlier. It will be remembered that Lauderdale, in his example of the capitalist farmer foregoing present consumption for the sake of accumulation, had maintained that this could lead to an immediate fall in the price of consumption goods as farmers realised they could not use all the capital equipment they had ordered. Now Malthus is also saying that accumulation will tend to lead to a future fall of price in that branch of production; but Lauderdale's reasoning was rooted in the notion of an absolute technical limit to the accumulation of capital, and ultimately this was what precipitated the general crisis, whereas Malthus's letters do not contain any suggestion of this, and seem to be based on the simple analogy with the production of one commodity within the framework of the whole economy.

Malthus's main work, and his first published writing on the question of gluts, is his *Principles of Political Economy considered with a view to their practical application*, the first edition of which appeared in 1820, and the second, posthumously, in 1836. The rest of this section is devoted to the ideas contained therein.

Malthus states in the Preface his disagreements with Adam Smith about saving. While he does not wish to deny that the conversion of revenue into capital is necessary to increasing wealth, nevertheless:

> It is quite obvious that (these propositions of Smith) are not true to an indefinite extent, and that the principle of saving, pushed to excess, would destroy the motive to production. . . . If consumption exceed production, the capital of a country must gradually be destroyed from its want of power to produce; if production be in a great excess above consumption, the motive to accumulate and produce must cease from the want of will to consume . . . it follows that there must be some intermediate point . . . where, taking into consideration both the power to produce and the will to consume, the encouragement to the increase of wealth is the greatest.[39]

But he does not imagine, like Lauderdale, that an increase in wealth can be achieved in some way other than by the accumulation of capital, or by saving.[40] His objection is only that it is possible to carry saving to excess.

Malthus's theory might be called "the theory of the golden mean". Accumulation is necessary and must exist, for otherwise there could be no increase in wealth, but at the same time it cannot be carried too far, or it will cut its own throat. In this respect Malthus sets the tone of all later underconsumption theories of the over-saving type (with the exception of Chalmers) in at once postulating the existence of this mean, and failing to give it any economic definition.

Malthus's ideas on saving and accumulation have been the subject of some debate. This is partly the fault of Keynes who, in his desire to rehabilitate those who had so often been maligned for their opposition to Say's Law, tended to minimise the faults in their argument and to present them almost as forerunners of himself. This is the train of thought taken up by Paglin, who maintains that Malthus does in effect distinguish between ex ante and ex post saving. He says:

> When Malthus deals with saving and investment in the ex ante sense of determining total output he clearly recognises that increased saving does not automatically create a demand for commodities but 'contributes to explain the cause of the diminished demand for commodities'.[41]

And on the next page, after giving his own statement in modern terminology of the Malthusian theory of events leading up to a period of stagnation:

> Although Blaug has correctly described the initial sequence in which all savings are invested, he makes a basic error of interpretation when he attempts to saddle Malthus with the view that savings are at all times automatically invested.
> While the Ricardian analysis . . . shows the stultifying effects of Say's Law, it is Malthus's great merit to have seen that at such a point consumption expenditure meant demand but that savings by no means guaranteed demand.[42]

The usual basis of such claims for the superiority of Malthus to Ricardo is that he recognises that the level of total output is not a given, but is a variable to be determined by the system. Here Paglin, in defence of this proposition, comes very close to suggesting that Malthus had the same insights as Keynes. In my view, this interpretation fails to take adequate account of the prevailing theoretical conceptions of the time and reads far too much into Malthus's own words. The simple fact is that the idea that savings were at all times automatically invested was a generally accepted assumption of this period, and it is not an idea which Malthus has to be saddled with, by Blaug or anyone else. Unless there is explicit proof to the contrary, we must assume that Malthus accepted this view. In truth, the weight of evidence is not on Paglin's side. In the very first chapter of the *Principles*, Malthus states unequivocally that "no political economist of the present day can by saving mean mere hoarding".[43] The central question therefore becomes: what happens to money that is saved and lent at interest? Is it automatically invested? Malthus quotes in full the following passage from Ricardo's *Principles*:

If £10,000 were given to a man having £100,000 p.a., he would not lock it up in a chest, but would either increase his expenses by £10,000, employ it himself productively, or lend it to some other person for that purpose; in either case, demand would be increased. . . . If he employed his £10,000 productively, his effectual demand would be for food, clothing, and raw materials, which might set new labourers to work. But still it would be *demand*.[44]

If he really disagrees with the notion that savings are automatically at all times invested, surely he must say so here. But in fact he does not challenge this assumption at all; he refers only to the transfer of economic activity to the production of necessaries, which would lead to a great development of agriculture and population. There is in fact no passage in the book which clearly postulates the possibility of a deviation of planned saving from planned investment other than by hoarding. Paglin does not have any difficulty in finding passages in which Malthus maintains that excessive saving could lead to a collapse of prices and a general glut. These passages abound. But they do not imply that these savings are not simultaneously invested.

There are two main arguments in the *Principles* for the proposition that there can be excessive accumulation. One, which we have already encountered in the correspondence with Ricardo, and which is clearly erroneous, is based on a direct analogy between supply and demand in the whole economy and supply and demand of an individual commodity. The other, which is also ultimately wrong but which does reveal some of the weaknesses of his opponents' conceptions, consists of an examination of the consequences when resources are transferred from consumption to investment.

An example of the first type of argument is the following:

In individual cases, the power of producing particular commodities is called into action, in proportion to the intensity of effectual demand for them; and the greatest stimulus to their increase, independent of improved facilities of production, is a high market price, or an increase of their exchangeable value, before a greater value of capital has been employed upon them. In the same manner, the greatest stimulus to the continued production of commodities, taken altogether, is an increase in the exchangeable value of the whole mass, before a greater value of capital has been employed upon them.[45]

Here Malthus presents the two cases as directly equivalent. Of course one wonders where this "increase in the exchangeable value of the whole mass" is to come from: it appears as if effective demand must come from somewhere outside the system. It is the great merit of Ricardo and Mill that they recognise that it cannot, and their objections are quite adequate as a reply to this argument of Malthus's.

Part of the responsibility for this mistake must lie with Malthus's theory of value. In Ricardo's theory, it was automatically assumed that the demand was there for the commodity to be produced, and demand played no part in determining the value of a commodity, so that such an analogy between the production of an individual commodity and of the whole mass of commodities would make no sense. But Malthus advocates a theory of value in which value is merely the outcome of the forces of demand and supply, and the natural price (or necessary price as Malthus prefers to call it) is simply the price necessary to induce a supply suited to the demand. Where for Ricardo the value resolved itself into wages and profits, for Malthus wages, profits and rent are the component parts of price which is now the sum of what has been paid out in these three forms. This involves a shift from a concept of distribution amongst social classes — for in Ricardo wages and profits are considered only on the level of the whole economy — to that of prices of factors of production — a concept which is not found in Malthus but which is there in embryo by virtue of his theory of value — and this shift implies necessarily the primacy of the individual commodity as the starting point for the analysis of the whole economy.

Thus, although Malthus's mistake is not a necessary deduction from his theory of value, this theory serves to give a plausibility to the analogy between the individual commodity and the whole

economy which plays such a large part in his argument, for in
imagining his commodity values jumping about in response to
every little change in demand and supply, he has lost sight of the
distribution of the product amongst the social classes and how
their incomes and expenditure relate to the cost of production.
In fact, Malthus's theory of value serves to obscure the real
issues in the general glut debate, and to distract attention from
the faults in his argument.

There are a few points in Malthus's argument, however,
where he does seem to have a deeper understanding of the
problem. On one occasion, after listing two rather trivial
objections to his opponents' arguments, he says:

> A third very serious error of the writers above referred to,
> and practically the most important of the three, consists in
> supposing that accumulation ensures demand; or that the
> consumption of the labourers employed by those whose
> object is to save, will create such an effectual demand for
> commodities as to encourage a continued increase of
> produce.[46]

It is clear that Malthus does not deny that accumulation
creates *some* demand, but he is convinced that it will be
insufficient, because it is equivalent only to the consumption of
the extra labourers employed.

He produces a similar argument at another point. He assumes
two branches of production, agriculture and manufactures,
exchanging with one another. If all producers now decide to
accumulate to a certain extent, consumption of capitalists will
fall, and the producers of goods for this market will find
themselves with a surplus. But the accumulation has meant
taking on new labourers, so

> An accumulation, to a certain extent, of common food and
> common clothing might take place on both sides; but the
> amount must necessarily be extremely confined. It would be
> of no sort of use to the farmer to go on cultivating his land
> with a view merely to give food and clothing to his
> labourers.[47]

In other words, the extra sale of wage goods can never bring
in more revenue than the cost of employing the extra labourers,
so where is the profit on the investment? Capitalist consumption

has fallen, to be replaced by consumption by newly employed labourers. The extra profits which must have been expected have not materialised. There is extra production, but no extra consumption.

This is in fact an extremely interesting argument. It should be noted that these extra labourers are not those employed on an investment project, in constructing a factory or in manufacturing machinery to be installed later, but are directly employed in production, in making the extra products which are the intention of the investment. This point is crucial: its importance cannot be overemphasised. It is a direct consequence of the prevailing classical conception of investment. (These points will be further elaborated in Chapter Five).

This conception saw investment essentially as the employment of more labourers, and imagined the increased production to result more or less immediately after the decision to invest. Although it was recognised that the labourers had to be provided with the implements and the means of labour, nevertheless the existence of a separate sector of production devoted to this was either not recognised or it was equated to the production of raw materials, ie it was just a stage in the production of a consumer good. The only equivalent to a sector producing means of production was the production of wage goods to be advanced to the new labourers — but this sector is not *physically* distinguishable from the consumption goods sector, and in most formulations of "Say's Law", which merely compare two static situations, the existence of this investment goods sector producing wage goods is not mentioned.

Thus it is easy to forget about the demand created in this way, and to portray investment as simply an increase in the production of consumer goods. But then the only extra demand is that of the labourers employed, and there is no extra demand which is sufficient to give a profit on this investment. In fact investment is bound to yield no profit at all! This is the trap into which Malthus falls.

But even if Malthus's argument were correct, still his solution to the difficulty is completely erroneous. He suggests three ways of stimulating the rate of consumption: a more equal distribution of landed property, the development of internal and external trade, so that consumption is encouraged by the greater variety of goods available, and the maintenance of unproductive consumers who will sustain demand when other classes are saving hard for the sake of accumulation. But just as the workers can only pay for goods equal in value to their total wages, so the unproductive consumers to whom Malthus appeals can only pay for goods equal in value to their own incomes, which are equivalent to rent, taxes and other expenses of capitalists, plus the portion of his profits that he spends on servants. It is impossible for them to realise the profits on investment as well, given the fact that no deviation of planned saving from planned investment is allowed. This is a very elementary mistake.

But although Malthus's attempt to justify the expenditure of the unproductive consumers can be dismissed out of hand, and in spite of the fact that much of his attempt to argue the case for the possibility of a general glut clarified nothing at all and indeed would have led the discussion off on entirely the wrong track, nevertheless his contribution is an interesting one since when he argues that investment only creates demand equivalent to the extra consumption of workers, he brings out a source of confusion in the classical conception of investment which the static analyses of Mill and Ricardo are not adequate to expose.

In sum, it is obvious that Malthus, in spite of his instinctive rejection of the idea that general overproduction was impossible, had great difficulty in developing an effective counter-theory. In his correspondence with Ricardo and in several places in the *Principles* he relied on an analogy between the economy as a whole and the production of one commodity within this whole, but this is obviously illegitimate since in the former case additional demand can come only from within the system whereas in the latter it can come from the outside. In the one case where Malthus does produce a significant objection, the logic of the argument is that any accumulation would lead to a glut, whereas he tries to argue only that beyond a certain point accumulation will cause a glut. This is indeed a problem not just with Malthus but with all those underconsumptionists who have argued that there could be excessive saving. Malthus's own solution, the consumption of the unproductive consumers, depicted as if the demand came out of nowhere and was not an element of the cost of production of commodities, only shows once again how far he was from an accurate conception of the movement and interrelations of the economy as a whole, and how far he was from a real solution to the difficulties he was presented with.

What, then, is the relationship between Malthus and Lauderdale and Spence? I have pointed out that Spence made a definite advance on Lauderdale, in putting forward a consistently underconsumptionist position. Spence, however, was unable to pinpoint any important difficulties in Mill's arguments. Malthus, at his best moments, and only in the *Principles*, comes close to doing this, but he makes the error of forgetting about the production of a stock of wage-goods to be advanced to the newly-employed workers. In any case, he is unable to propose a serious solution to the problem, and tends to mystify the discussion with the use of his theory of value. Nevertheless, "Say's Law" advocates could have learnt something from Malthus's book, since it might have led them to a more profound, dynamic analysis of the question.

THE FOLLOWERS OF MALTHUS

In 1822, an anonymous pamphlet entitled *Considerations on the Accumulation of Capital* was published, which essentially repeats the arguments of Malthus himself. The author states that:

> It is no doubt true, that a diminution of unproductive consumption may occasionally be essential to the increase of wealth; but, whenever such is the case, it will be found that its proportion has been previously unduly increased, and that commodities destined for productive consumption i.e. necessaries, are comparatively scarce and yield high profits.
> The errors of those who conceive that saving cannot be carried too far, consists in their not perceiving that excessive parsimony diminishes the demand for luxuries i.e. commodities of unproductive consumption, at the same time as it increases the supply of them.[48]

The author differs from Malthus, however, on one point: he makes a distinction within unproductive consumption, between money which is spent on the maintenance of unproductive labour and money which is spent directly on commodities. The aim of this distinction is to separate demand for commodities from demand for labour, productive or unproductive, because the author perceives a point of importance here. He claims that demand for labour is not demand for commodities, and that only "the revenue which is immediately exchanged for the produce of labour" creates a demand for commodities.[49] It appears as if he is suggesting that to employ a servant creates no demand for any commodities. The question is confused here by the author's tendency to use the term unproductive consumption to mean purchase and consumption of luxuries, and productive consumption to mean purchase and consumption of necessaries, or wage-goods, which although he is aware that this is strictly incorrect[50] he justifies on the grounds of "avoiding circumlocution". The problem is that the consumption of menial servants is now excluded from unproductive consumption, which is undoubtedly contrary to the regular use of the term.

But the author in fact sees the question of whether money is spent on commodities or on labour as the crucial question. He says that if the landlords stop spending their incomes on manufactures and prefer instead to maintain a set of idle retainers, there will be a big drop in the demand for these manufactures, and continues:

> It is important to remark that this falling off in the demand for commodities would not be compensated by an increase of demand in any other quarter. It would not be a mere transfer of demand from some particular species of commodities to others, but an utter annihilation of demand to the extent of the revenue to which this new direction had been given.[51]

On the argument that money employed as capital promotes demand just as much as money that is spent, the author admits that demand for food and necessaries is created by investment, but he claims that if the money is spent on commodities, the demand for these commodities will be in addition to the demand for necessaries for the labourers employed in their production. Thus in the second case there are two demands instead of one.[52] This is a simple mistake of double-counting.

Apart from this, the author's position is simply that investment reduces demand relative to supply and that to prevent a glut a certain level of unproductive consumption must be maintained — a position which we are familiar with from Spence and Malthus.

Ten years later, another parson, Thomas Chalmers, pub-

lished a book on *Political Economy*. He gives his statements about
the question of gluts an arithmetic precision which is notably
absent in Malthus. He says: suppose capitalists are laying out
£10m each year in trade, with a rate of profit of 10 per cent, so
that their annual revenue is £1m. If they save 1/5 of this and add
it to their capital, so that next year £10.2m is laid out, this will
have a terrible effect on the rate of profit:

> Anterior to the general saving that we now imagine,
> capitalists, for the prime cost of £10m, receive, in the whole
> price of their commodities, £11m. But since that saving, they,
> for the prime cost of £10.2m, receive the same sum of £11m.
> By the saving in question, they have become at once richer in
> capital and poorer in revenue. For the £200,000 which they
> have added to the one, they have sustained a greatly
> overpassing loss; for they have taken £200,000 and that
> yearly, from the other.[53]

Thus accumulation cannot take place, save at the expense of
the general revenue of capitalists, for an extra £200,000 laid out
has reduced their profits from £1m to £800,000.[54] Chalmers
seems to think that the capital laid out and the profits received
must necessarily add up to a fixed sum — so if the capitalists
accumulate all their revenue, they in fact find themselves with
nothing to live on! This apparently absurd conclusion is in fact
quite consistent with an interpretation of investment which
forgets, as Malthus appears to do, that wage-goods are *advanced*
to labourers and therefore have to be produced in the previous
period. If we do forget this, then investment simply consists of a
transfer of consumption from capitalists to the newly-employed
labourers plus an increment in production. Then expenditure
by capitalists on their own consumption is reduced by the
amount of the investment, so their profits must fall proportionately. This conclusion is a logical step from what Malthus
had said, but Malthus himself was obviously not prepared to
open himself up to ridicule by saying it.

Chalmers's book is the last contribution worthy of discussion.
There are occasional echos of the ideas of the underconsumptionists, as in the *Letters on the Rudiments of a Science* by Patrick
Plough, "a yeoman in the country" to his sons in town, which
vehemently attack the idea that parsimony is the road to wealth,
but they have no theoretical interest.

CONCLUSION

My conclusions are short, as they have been prefigured in the text.

The aim of this chapter was to show the development of the over-saving type of underconsumption theory in Britain in the early nineteenth century. The distinguishing feature of this type is the role ascribed to the level of savings. It is assumed by all the authors of this time that planned savings and investment move together and that hoarding is insignificant. If this were not so, the writers we have examined would not be underconsumptionists, since the demand for consumption goods would no longer play the unique central role. With these assumptions, the level of saving becomes the reverse side of the demand for consumption goods.

The general position of these writers is that there is a limit above which the rate of accumulation becomes dangerously high, threatening to precipitate a slump. But the logic of the argument as they develop it is that this limit is in fact a zero rate of accumulation, as is effectively pointed out by Chalmers. Thus they are caught in a trap, in which either they must draw back from the brink and discard part of their results, or they must openly state the absurdity of their conclusions. This impasse is partly the result of the prevailing conception of investment, although this conception does not necessarily lead to these conclusions. I shall discuss this fully in Chapter Five.

NOTES

1 A.Smith, *The Wealth of Nations*, pp.437–8.
2 R.L.Meek, *The Economics of Physiocracy*, pp.313–44.
3 F.Quesnay, *Analyse du Tableau Economique* (1766), translated in Meek, op.cit., p.120.
4 R.L.Meek, op.cit., pp.120–1.
5 Lord Lauderdale, *An Inquiry . . .*, pp.6–7.
6 ibid, pp.56–7.
7 ibid, p.27.
8 ibid, pp.111–2.
9 ibid, pp.208–9.
10 ibid, pp.214–5.

11 ibid, p.73.
12 ibid, pp.87–8.
13 ibid, p.220.
14 ibid, pp.221–2.
15 ibid, pp.245–6.
16 W.Spence, in *Spence and Mill on Commerce*, p.22.
17 ibid, p.33.
18 ibid, pp.33–4.
19 ibid, pp.34–5.
20 ibid, pp.36–7.
21 J.Mill, in *Spence and Mill on Commerce*, p.13.
22 ibid, p.23.
23 ibid, p.67.
24 ibid, p.70.
25 ibid, pp.71–2.
26 ibid, pp.81–2.
27 W.Spence, *Agriculture the Source of Wealth of Great Britain*, pp.108–9.
28 ibid, p.157.
29 ibid, p.158.
30 ibid, p.160.
31 ibid, p.161.
32 ibid, p.161.
33 By this I do not mean that other writers (eg Malthus) may not
    display Physiocratic influences but that these do not have the direct
    impact on their general glut theories that they do in Spence.
34 D.Ricardo, *Works*, Vol 6, pp.131–2.
35 ibid, pp.133–4.
36 ibid, p.134.
37 ibid, pp.131–2.
38 ibid, p.142.
39 T.Malthus, *Principles* . . . 1st ed, pp.8–9. There are some differences
    between this and the second edition as regards phraseology, and
    occasionally whole paragraphs have been left out or added in.
    However, no important changes were made on the subject with
    which we are concerned, and no significance should be attached to
    which edition is referred to.
40 ibid 2nd ed, p.314.
41 M.Paglin, *Malthus and Lauderdale*, p.116.
42 ibid, p.117.
43 Malthus, *Principles* . . . 1st ed, p.32.
44 Quoted in Malthus, op.cit. 1st ed, pp.359–60.
45 ibid 2nd ed, p.361.
46 ibid 1st ed, p.359.
47 ibid 2nd ed, p.364.

48 *Considerations . . .* pp.15–6.
49 ibid, p.45.
50 ibid, footnote p.9.
51 ibid, pp.48–9. There is a handwritten note in the British Museum copy which runs: "I have in fact expressed myself too strongly in this passage, because the surplus in the hands of the labourer might be so employed as to create a demand for commodities."
52 ibid, pp.42–3.
53 T.Chalmers, *On Political Economy*, p.88.
54 ibid, p.90.

3

J.C.L.SIMONDE DE SISMONDI

In 1848, reviewing the socialist and communist literature that had gone before them, Marx and Engels said:

> In countries like France, where the peasants constitute far more than half of the population, it was natural that writers who sided with the proletariat against the bourgeoisie, should use, in their criticism of the bourgeois regime, the standard of the peasant and the petty bourgeois, and from the standpoint of these intermediate classes should take up the cudgels of the working class. Thus arose petty-bourgeois socialism. Sismondi was the head of this school, not only in France but also in England.
>
> This school of socialism dissected with great acuteness the contradictions in the conditions of modern production. It laid bare the hypocritical apologies of the economists. It proved, incontrovertibly, the disastrous effects of machinery and division of labour; the concentration of capital and land in a few hands; overproduction and crises; it pointed out the inevitable ruin of the petty bourgeois and peasant, the misery of the proletariat, the anarchy in production, the crying inequalities in the distribution of wealth, the industrial war of extermination between nations, the dissolution of the old moral bonds, of the old family relations, of the old nationalities.
>
> In its positive aims, however, this form of Socialism aspires either to restoring the old means of production and of exchange, and with them the old property relations, and the old society, or to cramping the modern means of production and of exchange, within the framework of the old property relations that have been, and were bound to be, exploded by

those means. In either case, it is both reactionary and Utopian.[1]

This summary of Sismondi's contribution shows how different he is from his English contemporaries. The point of view expressed by the English underconsumptionists was very much that of the landed aristocracy: Spence wrote a pamphlet defending the Corn Laws, Malthus inveighed against the Ricardian idea that the interests of the landlord and those of the other classes in society are fundamentally opposed over the price of agricultural products, and all of them looked to the rich consumers to fill the gap left by excessive accumulation. It is Marx once again who has provided us with an accurate assessment of the significance of the English debates:

Malthus correctly draws the conclusions from his basic theory of value. But this theory, for its part, suits his purpose remarkably well — an apologia for the existing state of affairs in England, for landlordism, "State and Church", pensioners, tax-gatherers, tenths, national debt, stockjobbers, beadles, parsons and menial servants ("national expenditure") assailed by the Ricardians as so many useless and superannuated drawbacks of bourgeois production and as nuisances. For all that, Ricardo championed bourgeois production insofar as it signified the most unrestricted development of the social productive forces, unconcerned for the fate of those who participate in production, be they capitalists or workers. He insisted upon the *historical* justification and necessity of this stage of development. His very lack of a historical sense meant that he regarded everything from the historical standpoint of his time. Malthus also wishes to see the freeest possible development of capitalist production, however only insofar as the condition of this development is the poverty of its main basis, the working classes, but at the same time, he wants it to adapt itself to the "consumption needs" of the aristocracy and its branches in State and Church, to serve as material basis for the antiquated claims of the representatives of interests inherited from feudalism and the absolute monarchy. Malthus wants bourgeois production as long as it is not revolutionary, constitutes no historical factor of development but merely creates a broader and more comfortable basis for the "old" society.[2]

These two quotations speak for themselves.

From the point of view of the immediate history of underconsumption theories, the social aspects are of great importance: if one wanted to explain, for example, why Sismondi's ideas had a negligible impact in Britain, or why Malthusian theories had more or less died out by the 1840's, one could only do it by studying the history of Britain at this time in its wider aspects. Here, however, we are primarily concerned with theoretical history, and with the theoretical ideas of the underconsumptionists as such rather than with the explanation of the rise and fall of support for these ideas. If I have chosen to set aside Sismondi for a chapter of his own, apart from his contemporaries (for from a chronological point of view he should appear in the middle of the last chapter), it is because his is a very different type of underconsumption theory from theirs — one could say *the* other major type of underconsumption theory in the nineteenth century. These theoretical differences undoubtedly have an intimate connection with the differing social views of Malthus and Sismondi, and any history which failed to take account of them would be incomplete. But whilst recognising this it would be a great mistake to reduce the theoretical differences to epiphenomena of social ideologies, as if for instance Malthus's ideas were uniquely determined by the fact of his being an ideologist of the landed interest. For this reason I focus on the theories themselves, only drawing attention to their social implications and reflections in passing.

Sismondi himself, a Swiss by birth, was not, as he readily admitted, primarily an economist. He was an intellectual with a very wide range of interests who had written a 31-volume "History of the French People", and an equally impressive "History of the Italian Republics in the Middle Ages". Although he established great prestige for himself by this (see the list under his name on the title-page of the *Nouveaux Principes d'Economie Politique*), in economics he was always a maverick, lonely figure whom it is difficult not to compare to Hobson. He had a tremendous sympathy for and awareness of human suffering, and this is what brings him to a clash with the established truths of the science of political economy. He cannot accept that we are investigating the increase of wealth pure and simple, as if it had no relevance to the lives of our fellow men.

He had an enormous reverence for the works of Adam Smith,

and in 1803 he published a book entitled *De la Richesse Commerciale*, which made no pretence at all of originality but aimed simply to propagate the ideas of Smith on the Continent. Over the years, however, his attitude gradually changed. While he still regards Smith as the greatest contributor to political economy, to whom even the best of his predecessors bears no comparison, he can no longer share the great optimism with which Smith regarded a world based upon the freedom of trade and the accumulation of capital. But for a long time his attention was drawn elsewhere, and he did not find the time to work out fully his new opinions. "For more than 15 years since I had written on 'Commercial Wealth' ", he says, "I had read very few books on political economy; but I had not stopped studying the facts".[3] Nevertheless, things gradually clarified themselves in his mind, to the point where he felt he could see Adam Smith's mistakes:

> Some of them appeared to me foreign to the principles I had adopted. Suddenly they seemed to me to classify themselves, to explain each other, by the new development I gave to my theory. The more I progressed the more I persuaded myself of the importance and the truth of the modifications I brought to the system of Adam Smith. Everything which had up till now remained obscure in the science, considered from this new point of view, made itself clear, and my principles gave me the solution to difficulties which I had not dreamed of before.[4]

These new ideas got a first airing in an article entitled "Political Economy", written by Sismondi in 1815 for Sir Daniel Brewster's *Edinburgh Encyclopaedia.*[5] They only appear in a fully developed form, however, with the publication of the first edition of the *Nouveaux Principes d' Economie Politique* four years later. In this book he defines his relation to Adam Smith as one of developing and completing the latter's work. He accepts the essential features of his theory, but he feels that the experience of half a century since Smith's book was published has shown that his practical conclusions were erroneous, erroneous to such an extent as to be close to the complete opposite of what is correct. Sismondi says:

We profess, with Adam Smith, that labour is the sole original source of wealth, that parsimony is the only means of accumulating it; but we add that enjoyment is the sole aim of that accumulation, and that there is no growth of national wealth, except when there is also a growth of national enjoyments.[6]

This sentence expresses very well the humanist revulsion which Sismondi feels against Smith's mode of reasoning, once he had himself become convinced that the facts of life did not justify Smith's approach. He insists that the aim of government in economic matters is not just to ensure the accumulation of wealth and the increase of the powers of production — as was taken for granted by British political economy — but to ensure the happiness of the whole society, its poorest members included. He is severely impressed by the sufferings of the working class, as also by the misery of the peasants in the past and in the present where the organisation of agriculture is not to their advantage.

Sismondi's account of the development from the isolated hunter to modern society is different in emphasis from Smith's, in stressing the evolution of class divisions as it affects the labourer himself. Smith points out the role of the division of labour in the development of the productive powers of society. Sismondi draws out the social implications of these developments. He says: whereas the isolated hunter works in order to be able to rest, "social man" works only in order that someone else may rest; the efforts are separated from the rewards. The indefinite development of the productive powers of labour can result only in the increase of luxury and the enjoyments of the rich, since if this wealth was distributed evenly and the workers had a share of it, they would immediately prefer to work less and be a little less rich than to work as long hours as they do now. So, Sismondi concludes, the progress of industry can result only in increasing inequalities amongst men.[7] The only remedy for this is for the State to intervene to correct the situation, using legislation to equalise the distribution and reduce the working hours:

We have seen that the rich can increase their wealth, either by a new production, or in taking for themselves a greater part of what was formerly reserved for the poor; and, to regulate this division, to make it equitable, we almost always invoke that intervention of the government that Adam Smith rejected. We look to the government to be the protector of the weak against the strong, the defender of he who cannot defend himself, and the representative of the permanent but quiet interest of all, against the temporary but passionate interest of each.[8]

This is where Sismondi's practical conclusions diverge from those of British political economy.

He expresses similar sentiments on agricultural questions. Here he is a partisan of "patriarchal cultivation" — individual peasant agriculture. This is the form which produces the best results in terms of efficient use of the soil, for because the producer does not share the product with anyone else, he takes much greater care of the land. Knowledge of the characteristics of each particular field is passed on from father to son. Furthermore, the moral character of the individual landholder is much superior to the rest of the agricultural population, because of the habits of order and economy induced by the possession of property. In short, "no social organisation guarantees more happiness and more virtue to the most numerous class of the nation, more opulence to all, more stability to the public order."[9]

So the division of society into rich and poor is the central theme of Sismondi's work, and it is to this that he attributes the root cause of crises. The workers are too poor to buy their own product. This argument is fully elaborated only in the *Nouveaux Principes*, but by 1815 we can already see some movement away from Smithian formulations of the problem, and a search for a new approach. In his Encyclopaedia article he says:

By a circular concatenation, in which every effect becomes a cause in its turn, production gives revenue, revenue furnishes and regulates a consumable fund, which fund again causes production and measures it. The national wealth continues to augment and the state to prosper, so long as these three quantities, which are proportional to each other, continue to augment in a gradual manner; but whenever the proportion among them is broken the state decays.[10]

To cause distress in the state, it is enough that this equilibrium
be broken. Production may diminish because capital is consumed; consumption may diminish because of the poverty of the
labourers; revenue may diminish because production creates
less revenue than usual. So nations can fall into ruin equally by
spending too much or by spending too little, because equally
they destroy the equilibrium between production, revenue and
consumption.

Suppose there is a shift of funds from unproductive to
productive consumption.

> This employment of the national produce in giving move-
> ment to new labour, though it does not destroy the balance
> between production and consumption, renders it much more
> complex. The new produce thus obtained must at last find a
> consumer; and though it may be generally affirmed, that to
> increase the labour is to increase the wealth, and with it in
> similar proportion the revenue and the consumption; still it is
> anything but proved, that by the increase of its labour, a
> nation may not altogether deviate from the proper rate of
> consumption, and thus ruin itself by economy as well as by
> prodigality. Happily, in most cases, the increase of capital, of
> revenue, and of consumption requires no superintendence;
> they proceed of their own accord with an equal pace; and
> where one of them at any time, happens to pass the others for
> an instant, foreign commerce is almost always ready to restore
> the equilibrium.[11]

That is as far as he goes in the *Encyclopaedia* article. The most
striking thing about it is its vagueness: he talks about the
equilibrium between production, consumption and revenue and
the "circular concatenation" linking them, but exactly what the
relation between them is he never specifies. We can recognise
something of Adam Smith in it: in the discussion of the relation
between production and consumption such that if the latter
exceeds the former the country is living off its capital. But there
is much more in these passages than that. Let us start with the
first quotation. Sismondi does not just take production and
consumption but includes a third term, revenue, as well. It is
necessary that they should be kept in strict proportion for
"whenever the proportion among them is broken the state
decays". But he gives no indication as to what the relation

between these three variables is, and in particular we may ask how it is possible for revenue to diverge from production. In 1803 Sismondi had said quite definitely that the annual product of labour must comprise the whole national revenue,[12] but now he is worried about the consequences if "the production give a revenue smaller than usual, in which case a part of the capital must pass to the fund of consumption".[13] Here we can imagine a single capitalist who has to sell at a loss being forced to touch some of his reserves in order to live as comfortably as before, but the precise meaning of this on the scale of the whole economy as opposed to the single individual is by no means clear.

The second passage discusses the problem of accumulation. There is a definitely Malthusian air about the speculation that a nation may ruin itself by economy as much as by prodigality because of a deviation from the proper rate of consumption, but Sismondi seems content to assert that his three variables will increase at roughly an equal pace, without discussing what determines the pace at which they increase. Indeed the whole article suffers from total vagueness in this respect. Sismondi is so bemused by his "circular concatenations" that he is unable to give an exposition of what precisely the relation between the variables is.

THE 'NEW PRINCIPLES'

The same ideas are repeated in Book 2 Chapter 6 of the *Nouveaux Principes.* Revenue determines expenditure; expenditure must absorb the whole of production; the absolute consumption determines whether production next year is equal or greater, and revenue is born out of this production. Wealth increases, so long as the absolute consumption determines always a higher reproduction, and so long as the other parts of wealth follow it at an equal pace. But if the proportion is broken, a crisis ensues. Suppose that the rich save a little to add to their capital, so that production is increased. The saving done last year creates new revenue this year. But to do this too much would be ruinous, for:

It is the revenue of last year which must pay for this year's production; it is a predetermined quantity which serves as a measure for the indefinite quantity of labour to come. The mistake of those who urge unlimited production comes from their confusion of past revenue with future revenue. They have said that to increase the labour, is to increase the wealth, and with it the revenue, and hence the consumption. But one only increases the wealth in increasing the labour demanded, the labour which is paid for at its proper price; and this price, fixed in advance, is the pre-existing revenue. In the end one merely exchanges the totality of this year's production against the totality of the previous year's.[14]

Malthus thought this was a valueless piece of analysis; but Jean Weiller, in his introduction to the 1971 edition of Sismondi's book, follows Schumpeter in seeing in this the essence of a truly dynamic analysis of a sort which Sismondi's contemporaries had not produced, since it recognises that the income expended in period t was produced in period $t-1$, while the income corresponding to period t becomes available only in period $t+1$.[15] In my view it is right to point out the dynamic aspects of this analysis, for the usual formulation of "Say's Law" at this time ran purely in terms of comparative statics, with no indication of how the progress from one situation to the other was achieved. It is therefore a step forward to look closely at the relation between successive time-periods. But the value of the passage should not be exaggerated. For instance, the period taken by Sismondi is one year, and yet no one could have been more aware than himself that a worker must spend his income within a week after he first receives it, since this is his only basis of survival. The worker clearly pays for this year's product with this year's revenue.

If Sismondi is saying here that if all profits are invested, then the amount of investment is measured by the level of profits just received, this is acceptable; but it is not correct to present this as an exchange of this year's production against last year's, since firstly, the profits do not represent the whole of last year's production, and secondly, for the statement to be true, there would have to be no profit on this year's production. What we can note, however, is that Sismondi has taken the crucial step of asserting that it is production that depends on consumption: "the absolute consumption determines an equal or superior reproduction". In making consumption the variable that decides the course of national wealth, he has decisively reversed the formulation of Mill and Ricardo.

We should not move on without mentioning the following passage:

> Production is stopped as soon as it can no longer exchange against revenue. If suddenly the whole rich class resolved to live from its labour like the poorest, and to add all its revenue to its capital, the workers, who counted on this exchange for their living, would be reduced to despair and would die of hunger.[16]

This sounds very Malthusian; but actually it says nothing specifically about accumulation, and since he is assuming that the rich suddenly decide to become workers, it is likely that he has in mind that they simply hoard the money which they no longer spend.

Later on in the book, in Chapter 4 of Book 4, entitled "How Commercial Wealth follows the Growth of Revenue", Sismondi produces a theory of crisis based on the increasing inequality of distribution already mentioned. The crucial question, he says, is the distribution of income: "The equality of enjoyments must always have as a result the continual extension of the market for the producers, their inequality must always make it shrink."[17] This is so because:

> The same revenue is indeed used by the rich and the poor, but it is not used in the same fashion. The first replaces much more capital and much less revenue than the second; he aids the population much less, and consequently is much less useful to the reproduction of wealth.[18]

The same total revenue, when very unequally distributed, is spent on a very different collection of products from when it is more or less equally distributed. With very unequal distribution, the mass of poor can afford only essentials and do not provide much of a market for manufacturers, while the few rich, rather than buying a vast mass of goods with their wealth, go for quality — the better-worked, more finished goods — and will spend a lot of money on foreign luxuries. Thus the vast majority of manufacturers, who had a good market for their products with equal distribution of incomes, now find themselves out of work. It is one of the inherent contradictions of the growth of large-scale industry, that, by replacing a man-made product by a necessarily inferior machine-made one, it excludes its own products from the consumption of the rich.

> Thus by the concentration of fortunes in the hands of a small number of owners, the internal market is all the time shrinking, and industry is more and more reduced to looking for outlets in foreign markets, where it is threatened by greater revolutions.[19]

This is the fundamental force behind the explosion of English commerce, and the sale of English manufactures all over the world. However, if this is the explanation of the intensity of commercial rivalry, nevertheless Sismondi is not under the impression that from the point of view of the world economy this represents a solution to the problem he has highlighted.

Everywhere, says Sismondi, the quantity of goods for sale is greater than the number of people who want to buy them. This fact shows itself in many ways, in many places. Why is it that the philosophers do not want to see what stares the common man in the face? Their mistake is that they are trapped by the false principle that the annual production is the same thing as the annual revenue. Both Say and Ricardo think that there is no capital that cannot be employed in a country, because the only limit to demand is production, and so the additional capital effectively creates the demand for its own products. With this principle, one cannot possibly explain the most obvious fact of the history of commerce, the glutting of markets.

So it is the inequality in the distribution of income, and in particular the restricted consumption of the masses of the population, that forces industry to look for markets abroad. This is Sismondi's explanation of crises.

Is this an acceptable theory? We can see in it the germ of present-day debates on the relation of the distribution of income to the possibilities of development of a country, and certainly Sismondi is not the last person to present this kind of argument. But Sismondi does not elaborate his theory rigorously enough, and in particular he fails to separate the question of overproduction from that of the demand for labour. When he first mentions the problem he discusses the fact that a rich man likes much more finished, more precious products than his poorer counterparts, and tends to favour the existence of a few highly skilled, highly paid labourers. Thus a less equal distribution of income will give employment to fewer labourers in toto. In addition, he says, it is the rich who are responsible for so many workers being active in unproductive occupations, which add nothing to the national wealth. In this way he tries to give the impression that a more equal distribution of income is more favourable to the increase of wealth because more people are employed in productive occupations such as manufacturing. This argument is insufficient because he fails to show the relation between the distribution of the working population and the level of accumulation of capital, which is the important variable from the point of view of the growth of national wealth.

The chief defect of Sismondi's analysis is that he does not consider the circulation of money and goods and the economic relations between the various classes of the population in sufficient detail. For instance, in the example just mentioned, the highly skilled, highly paid artisans represent precisely the kind of consumer that Sismondi maintains is necessary to the growth of large-scale industry, and yet he does not consider the demand which they constitute at all. The same defect applies to his assertion that the growth of large-scale industry undermines its own market. To illustrate: suppose, following Sismondi's example, we assume that workers spend all their money on goods produced in the capitalist sector of the economy, while the capitalists spend all their money with the artisan sector. Like Sismondi, we leave investment out of account (that is, net investment equals zero). Now the expenditure of the workers accounts for their own wages only, so that unless other buyers can be found for the products of the capitalist sector, there will be no profits. The artisans live off the expenditure of the capitalists. They can either spend their money amongst themselves or they can spend it with the capitalist sector. The degree to which artisans spend amongst themselves in fact makes no difference to the issue, and so the source of profits is in fact, contrary to first appearances, the expenditure by the capitalists with the artisans. So Sismondi's argument is incorrect insofar as this is the basis of it, while his point about the tendency of the rich to buy foreign goods is irrelevant on a world scale. His position is superficially appealing but is really based upon an elementary mistake, as Malthus was the first to recognise.

The essence of Sismondi's position is that it is the poverty of the workers which is responsible for crises. This is what distinguishes him theoretically from the early British underconsumptionists, for their theories were always based on the possibility of an excessive degree of saving, and since it was generally accepted that workers did not save, the important classes were therefore the capitalists and the landlords. To an important degree, these represent the two basic types of underconsumption theories, since in the period with which we are concerned the fundamental premise of any writer can be put down to one of these types.

DEBATE WITH MCCULLOCH AND RICARDO

McCulloch attempted to refute Sismondi's arguments in an article in the *Edinburgh Review*. He said:

> Demand and supply are truly correlative and convertible terms. The supply of one set of commodities constitutes the demand for another.[20]

Suppose a cultivator advances food and clothing for 100 labourers, who raise for him food for 200 labourers, and that a manufacturer likewise advances food and clothing for 100 labourers, and gets back clothing for 200 labourers.* Then they will exchange, and how can there possibly be a glut? McCulloch then multiplies the figures by 1,000 to give a whole society, and asks what happens if 1,000 new capitalists with 100 labourers each appear in agricultural production. Then there will be a glut in agriculture, but a corresponding boom in manufactures, and as soon as half of these new capitalists shift into manufactures, equilibrium will once again be restored.

Now suppose because of the introduction of new machinery productivity and output is doubled in manufacturing. Then manufactures will halve in value relative to agricultural products, and so the doubled quantity of manufactures is exactly equal in value to the former quantity. Hence there can be no glut.

> Demand will increase in the same ratio with supply, and the power of consumption keep pace with the power of production.[22]

---

*This example is in fact absurd because the labourers consume all the product and the capitalists starve!

Sismondi wrote a reply the following year.[22] He protests first of all that McCulloch has assumed precisely what is in question with regard to price, by talking only of cost of production. The real question, he says, is whether goods can be sold at the cost of production.[23] He produces a counter-example, the Leipzig book trade. Each merchant brings to Leipzig each year 40 or 50 copies of each of the 4 or 5 books he has printed, and goes home with as many books, but each of them different. This is the demand and the production, which, according to McCulloch, are correlative and convertible. But the point is this: he who brings a bad book, or one which everyone bought the year before, will find himself at the end with his book unsold; there will be no demand for his product.[24] Now, what does this example of the Leipzig book trade amount to theoretically?

It could be seen as a very good example of what McCulloch is saying; for if each merchant brings the right books everything goes smoothly and there is no interruption in the circulation. Bringing the wrong books amounts simply to not adjusting the production to the demand.

But there is a deeper aspect to it. If one merchant brings a book which he cannot sell, he is also unable to buy; as a result, a larger number of merchants (those who would have sold him a book) find themselves with an unsaleable surplus product. The bad judgment of one producer has provoked a general crisis. The significance of the example is that it highlights the uncertainty with which the producer of commodities is always faced, in that he can never be sure of his market. There are bound to be errors, and these errors have ramifications throughout the whole economy.

Say, Mill, Ricardo, McCulloch: they all present the question as if the smooth adjustment of production to demand is a minor irritant. Sismondi does not accept this, and although his example does not directly refute the theory of the impossibility of general overproduction since it could be explained as a simple demonstration of the consequences of producing the wrong goods, it nevertheless shows a sharp awareness of what Marx called the anarchy of capitalist production: the uncertainties which the producer faces are always considerable and the problems of adjustment may thus become extremely complicated. In other words, Sismondi is challenging the idea of the "invisible hand" by whose grace capitalist production manages to run smoothly and without fundamental difficulties.

In 1823, Sismondi had the opportunity to discuss these matters for a few days with Ricardo, and in an article entitled *Sur la Balance des Consommations avec les Productions* published the following year, he tries to give an overall view of the debates. Say and Ricardo, he says, have maintained that the economist need only concern himself with the production of wealth, because they see consumption as following production, and as always being sufficient to prevent a glut on the market. Malthus and Sismondi, on the other hand, have maintained that consumption is not at all the necessary consequence of production, and that the most obvious sign of prosperity is a growing demand for labour.[25] He then goes into a long example. Take a farm employing 10 labourers, and suppose productivity is increased by 50 per cent. The farmer can now sell the same quantity of corn as before (plus a bit more) at the same price, while ridding himself of three of his workers and correspondingly reducing his expenses. The industries producing manufactures consumed by workers will experience a loss of demand, while the industries producing luxury goods will experience a boom, because of the increase in the farmer's profits. Workers shift from one industry to the other, and at the end of the adjustment, we arrive, like Ricardo, at the conclusion that production has created a consumption. But, says Sismondi, we have abstracted completely from time and space, and from all the obstacles to this adjustment.[26] Yet these are precisely the important elements. Machines have to be built in the luxury industries. Where does the capital come from to pay for them? And what happens if the labourers thrown out of work in agriculture are unfit for any other occupation? They will stay in agriculture and wages there will be forced down, thus aggravating the situation.

This amounts to an explicit statement of what is implied in the example of the Leipzig book trade.

Sismondi gives the impression of profound insight buried in the midst of considerable confusion. It is some years, basically until the publication of the 1824 article we have just examined, before he can work out thoroughly what his criticisms of the "Say's Law" proposition are, and his early attempts — especially the *Encyclopaedia* article — are worth very little indeed. In the end, his critique has two prongs:

(a) the difficulties of adjustment, which mean that a sudden change can precipitate what can only be called a general crisis;

(b) the theory expounded in the *Nouveaux Principes*, based on the inequality of the distribution of income associated with large-scale manufacturing production.

These two lines of attack work on different levels. The first is not so much a theoretical critique as a challenge to the conception of capitalist production which is implied in the propositions of Mill and McCulloch, as a harmonious smoothly-running economic machine. Fundamentally, this conception is as common to Spence and Malthus as it is to Ricardo. The second line is definitely a theoretical critique, in the sense that it attempts to prove theoretically the possibility of a general glut, and therefore to disprove directly the opponents' arguments. Here his theory is based on the poverty of workers, whose income is pressed down to the minimum required for them to live and raise a family. With the development of the powers of production, and especially with the transition from individual artisan to capitalist machine production, income distribution becomes more and more unequal, but the sale of the products of machine industry requires a relatively equal distribution. Hence the growth of capitalist production is accompanied by a glutting of markets and increasingly fierce competition between the various capitalist nations.

The implication of Sismondi's theory is that capitalist production cannot last as it is since it "cuts its own throat", and the only solution is for the government to intervene radically in the economic sphere. These practical conclusions run right against the accepted truths of contemporary political economy.

The historical significance of Sismondi (from a theoretical point of view) is that he is the first person to elaborate an underconsumption theory based on the distribution of income between workers and capitalists.

NOTES

1 K.Marx and F.Engels, *Selected Works*, pp.55–6.
2 K.Marx, *Theories of Surplus Value Part III*, pp.51–2.

3 J.C.L.Simonde de Sismondi, *Nouveaux Principes d'Economie Politique* (NPEP) 1st edition, Vol 1, p.iii.
4 ibid, pp.iii–iv.
5 Sir D.Brewster's *Edinburgh Encyclopaedia*, Vol 17, pp.37–78.
6 NPEP 1st ed, Vol 1, p.52.
7 NPEP Book 1 Ch 3.
8 NPEP 1st ed, Vol 1, pp.54–5.
9 NPEP Book 3 Ch 3.
10 *Edinburgh Encyclopaedia*, Vol 17, p.44.
11 ibid, p.45.
12 *De la Richesse Commerciale*, Vol 1, p.85.
13 *Edinburgh Encyclopaedia*, Vol 17, p.44.
14 NPEP 1st ed, Vol 1, p.112.
15 NPEP ed J.Weiller, p.16.
16 NPEP 1st ed, Vol 1, p.82.
17 ibid, p.331.
18 ibid, p.331.
19 ibid, p.336.
20 J.R.McCulloch, *Mr. Owen's Plans for Relieving the National Distress*, in *Edinburgh Review* Vol 32 No 54, p.470.
21 ibid, p.473.
22 published in *Annales de Jurisprudence* 1820, reprinted in NPEP 2nd ed, Vol 2.
23 NPEP 2nd ed, Vol 2, pp.379–80.
24 ibid, pp.381–2.
25 This article, which first appeared in *Revue Encyclopédique* in 1824, is reprinted in NPEP 2nd ed, Vol 2.
26 NPEP 2nd ed, Vol 2, p.424.

4

RODBERTUS

Rodbertus (Dr.Karl von Rodbertus-Jagetzow) postdates the writers considered above by a clear generation. His *Soziale Briefe an von Kirchmann*, which are the relevant texts for us, appeared only in 1850. An English translation of the second of these letters was published in 1898 by J.B.Clark, under the title *Overproduction and Crises*. An interesting point about this letter, which gives an exposition of von Kirchmann's views as well as Rodbertus's own, is that the discussion amounts to a comparison of a Malthusian with a Sismondian view of crises.

Rodbertus is clearly of the Sismondi rather than of the Malthus school; that is, he sees the insufficient incomes of the workers as the root cause of overproduction. He says to von Kirchmann:

> You, like myself, honoured friend, recognise that it is pauperism and a glutted market that lie at the root of the economic distresses of the time; and no one, I should think, who has sufficiently reflected upon the subject, can fail to perceive this.[1]

But it is not clear that this is in fact correct, to judge by Rodbertus's own account of von Kirchmann's ideas. von Kirchmann argues as follows: he sets up an example of a society with 903 inhabitants, 3 capitalists each employing 300 workers, in which the capitalists take exactly half the annual product. If they all produce wage-goods, they will find themselves unable to sell half their product, for they themselves do not want wage-goods but luxuries. The solution, therefore, is for 450 of their workers to be shifted into luxury production. Now there will be no overproduction. Everything is splendid, until the capitalists decide they want to accumulate. If they invest in the production of wage-goods, obviously they will get the same problem as before: how do they sell the goods that are not bought back by their own workers? But what if they invest in the production of luxuries? The first year they set up and arrange everything, and the second year they start production. But they still find no buyers, because there could be no buyers, except each other, and they do not wish to buy all these extra luxuries because they have decided to save.

> The population is always confronted with this dilemma; the three entrepreneurs must either expend their income to the last penny in comforts and luxuries of every description, in which case all the 900 workmen will at least be able to make a living, even though a miserable one, or if they curtail their luxuries and determine to save, they find no market, the goods accumulate, and part of the workmen will have no work and therefore no means of subsistence.[2]

The affinity of this argument to those of the English underconsumptionists is obvious. It was not, according to von Kirchmann, the only cause of crises, but one of the important ones.[3]

The one substantial difference from the Malthusian argument is that von Kirchmann assumes that a certain amount of time is necessary for investment before production can start; but this only makes all the more glaring his lack of any conception that investment means expenditure on labourers and commodities before any product is produced and therefore represents costs other than the immediate cost of production. It is not even clear that he realises that accumulation creates a demand for labour, but it is extremely unlikely that he does not. The absence of any consideration of the demand created by the act of investment, even though he does take the step — abnormal for early nineteenth century political economy — of recognising that a time period must be allocated for it before production starts, reflects the problems involved in the conception of investment that prevailed at this time. I shall discuss this question fully in the next chapter.

Rodbertus goes back to the labour theory of value. He says:

> All commodities economically regarded must be regarded solely as the product of labour, as costing nothing but labour.[4]

According to him, it follows directly from this that pauperism and crises result from the fact that:

with increasing productiveness of the labour of society, the wages of the labouring classes become an ever smaller portion of the national product.[5]

He is interested above all in relative shares of the national product. The reason for the fall of the workers' share is their lack of bargaining power — due to the proximity of hunger and the competition of their fellows. Thus, when the productiveness of labour is increased, the worker cannot manage to sell his labour-power at a sufficiently increased price for his share of the total product not to fall. Rodbertus, like Sismondi, also looks back nostalgically at the independent artisan.

If every participant in exchange always retained the entire product of his labour, if his purchasing power, therefore, consisted in the market value of the entire product . . . then no glut could arise from an increase in productiveness, either in respect to any *one* or to *all* commodities, until all the participants had received enough of them for their use, until more of them had been produced than is required by society.[6]

There could not possibly be any overproduction in this case. In fact overproduction is not to be expected even when society is divided into three classes: workers, capitalists, landowners — so long as each class always retains an equal share of the product as it increases. But if we leave the "natural" laws of competition to themselves, this will not happen, for the share of the workers will gradually fall:

The purchasing power of the greatest part of society diminishes in proportion to increasing productiveness; and society is placed in the position of producing value-in-use which is no longer market value and purchasing power, while yet the need for it is, in the case of most people, unsatisfied.[7]

In Rodbertus's opinion, then, the fall of the workers' share in the product is the fundamental cause of crises.

But the problem with Rodbertus's theory is: what is the mystique that has attached itself to constant relative shares? Why should it make any difference if they change? Why can the distribution of production not adapt itself accordingly? Rodbertus gives no answer to these questions. The best summary is perhaps a quote from Clark's introduction:

Rodbertus's own theory of gluts reduces them to misdirected production, however little his own language and thought may have made such a reduction. We have only to create, in imagination, the condition that Rodbertus describes — that of a society devoting a fixed fraction of its productive power to making goods for labourers, while the labourers are able to buy and pay for a diminishing share of these goods — in order to see that the trouble would be relieved if a certain portion of the productive power were used for making what other classes desire.[8]

Rodbertus follows Sismondi's idea of increasingly unequal distribution of income, but without Sismondi's explanation of why this is important. In Sismondi the central theme was the contradiction between the growth of large-scale machine industry, and the effects of this in terms of demand for its own products. Rodbertus leaves this part of the argument out, and puts nothing in its place. It is interesting that von Kirchmann and Rodbertus reproduce the conclusions of Malthus's and Sismondi's ideas on crises respectively, without being able (or perhaps without feeling the necessity) to give any theoretical justification for these conclusions. In one sense this is revealing since in both cases it throws into sharp relief the inability of these authors, or any of the underconsumptionists of this period, to understand some of the elementary relations in the general production and circulation of commodities, but in another sense it is a vulgarisation, since Sismondi at least, in his particular way, had important insights into the difficulties of the classical formulation of these problems.

NOTES

1 K.von Rodbertus-Jagetzow, *Overproduction and Crises*, p.19.
2 ibid, p.51 (quoted).
3 ibid, p.68.
4 ibid, p.70.
5 ibid, p.71.
6 ibid, pp.127–8.
7 ibid, pp.130–1.
8 ibid, pp.3–4.

5

RETROSPECT ON THE
EARLY NINETEENTH CENTURY

THE PHYSIOCRATIC LEGACY

In studying the history of underconsumption theories in the first half of the nineteenth century, I have in fact discussed all the major contributions on one side of the debate over the possibility of general overproduction. In this chapter I shall try to explain why it was that those who believed that general overproduction was possible should fall back on an underconsumptionist theory.

The explanation runs in terms of the conceptions current in economic writings of the time, of all shades, in the wake of Adam Smith. In particular I want to stress the retention of the Physiocratic division of the major sectors of the economy by later writers, the classical conception of investment, and the lack of identification of any portion of the national product to be set aside for replacement of worn-out means of production.

The Physiocrats have often been cruelly neglected by British historians of economic thought, but their importance is considerable. Here it is their understanding of the economy as a whole, as a total entity, and of the significant divisions and categorisations of the various branches of production and the inter-relations between them which is relevant. For they achieved a relatively coherent system of theory, some of the assumptions of which were never completely overthrown by Adam Smith and his followers, and it is precisely the incompleteness of the theoretical revolution marked by the publication of *The Wealth of Nations* that lies at the root of the question of underconsumption theories at this time. In this chapter, I shall start by looking at the Physiocratic system, pass on to Adam Smith's attempts to grapple with this heritage and the perspectives opened up by his own theoretical innovations, and then analyse how the degree of success (or failure) of Smith's struggles has determined firstly the specific form in which the "Say's Law" proposition was understood and publicised, and secondly the form of the attempts to challenge it.

The Physiocrats are the first people in the history of economic thought who can be regarded as having founded a system of theory, in the sense that their ideas can be put together into a framework of concepts and of theoretical propositions which together make up a relatively coherent whole. In a sense the proof of this is the *Tableau Economique,* since this manages to express in diagrammatic form the whole Physiocratic conception of the economic aspects of society. The brilliance of this construction is all the greater since earlier political economy had not produced anything in the way of a "rough draft", for the *Tableau Economique* is by no means a mere tabulation of the various economic activities of the country, but is intended to capture in a simple illustration the relations between the various parts of the economy. Of course this does not mean that the Physiocrats dropped out of the blue, in the sense that no elements of their system can be discerned in earlier writings — for no theoretical revolution has ever been accomplished in this way — but their own achievement is that they did create the system in comparison to which earlier writings can only be judged as rudimentary fumblings enlightened by occasional brilliant insights. So if, as Meek has rightly stated, the Physiocrats were taken very seriously by all economic writers in the late eighteenth and early nineteenth centuries, it is because they had earned that attention by their contribution to the foundation of an economic science.

The distinctive feature of the Physiocrats is the role played by agriculture in their system. Agriculture, including also mining and fishing, is regarded as the only economic activity which is ultimately productive of wealth, while other activities, such as manufacturing and commerce, only change the form of objects into something more suitable for human consumption, but they do not in any way add to the value embodied in these commodities or to the total wealth of society. The special role which is attributed to rent in the Physiocratic system is directly linked to the importance of agriculture, because rent is the revenue resulting from the ownership of property in *land,* and is therefore intimately associated with agricultural production. In fact the Physiocrats measured the wealth of a nation by the level of the "net product" accruing to the proprietors of the land after all the expenses of cultivation had been paid, i.e. rent was synonymous with national wealth.

As far as the sovereign and the nation were concerned, therefore, what was demanded of agriculture was that it should produce as large a net product as possible. The Physiocrats had very clear ideas as to how this was to be done: they were unashamed partisans of the development of capitalist agriculture. One of the very first Physiocratic writings, the Encyclopaedia article *Fermiers* written by Quesnay in 1756, is devoted to precisely this point, and in it Quesnay tries to show how much more productive capitalist agriculture is than individual peasant cultivation. The basic argument is that peasants are too poor to be able to obtain the means of production necessary to get the most out of the land — in particular they commonly use oxen where horses are much more productive — and that only a rich farmer has the necessary funds to remedy this.

> The richer the farmers, the more they increase by their resources the product of the land and the power of the nation. A poor farmer can cultivate only to the disadvantage of the State, because he cannot obtain by his labour the production which the soil accords to a wealthy cultivation.[1]

The *Tableau Economique* assumes the predominance of capitalist relations in agriculture, for although much Physiocratic writing is concerned to prescribe measures necessary to ensure the best possible economic organisation of the country, the *Tableau* seems to be based on a world in which these reforms have already been carried through. Nevertheless the profits of the farmer do not form part of the surplus product ("net product") which is the basis of the nation's wealth, and although there are very occasional passages in which Quesnay does seem to include profits in the net product,[2] there is no doubt that fundamentally he conceives it as consisting only of rent. The question of agricultural relations is therefore treated exclusively from the point of view of the landed proprietors, with regard to which kind of tenancies create the greatest surplus over and above what remains to the producers themselves.

By contrast, manufacturing is regarded by Quesnay as the domain of independent artisans, each working on his own

account and earning a subsistence from working up raw
materials bought from the farmer into products saleable to
whoever wants to buy them. To the Physiocrats, the value of the
finished product is exactly equivalent to the value of the raw
materials consumed and the expense of the artisan's own
consumption, so that no surplus value is produced. If by any
chance one manufacturer manages to accumulate wealth, he has
achieved this only by suppressing the consumption of his fellows
and appropriating a bit of each of their own subsistence to
himself, or by charging an excess price to the buyer. But in each
case there is only a transfer of wealth, and not the creation of
new wealth. Similarly with interest on money: a merchant who
earns interest on money lent to a landowner appropriates a slice
of the net product to himself, but the net product is not in any
way increased by the act of lending.

Consistent with this analysis, Quesnay depicts three basic
classes in society; the proprietors of the land, the productive
class (those active in occupations that are productive of wealth —
farmers and labourers alike), and the sterile class (those active in
occupations non-productive of wealth). Each of these classes
stands in a different relation to the production of wealth.

The *Tableau Economique*, which was actually one of the first
Physiocratic productions, was their highest theoretical achievement. It depicts the flow of commodities between the various
classes in production: the farmer pays rent to the proprietor; the
proprietor buys equal quantities of commodities from the
farmer and the sterile class; the sterile class buys from the
farmer, and the farmer from the sterile class. In this way the
Physiocratic conception of the economy is theoretically pictured,
and this picture is made possible by the existence of two distinct
sectors of production — the productive and the unproductive —
differentiated by their economic characteristics. Quesnay quite
rightly omits the exchanges within the productive class and
within the sterile class, for these are secondary and would only
obscure the more important features.

Quesnay's treatment of the farmer-capitalist is interesting. He
never properly recognises the mobility of capital from one
employment to another, and so he treats the farmer-capitalist as
a category in his own right: a farmer motivated by profit, but
always a farmer. One never gets the impression with him that
capital flows into and out of agriculture, which is of course quite

consistent with his assumption that capitalist relations are almost non-existent in other occupations. Later on, this becomes a source of paradox in the Physiocratic system, for the general predominance of capital in reality becomes more and more clear. No one goes so far as to suggest that profits actually represent an addition to the net product — for it would be difficult to do this without bursting out of the Physiocratic system altogether — but the mobility of capital must call into question the accuracy of the Physiocratic conception that agriculture alone is productive. In this respect it is Turgot who goes furthest along the road towards Adam Smith.

Turgot points out that many industrial projects — the building of canals, for example — require the co-ordination of large quantities of labour, and lend themselves naturally to capitalist organisation. He subdivides the whole sterile class into two orders: employers, living off the profit from their capital, and simple artisans of no property who live by their daily labour. Thus he overthrows Quesnay's conception of the non-capitalist nature of manufacturing.

Turgot goes on to enumerate five different employments of capital — the purchase of land, the advances of manufacturing and industrial enterprises, advances for undertakings in agriculture, advances for commercial undertakings, and the lending of money at interest — amongst which there must be a general rate of profit because of the possibility of flow from one to another. The measure of this general rate of profit is the rate of interest. Although Turgot does not take it any further, this line of thought can only end by questioning the privileged position of agriculture; for is it not just another line of capitalist enterprise?

ADAM SMITH

And so we come to Adam Smith. As we have seen, Physiocracy was in essence a conception of a capitalist economy, since capital is the moving force behind the whole process of production,* but in it capitalism was confined within a shell of feudal assumptions. The unique role of agriculture, the duties of the

---

*"But as a matter of fact the system of the Physiocrats is the first systematic conception of capitalist production. The representative of industrial capital — the class of tenants — directs the entire economic movement." Marx, *Theories of Surplus Value, Part I*, pp 343–4.

landed proprietors, upon whom was conferred the privilege of determining by their expenditure the direction of the whole economy, but who suffered also the burden of paying all the taxes, and in Quesnay at any rate the very static vision of the social orders — in all these ideas are feudal in origin. It was the achievement of *The Wealth of Nations* that it broke the chains of these backward-looking conceptions by elaborating a theory which started from the process of labour in general, in whatever form, and by building upon that to present an analysis of an economy assumed to be dominated by capitalist relations, in which not only does the capitalist play the directing role in production but the accumulation of capital is isolated as the determining force in the development of a country. The Physiocrats could never reach this point because their net product consisted only of rent.

Adam Smith develops a new conception of the classes in society. We have the labourer, employed by capital for a daily wage and set to work with the object of creating a greater value than was originally laid out. We have the capitalist, the owner of capital, who lives off the profit of his advances. And we have the landowner, with none of his grandeur of former times, whose rent is nothing but an expense to the capitalist extractable by virtue of his monopoly of the land. His wealth is no longer god-given, but depends upon particular social institutions that allow him to appropriate a portion of the labour of others.

> As soon as the land of any country has all become private property, the landlords, like all other men, love to reap where they never sowed, and demand a rent even for its natural produce. The wood of the forest, the grass of the field, and all the natural fruits of the earth, which, when land was in common, cost the labourer only the trouble of gathering them, come, even to him, to have an additional price fixed upon them. He must then pay for the licence to gather them; and he must give up to the landlord a portion of what his labour either collects or produces.[3]

The Physiocratic conception of productive and sterile classes is thus overthrown. I have spent a little time discussing this overthrow, because it is necessary to have an accurate idea of precisely how far Adam Smith did go, in order to see where he stopped short.

The question of investment and consumption becomes more clarified in Adam Smith. He distinguishes the example in which a capital is accumulated, in which case an additional portion of the commodities produced re-enters and is consumed in the process of production, from that in which a capital is spent as revenue, in which case this portion is simply consumed by individuals. In the Physiocrats, the position is rather more complicated. On the one hand, as I have already indicated in Chapter Two, they do not make any distinction between investment and consumption in the expenditure of the proprietors, considering the only important aspect to be whether this expenditure acts to the benefit of agriculture or to the benefit of manufacturing. But on the other hand, when they consider the advances of the farmer, there cannot but be a distinction. They recognise that a certain proportion of the product of each harvest has to be set aside as seed and as subsistence for the labourers for the next year (*les avances annuelles*), so that a choice has effectively to be made as to precisely how much of the product is to be kept for advances and how much is to be put on the market. Here the farmer chooses between investment and consumption. But since the farmer is merely setting aside part of his own product and not going out to buy commodities on the market, the Physiocrats never realise the distinction at the level of expenditure. It is only with Adam Smith that the accumulation of capital becomes a creation of demand for commodities. Taking this a bit further, we can see that when it comes to the development of the productive powers of the nation, the distinction between expenditure on agriculture and on manufacturing was indeed the crucial one for the Physiocrats, since only agriculture was the source of wealth. But on the basis of Adam Smith's innovations, the central distinction must now be between investment and consumption out of the revenue of capitalists, since only the former represents the accumulation of capital. When they come down to purely capitalist relations, this is indeed the distinction that the Physiocrats make.

But if Smith recognises the distinction between accumulation of capital and consumption when it is a matter of the choice of the capitalist, he does not go on to distinguish two sectors of production on this basis — a sector producing consumption goods and a sector producing investment goods. Moreover, his

conception of investment is of advances made for the employment of labour and the buying of raw materials and ancillaries
for that labour. Since the emphasis in this conception of
investment is on the employment of new labour, producer goods
are not even distinguished *physically* from consumer goods —
since they will consist of food and clothing for labourers.

This idea of investment as consisting fundamentally of
advances to workers, together with the conception of the basic
sectors of the economy as agriculture and manufacturing, does
not have any serious consequences provided it is based on a clear
idea of the role of time in the whole process. If investment is
conceived to mean the production of extra wage-goods in the
present period and their advance in the next period, then there
are no difficulties. It is possible to set up a diagram analogous to
Marx's reproduction schemes based on the distinction between
an investment and a consumption goods sector, even though the
products produced are not physically but only economically
distinguishable. In this case the verbal stress on the division
agriculture/manufacturing is unimportant *in practice*. The great
mistake of Malthus and his followers, however, is that they do
not clearly separate time-periods in this way, thus effectively
imagining all the consequences of investment in period t to
appear in period t.

Now I want to look in more detail at Smith's attempts to
grapple with the problems of depreciation and the production
of investment goods. He comes closest to a correct appreciation
of the problem when he discusses fixed capital. Fixed capital is
precisely that portion of capital which remains fixed in form as
buildings, machinery, tools etc., whereas circulating capital starts
off as raw materials or labour power and transforms itself into
the finished commodity that appears on the market. Smith says:

> Some part of the capital of every master artificer or
> manufacturer must be fixed in the instruments of his trade.
> This part, however, is very small in some, and very great in
> others.[4]

He recognises implicitly the connection of the growing importance of fixed capital with the development of factory
production and mechanisation in the contrasting examples he
gives, for he quotes by way of a low proportion of fixed capital
the capital of a master artificer such as a tailor, a shoemaker, or a

weaver, and by way of a high proportion a great iron-work or a coal-mine.[5] He continues:

> Every fixed capital is both originally derived from, and requires to be continually supported by a circulating capital. All useful machines and instruments of trade are originally derived from a circulating capital, which furnishes the materials of which they are made, and the maintenance of the workmen who make them. They require, too, a capital of the same kind to keep them in constant repair.[6]

This last sentence admits that fixed capitals demand labour and therefore expense for their upkeep. Smith is clear about the consequence of this for the individual capitalist; he says:

> The gross rent of a private estate comprehends whatever is paid by the farmer; the net rent, what remains free to the landlord, after deducting the expense of management, of repairs, and all other necessary charges; or what, without hurting his estate, he can afford to place in his stock reserved for immediate consumption, or to spend upon his table, equipage, the ornaments of his house and furniture, his private enjoyments and amusements. His real wealth is in proportion, not to his gross, but to his net rent.[7]

These necessary charges are nothing other than the expenses of upkeep of the fixed capital invested by the owner in his land, or in other words the depreciation.

For society as a whole, Smith defines the gross revenue as the total annual produce, and the net revenue as what remains to the inhabitants after deducting the expense of maintaining first their fixed and second their circulating capital. Finally he says:

> The whole expense of maintaining the fixed capital must evidently be excluded from the net revenue of the society. Neither the materials necessary for supporting their useful machines and instruments of trade, their profitable buildings, etc., nor the produce of the labour necessary for fashioning those materials into the proper form, can ever make any part of it.[8]

All this seems to indicate a clear understanding that part of the total labour of society must be devoted to the replacement of used-up means of production. But in fact, when his attention is

not riveted directly on the problem of fixed capital, Adam Smith
lets the whole question of the repair, replacement and production of machinery and buildings fade out of his mind. For
instance, when he makes a distinction between gross and net
profit, it is not depreciation but insurance that he is referring to:
the need to set aside a fund as a guard against extraordinary
losses.[9] Even more important, he maintains resolutely that the
total product immediately divides itself entirely into wages,
profit and rent. In the price of corn, he says, one part pays the
rent, another the labourer's wage, and the third part the
farmer's profit.

> A fourth part, it may perhaps be thought, is necessary for
> replacing the stock of the farmer, or for compensating the
> wear and tear of his labouring cattle, and other instruments
> of husbandry. But it must be considered that the price of any
> instrument of husbandry, such as a labouring horse, is itself
> made up of the same three parts; the rent of the land upon
> which he is reared, the labour of tending and rearing him,
> and the profits of the farmer who advances both the rent of
> this land, and the wages of this labour.[10]

It is all the more surprising that Smith should say this since the
Physiocrats had so clearly pointed out the necessity of laying
aside a part of the harvest as seed, and this part could not
possibly be resolved into wages, profit or rent. The implications
of this statement are extremely important, for it amounts to
saying that the whole produce is ultimately consumed by
someone, that there is no steady demand for investment goods
(to make up for depreciation) and consequently that this sector
has no basis for being regarded as theoretically important.

Such a theoretical devaluation helps to induce the idea that
this sector has no independent significance, and this is a notion
which is an important component of underconsumption theories, where it is used to justify the assertion that investment
demand cannot make up for a lack of consumption.

Other statements in *The Wealth of Nations* show the subordinate position which Smith attributes to the investment goods
industries. At one point he says:

> Those machines and instruments of trade, etc., require a
> certain expense, first to erect them, and afterwards to

support them, both which expenses, though they make a part of the gross, are deductions from the net revenue of the society.[11]

Here it is not just depreciation costs but also the whole investment goods sector which is excluded from the net revenue. It seems to me that this implies a lack of recognition of this sector as an important area of capitalist enterprise. A clearer case, though, is the chapter on "The Different Employment of Capitals". Here Smith enumerates four different ways of employing a capital: in "procuring the rude produce annually required for the use and consumption of the society" (i.e. in agriculture, fishery and mining); in manufacturing; in transport from the place of production to the place of consumption; and in retailing, the breaking down and division of the product into a form suitable for consumption. The production of means of production does not appear in this list, and the only reference made to it is the following:

> Part of the capital of the master manufacturer is employed as a fixed capital in the instruments of his trade, and replaces, together with its profits, that of some other artificer of whom he purchases them.[12]

The real difference between the production of means of production and the production of consumption goods is that while the former are sold to another capitalist, the latter are sold to consumers. Smith's different ways of employing a capital in reality amount to different stages in the production of a consumer good, as is clear from the manner in which he describes them, and it would be equally true to say, as Smith says of the elements of fixed capital, that a manufacturer in buying raw materials from a farmer is replacing that farmer's capital, together with its profits. So it is by no means clear why the production of machinery should not be treated on the same level as agriculture, as a branch of production in its own right, and it reflects the muddle in Adam Smith's mind on these questions that he can at once mention the problem, and simultaneously leave it out of account.

It is important to note also how Smith conceives the act of investment, because his conception of it permeates the writings of all his followers. The primary thing is always the taking on of more labourers, who then receive as advances the elements of their own consumption, the raw materials which they are to work up, and the implements to work with. This contrasts quite strikingly with modern conceptions of investment, which stress the construction of plant and machinery.

At the beginning of Book II of *The Wealth of Nations*, Smith says:

> The person who employs his stock in maintaining labour, necessarily wishes to employ it in such a manner as to produce as great a quantity of work as possible. He endeavours, therefore, both to make among his workmen the most proper distribution of employment, and to furnish them with the best machines which he can either invent or afford to purchase. His abilities in both these respects are generally in proportion to the extent of his stock, or to the number of people whom it can employ.[13]

Here the emphasis is on the maintenance of labour, which is then "furnished with machines". One of the consequences of this conception is that investment is not regarded as requiring any time; the increase in production happens more or less immediately. This is an important point because it creates a trap which Malthus and his followers fall into, as I shall explain later. Although in the above passage Adam Smith uses the word 'machines', often he refers simply to 'tools',[14] and this is symptomatic of the lack of significance attached to the production of means of production already discussed. It clearly shows his conception of means of production as adjuncts or ancillaries to the labour process.

THE SECTORAL DIVISION OF THE ECONOMY

The importance of *The Wealth of Nations* in making a decisive break with the feudal conceptions of Physiocracy has long been recognised, and I have tried to show the connection between this and the development of the distinction between investment expenditure and consumption expenditure, a distinction which is presented for the first time by Adam Smith. Smith overthrew the idea that agriculture was the only productive activity and that rent was the only surplus product. He established labour in general as opposed to merely agricultural labour as the basis of value and he also established the accumulation of capital as opposed to the expenditure of landowners as the basis of economic development. But he could not escape altogether from the Physiocratic tradition. Much of the Physiocratic influence in *The Wealth of Nations* is obvious and has long been recognised — I am thinking for example of the reiteration of the inherent superiority of agriculture because it repays not only the wages of labour and the profits of capital but also the rent of land — but there is one particular aspect which seems to have passed unnoticed but which is highly relevant here. It relates to the conception of the basic divisions of the economy.

In the Physiocratic system, as has already been said, it is natural to divide the economy into agricultural and manufacturing sectors, because the economic role ascribed to each of these sectors by the Physiocrats is fundamentally different. One is the productive sector, the other the unproductive sector. However, once the basic Physiocratic assumptions have been overthrown, this is no longer true. To divide the economy in this way has no particular significance. On the basis of Adam Smith's innovations, the logical division is into a sector producing consumption goods and a sector producing investment goods. One sector provides for present consumption, the other provides the material basis for the accumulation of capital. This is a distinction which has meaning in a theoretical framework which recognises that the labour of all sectors is productive, but that not all of it serves the immediate purpose of the accumulation of capital. But Smith himself, as I have tried to show, does not make this basic division. He attributes only a very minor role to investment goods production, and when describing the main branches of the economy he retains the Physiocratic division of agriculture and manufacturing. Even Ricardo, who in other respects was a highly systematic expunger of Physiocratic influences in Smith's work, fails to recognise the Physiocratic basis of this division and reproduces it as before. Only with Marx is a correct definition of the departments of a capitalist economy finally achieved.

There are two basic reasons why Smith fails to develop the necessary division of the economy. Firstly, he retains a conception of investment in which expenditure on the acquisition and maintenance of the instruments of labour is of little significance compared with the expenditure on the labour itself, so that although when directly discussing fixed capital he acknowledges the expense of maintenance, the buying of the elements of fixed capital retains a very subordinate position in his understanding of investment itself. This is reflected in his discussion of the different employment of capitals, in which the production of instruments of labour is basically forgotten and only brought in as an appendage to the manufacture of consumption goods. Secondly, he conceives the total product as resolving itself entirely into revenue, into wages, profit and rent, so that there is no independent sphere of activity for the investment goods industries — whose products would exchange against the depreciation fund — and the whole output must necessarily be consumption goods. So the notion of the necessity of an independent investment goods sector is never grasped by Adam Smith, and when dividing the economy into various sectors he necessarily falls back into the identification of different types of consumption goods, and thus into the old split between agriculture and manufacturing made famous by the Physiocrats.*

This had a profound influence on the general glut debate of the early nineteenth century. Those who maintained that only partial gluts were possible did so by arguing that the production of a commodity created the purchasing power sufficient to buy the whole output, and since it was assumed that hoarding was insignificant and that all savings were invested, the demand exactly compensated the supply. This is obvious if we think of just one line of industry, in which the producers live entirely off their own product. But if we want to extend it to a multi-product economy, there are no special complications, for it is exactly as if the producers bought only their own products, and then exchanged them directly with one another. It is in this way that the analogy with barter grew up, and the view that the intervention of money changed nothing. In this conception, if we want to consider the effects of an increase in production, there are no particular problems, for an exactly equivalent increase in purchasing power is simultaneously produced, and provided the supply of the various products is appropriately

---

*"Smith was concerned with a basically two-sector case (agriculture and manufacture)." A.Skinner — Introduction to the Penguin edition, p.43.

proportioned to the desires of consumers, nothing is changed. All this is expressed in the passages quoted from James Mill in Chapter Two.

What is interesting is that this way of examining the problem is completely static. Basically it says that an economy of a certain level of production can create the demand for its total product without any problem, and so can an economy of any other level of production, so how can there possibly be any difficulty in getting from one to the other? This is best expressed by McCulloch in his *Edinburgh Review* article, where having imagined 1,000 capitalists in agriculture and 1,000 in manufacturing satisfactorily exchanging with one another, he suddenly brings in 1,000 more out of nowhere to operate in agriculture. Alternatively, he says, we can imagine a doubling of the productivity of all machinery. Both these suggestions amount to conceiving accumulation as merely an increase in output.

The roots of this conception are in the features of *The Wealth of Nations* that we have just observed. It is based on the idea of consumption goods making up the entire product, and agriculture and manufacturing being the two fundamental sectors of the economy. This excludes the one factor which would give the analysis a dynamic component — an investment sector. None of the defenders of "Say's Law" ever produced the demonstration of the relations between investment and consumption which could have exposed the errors of their opponents, because Adam Smith had not indicated to them the importance of a non-Physiocratic conception of the divisions of the economy for the creation of a non-Physiocratic *Tableau Economique.*

Of course not all of them used examples quite as grotesque as McCulloch's. James Mill, for instance, in his reply to Spence, focusses on one time-period, and points out the two possible destinations of the product — individual consumption and productive consumption. But he does not get beyond the mere *assertion* of the fact that it makes no fundamental difference how much investment there is from the point of view of aggregate demand to the *demonstration* of the relations between the two sectors; of particular importance, in the light of Spence's ideas, is to show how investment in this period does not create problems of overproduction in subsequent periods. What was required was an equivalent to Marx's expanded reproduction schemes. The failure to create this, in my opinion, can very largely be attributed to Smith's neglect of an investment sector, to his conception that the whole product resolves itself immediately into revenue, and to the consequent retention of the Physiocratic division agriculture/manufacture.

The same factors are largely responsible for the predominance of underconsumption theories on the other side of the debate. Adam Smith suggests that the whole annual product is distributed as wages, profits and rent. I have already pointed out that this implies a subordinate role for the producer goods industries, since they are not seen as an independent and relatively autonomous sector of the economy, and that there are passages in *The Wealth of Nations* which definitely indicate that Smith thought of their role as a subordinate one. In the limiting case, these industries could be regarded as equivalent to raw materials industries, expanding only in response to an already existing increase in final consumer demand — and this is indeed how Malthus conceives it.

The most important direct implication of this idea of Smith's, though, is that all effective demand is demand for consumption goods, and so it is only natural that those of his followers who were looking for an explanation of what they saw as deficient effective demand should look at consumer demand for the cause of it. For if the whole output consists of consumption goods, any problem of effective demand must come down to insufficient expenditure on consumption by some class or other of the population. For Sismondi it was the workers; for Malthus the unproductive consumers. After all, if depreciation is forgotten, there is no investment sector at all in a static economy — and this alone makes it difficult to think of it as important. Against this the defenders of "Say's Law" did not fundamentally assert the independence of the investment sector; all they were concerned to prove was that investment could never create a problem of effective demand.

The conception of investment was also a contributory factor. It emphasised above all the employment of new labourers, and quite often the demand for implements and machinery was altogether forgotten; Malthus is a good example of this. Then investment goods are even physically indistinguishable from consumption goods.

So political economy in the early nineteenth century exhibited a number of features — the lack of recognition of depreciation and the need for continuous replacement of worn-out plant and machinery, a conception of investment which minimised the demand for these goods, and a lack of identification of an investment sector as a separate sector of the economy — which worked against the creation of anything equivalent to Marx's reproduction schemes, in which the production of investment goods stands as an equal side by side with the production of means of consumption. Overwhelmingly, aggregate demand was thought of as consumer demand, and the lack of physical distinction between investment and consumption goods implied in the conception of investment only reinforced this. As already pointed out, this need not have led to mistakes, but it undoubtedly does explain both the static framework of the "Say's Law" arguments and the prevalence of underconsumptionism amongst the opposition.

What light does this throw on the underconsumption theories themselves? In Sismondi's case, the striking characteristic is that investment is ignored altogether. This is true also of Rodbertus, and essentially true of the Narodniks as well. None of them come to grips with the problem of why investment cannot solve the difficulty. Here the assumption of the subordinate role of investment seems to have eliminated even the need for discussion of the possibility.

In the British type of underconsumption theory investment cannot be ignored in this way since the level of accumulation is at the centre of the theory. It seems that in this theory, a muddled understanding of the role of time is at the root of the mistakes. The act of investment and the increased production resulting from it are collapsed into one time-period, so that the increased supply and reduced consumer demand create the appearance of overproduction. Let us look more closely at the implications of the classical conception of investment as essentially the employment of more labourers, in the way that it is understood by Malthus and his followers.

If the existence of an investment goods sector is ignored, and if we assume that society consists only of capitalists and workers and that workers spend all of their income, then Wages = consumption of the workers, and Profits = consumption of the capitalists. We can imagine a stationary economy of this kind simply enough. But what happens if capitalists decide to increase their output? Still keeping to classical assumptions, we must take it that they can only do this by reducing their consumption. There is a transfer of purchasing power from capitalists to workers, and an increased output is produced, but profits fall, because capitalists' consumption has fallen. Profits need not fall if capitalists increase their consumption, but according to our rules this is not allowed. Profits must therefore fall, as Chalmers suggested, in a one-to-one correspondence with the increase in investment. The logical result of this is that any accumulation at all must precipitate a crisis.

We have already seen, in Chapter Two, that Malthus grasps this difficulty (which he thinks disproves his opponents' arguments), but being unwilling to take it, as Chalmers does, to its logical, absurd conclusion, he leaves himself in the very vague position of saying that there is a point, albeit undefined, above which accumulation can be excessive. As a consequence, his argument lacks conviction. The theoretical mistake here is that it has been forgotten that investment creates demand for wage-goods to be advanced in one period, but the increased production occurs only in the next period. Once we confine ourselves to looking strictly at one time-period, the overproduction disappears.

But although the mistake is one of confusion over the action of time, the prevailing conception of investment must bear considerable responsibility for generating it. If today the emphasis on construction makes it natural to think of gestation periods of investment, then the classical emphasis on increased employment has the opposite effect of creating the idea that so long as the labourers can be found there is very little lapse of time between the decision to invest and the start of production. With this idea in mind, it is only too easy to make the mistake which Malthus makes.

In this chapter I have tried to show that the heritage of Adam Smith had profound effects on the general glut debate of the early nineteenth century, although it affected the two sides in different ways. To a significant extent, this reflected Smith's inability to make the complete break with Physiocracy that was demanded by his basic theoretical innovations, and a lack of understanding of the production of investment goods as a vigorous independent sector of the economy. In the next chapter, I shall show how Marx cut through the old ideas and developed a more profound analysis.

NOTES

1 F.Quesnay, *Oeuvres Economiques*, pp.174–5.
2 For a discussion of this see R.L.Meek, "Physiocracy and the Classical Conception of Profit", in *Economics of Physiocracy.*
3 A.Smith, *The Wealth of Nations*, pp.152–3.
4 ibid, p.374.
5 ibid, pp.374–5.
6 ibid, p.378.
7 ibid, p.382.
8 ibid, p.382.
9 ibid, p.199.
10 ibid, p.153.
11 ibid, p.385.
12 ibid, p.462.
13 ibid, p.372.
14 eg ibid, p.392.

6

KARL MARX

Some people have suggested that Marx had an underconsumptionist theory of crisis, and one of the aims of this chapter is to discuss this question. But in the wake of the points that were made in the last chapter as to the relation between the development of underconsumption theories in the early nineteenth century and the ideas of *The Wealth of Nations,* a study of *Capital* acquires a deeper significance. For Marx is the first person to challenge openly and explicitly the conception of investment current in Adam Smith and his successors, and to produce a thorough-going critique of Smith's views on these questions. A treatment of these aspects of Marx's work serves the double aim of clearing the way for a sound discussion of whether Marx himself can be classed as an underconsumptionist, as Paul Sweezy in particular has argued, and of rounding off the inquiry developed in the last chapter by showing the different perspectives opened up by Marx's innovations.

The differences are already apparent in Marx's discussion of value, for it is here that he distinguishes a separate portion of the value of a commodity which is due not just to the labour employed in production or to the value of the raw materials, but is due to the gradual wearing-out of the machinery used. In Ricardo the problem of what Marx calls constant capital is treated simply as an addition to the total of advances for the payment of labour, and since this advance also must be rewarded with profits at the normal rate, the total value of the product must be augmented appropriately. Ricardo gives the illustration of two capitalists, each employing one hundred men a year at a rate of £50 per annum, one of whom uses his labour for two years in producing two crops of corn, and the other of whom uses his labour the first year to build a machine, and the second year to make cotton goods with the help of this machine. In the first year each lays out £5,000, which at a rate of profit of 10 per cent yields a product of the value of £5,500. The farmer lives off his profits and in the second year only lays out £5,000, as he did in the first year, and again produces a value of £5,500. Over the two years the total value produced is £11,000. The cotton manufacturer, however, lays out £10,500 in the second year — £5,000 in labour and £5,500 in machinery — which at 10 per cent yields him a value of £11,550 by the year's end — £5,500 in machinery and £6,050 in cotton goods. The employment of fixed capital has augmented the value of the product of two years' labour by £550. Here fixed capital is regarded simply as past labour which has been stored up, and accumulated profits as a result; it is these accumulated profits which are responsible for the augmentation of value. This, however, is simply a reward for waiting, in the sense that it is purely a consequence of the fact that the capital has been invested for two years instead of one, as Ricardo himself noted, so that compound interest has been gained on it.

At another point Ricardo mentions the labour required for the maintenance of machinery. In his view, as also in Marx's, this must be regarded simply as labour bestowed on the production of the commodity itself. He says:

> If the wear and tear of the machine were great, if the quantity of labour requisite to keep it in an efficient state were that of fifty men annually, I should require an additional price for my goods, equal to that which would be obtained by any other manufacturer who employed fifty men in the production of other goods, and who used no machinery at all.[1]

The problem of depreciation, though, is not touched upon as such by Ricardo, for he regards a machine as a piece of capital invested in the past which by now must represent so much value at compound interest, and he forgets that sooner or later the useful life of the machine must come to an end so that all this value, if it exists in reality, must somehow or other have been transferred to the product. The mechanism of this transfer is not discussed at all by Ricardo.

For Ricardo, therefore, the question of machinery is simply one of stored-up labour, and products exchange in proportion to the total labour employed in their production, modified according to the relative proportions of fixed and circulating capital involved. Marx has a different approach. In particular, he rigorously distinguishes between the "dead" labour and the "living". He does so by making two innovations: firstly he distinguishes between surplus value and profit, and secondly instead of the categories of fixed and circulating capital he introduces the more fundamental ones of constant and variable capital. In Marx, fixed and circulating capital are simply varieties of constant capital, distinguished by their rate of circulation.

It is obvious that in Adam Smith and Ricardo there is something paradoxical in the use of labour as a measure of value, for both of them realise that as soon as society develops beyond the stage of the salmon and the beaver hunter and stock is accumulated, products no longer exchange exactly in proportion to the quantity of labour embodied in them and the law must be modified accordingly. But if these modifications are necessary, what is the point of taking labour as a measure of value at all?

In Marx it is the distinction between surplus value and profit which answers this question, for by this means he splits off the issue of the existence of a general rate of profit, of capitalists receiving profit in proportion to their capital laid out, from that of the extraction of surplus labour. In Volume I of *Capital* he talks of commodities exchanging at their values, according to the labour-time embodied in them, because here he is trying to analyse the production process of capital, the class relations implicit in the capitalist mode of production, and the mechanism of the extraction of surplus labour in this mode. He talks about a rate of surplus value. This exists on a social level, rather than on the level of the production of an individual commodity, for exploitation in Marx is a matter first and foremost of relations between classes and not between individuals; this is why he does not bring in the problem of a deviation of relative prices from relative values in the first Volume, for this problem concerns only the distribution of the total surplus value amongst the individual capitalists, which is secondary to the problem of the appropriation of this value. In Volume I we meet the industrial capitalist as the immediate appropriator of surplus labour. Thus in Marx the "labour theory of value" is separated from any attempt to explain the price of an individual commodity.

The switch from the idea of fixed and circulating capital to constant and variable capital reflects these changes. Although there was a technical basis to the idea, fundamentally fixed and circulating capital were distinguished by the rate at which the capital circulated and was realised once again as money: fixed capital only slowly, and circulating capital relatively quickly. In other words it was geared to the idea of capital generating profit at a certain rate. But Marx's constant and variable capital are distinguished by their relation to the production of surplus value: Marx conceives human labour as the only source of value, so he makes the distinction between capital as labour-power (variable capital) and capital as objects and means of production (constant capital). Only labour-power, when expended in production as labour, creates value, while the value of constant capital is transferred to the product without quantitative alteration. Of course within these categories capital may circulate at different rates, but this is no longer the basic issue.

The significance of the inclusion of depreciation of means of production is that when we transfer from the individual capital to the total social capital, although raw materials are eliminated, the question of replacement of means of production used up still remains, and a certain portion of the total social labour must be devoted exclusively to this. Thus Marx arrives at the two departments of his reproduction schemes, that producing means of production and that producing means of consumption. It should be noted that Marx could have slipped back into classical assumptions by thinking of constant capital simply as raw materials. Then, on the level of the whole economy, his Department One would have been eliminated, but so long as the system is growing there is still the production of stocks of materials and wage-goods to be laid out in the next period, which, since the advances are increasing from period to period, do not exactly match present consumption of these goods — so there still exists a separate investment sector, and a reproduction scheme could be constructed.

Equally, it should be noted that there is no intrinsic reason why the transfer of a certain portion of the value of the means of production to the product should not be recognised in Ricardo's theory. It is sufficient to assume that the value of machinery is steadily diminished until it reaches zero when it is worn out, and that the value of the product each year is augmented by exactly the same amount. Thus, although Marx's reproduction schemes are elaborated in terms of constant capital, variable capital and surplus value, political economy was not obliged to await these conceptual innovations in order to produce such a diagram of a capitalist economy.

What are the implications of such a diagram for the "general glut" question? It obviously does not solve the problem of the industrial cycle, since a diagram can never present an explanation, but by correctly formulating the sectors of the economy and their inter-relation, it creates the possibility of a correct explanation which did not exist before. To be precise, it is not that the formal possibility of a correct explanation had not existed, but the reproduction schemes set up a ready critique of the wrong explanations that had been offered previously and establish a framework for a rigorous analysis of the question, so that in fact they represent a great step forward, given the situation as analysed in the last chapter. In treating of simple reproduction, Marx gives us the following example:

I. $4,000c + 1,000v + 1,000s = 6,000$
in means of production;

II. $2,000c + 500v + 500s = 3,000$
in means of consumption;

Total produced $= 9,000.$

In simple reproduction he assumes that all plant and machinery wears out in one year, so that it has to be entirely replaced every year. He also assumes that surplus value is entirely consumed and none saved, and that net investment is zero. Under these assumptions the condition of balance of the two sectors, given by equating the demand to the supply in either one of them, is that $IIc = I(v + s)$. The reason why everything reduces to this one equation is that Marx retains the classical assumption that intended savings are exactly equal to intended investment, for this assumption means that the total demand exactly compensates the total supply, and the only problem that can arise is that of the distribution of this demand between the two sectors. In this sense, the reproduction schemes could be regarded as a more sophisticated formulation of Say's Law, as indeed was claimed by Rosa Luxemburg. But at the same time, any serious consideration of the diagram must raise some basic questions. The existence of a banking system, paper money and credit facilities means that a capitalist can extend his production without proportionately cutting back on his own consumption, or that of his fellows. If this happens, a situation of excess demand is created, which must create a boom in profits either in higher prices or in greater capacity utilisation, for the surplus value which it is planned to spend is now greater than the quantity being produced. So the question of the adjustment of planned saving to planned investment is immediately raised.

The most significant point about the reproduction schemes, although Marx does not depart from the usual classical assumptions on these questions, is that they lead logically to the Keynesian solution to this problem. The neoclassical answer was that the adjusting force was the rate of interest, which could be considered as the price of savings, while planned investment could be seen as the demand for savings and planned saving as the supply of them. The Keynesian solution is that the level of national income, acted upon by the level of effective demand, alters in such a way as to bring planned saving into line with planned investment — in other words fundamentally it is saving which adjusts itself to investment, as opposed to an equilibrium price being reached to balance the two forces, as in the neoclassical conception.

The reproduction schemes tend naturally towards the Keynesian formulation, not just because they make no reference to the rate of interest or to what determines the level of planned saving and investment, but because they throw to the forefront the level of output and its relation to effective demand. Marx's balancing equation $IIc = I(v + s)$ represents the condition of balance of demand to supply in each of the departments. If we throw out the assumption of the necessary equality of planned saving and planned investment, the problem of the absolute level of effective demand has to be considered in addition to its distribution between departments. If there is excess effective demand, either capitalists find themselves unable to supply the demand (if prices are maintained) and start to take on more labourers and increase production and hence profits, or they raise their prices and make more profit per unit of output. In my opinion, it is no accident that Kalecki, starting from a model based on Marx's reproduction schemes, should arrive at the same results as Keynes in so far as the kernel of his ideas are concerned (for the framework within which they are set is different) and without the tortuous rejection of received notions that Keynes had to go through, for the reproduction schemes are an accurate formulation of the major divisions of a capitalist economy, and constitute a natural starting-point for an analysis of its development.*

It has been said that Mill and McCulloch failed to produce an entirely convincing refutation of underconsumptionist arguments, because of the limitations of their conception of investment and of the basic sectors of the economy. The reproduction schemes remedy these defects, and it is very easy to use them to demolish the ideas of Sismondi and Malthus, for it is clear that workers can only consume the portion of the output represented by 'v', and that landlords etc. can only consume the portion represented by that part of 's' that falls to their lot. Marx explicitly criticises these ideas at one point in Volume II of *Capital*:

> It is purely a tautology to say that crises are caused by the scarcity of solvent consumers, or of a paying consumption. The capitalist system does not know any other modes of consumption but a paying one, except that of the pauper or of the "thief". If any commodities are unsaleable, it means that no solvent purchasers have been found for them, in other words, consumers . . . But if one were to attempt to clothe this tautology with a semblance of a profounder justification by saying that the working class receive too small a portion of their own product, and the evil would be remedied by giving them a larger share of it, or raising their wages, we should reply that crises are precisely always preceded by a period in which wages rise generally and the working class actually gets a larger share of the annual product intended for consumption. From the point of view of the advocates of "simple" (!) common sense, such a period should rather remove a crisis.[2]

Superficially it seems somewhat of a paradox in Marx that his reproduction schemes should tend to reinforce the arguments of the "Say's Law" advocates at the same time as he himself

---

*This does not of course mean that the terminology 'c + v + s' etc. is essential to the inquiry.

regarded their ideas as "childish babble" and was more in sympathy with their opponents. When he himself discusses the question of crises, he traces the possibility of them back to the characteristics of commodity production in general, to the fact that products no longer exchange directly with one another, but against money. Thus production is no longer just the production of a useful object, a use-value, but functions as an element of the total social labour, determined by the laws of the market. The product must be sold for money before the producer can buy in order to satisfy his own needs. The whole process can be described in the formula C-M-C, where C represents a commodity and M money. The circulation of commodities in fact splits itself into two distinct part, C-M, the sale of a commodity, and M-C, the purchase of a commodity. It is this split which creates the possibility of a crisis:

> If the interval in time between the two complementary phases of the complete metamorphosis of a commodity becomes too great, if the split between the sale and the purchase becomes too pronounced, the intimate connection between them, their oneness, asserts itself by producing — a crisis. The antithesis, use-value and value, the contradictions that private labour is bound to manifest itself as direct social labour, that a particularised concrete kind of labour has to pass for abstract human labour; the contradiction between the personification of objects and the representation of persons by things; all these antitheses and contradictions, which are immanent in commodities, assert themselves, and develop their modes of motion, in the antithetical phases of the metamorphosis of a commodity. These modes therefore imply the possibility, and no more than the possibility, of crises.[3]

In essence, behind all the flowery language, Marx's general possibility of crises amounts to no more than had been implied by Sismondi in his example of the Leipzig book trade. It relies on the effect that a commodity produced may for some reason or other not be able to find a buyer, and that a producer who has already sold may for some reason or other not want to buy again immediately. In other words it is based on the idea that commodity production is at the same time interdependence and anarchy — interdependence because each producer has to rely on the demand provided by someone else, and anarchy because each producer is left to decide for himself what it is best to produce. These are points already made by Sismondi, although not on the same level of abstraction; it is a challenge to the idea of harmonious and speedy adjustment to dislocations that is implied in the "Say's Law" argument.

CRISES AND CYCLES

In addition to this, Marx gives us a theory of the industrial cycle. This is an advance on Sismondi, who thought in terms of the final collapse of large-scale industry rather than in terms of cycles. The basis of Marx's cycle is the fluctuation in the rate of investment. The boom is characterised by a high rate of investment, and a rising demand for labour. As a consequence of this, wages rise, and the rate of surplus value falls. After a certain time the fall in profits has its effect on the rate of investment, which declines precipitately. With the decline competition between the workers starts to make itself felt once again, and the rate of surplus value rises once more. The conditions are created for a new spurt in investment.

What is noticeable in this theory, and what separates Marx from the underconsumptionists, is the stress on the rate of accumulation as the variable whose fluctuations have the decisive effect on aggregate demand. As was said in Chapter One in giving a definition of underconsumption theories, one of their significant characteristics is the belief that the slump cannot be treated just as a part of the trade cycle, but that it reflects deeper problems in a capitalist economy that are always tending to drag it down towards stagnation. Furthermore, since this tendency is due essentially to a lack of demand for consumption goods, it is a more or less necessary concomitant of the theory that it should deny any relatively independent role to investment — for otherwise the lack of consumer demand could always be replaced by a high rate of investment.

On both of these issues — the independent role of investment and the stagnationist tendency of capitalist production — Marx's position is almost diametrically opposed to the underconsumptionist one. Indeed one of the striking characteristics of his work is the stress that he puts on the inherent dynamism of capitalist production, of how the capitalist is merely a functionary of capital and exists primarily in order to accumulate capital rather than to live in luxury: "Accumulate, accumulate, that is Moses and all the prophets", as he puts it. While seeing crises as the expression of the contradictions of capitalist production, Marx is very clear that they represent only a temporary break in the drive to expansion, a recreation of the conditions of that expansion which have temporarily broken down, rather than a manifestation of a tendency to stagnation.

So Marx's conception of a capitalist economy is very different from an underconsumptionist one. Furthermore, his reproduction schemes, which are a definite theoretical advance on anything produced by his predescessors, show up clearly the mistakes in the arguments of Sismondi and Malthus. This must be borne in mind when examining the passages but together by Sweezy as evidence that Marx had a fundamentally underconsumptionist theory of crisis.

Sweezy's argument is set out in his book *The Theory of Capitalist Development* — subtitled "Principles of Marxian Political Economy" — first published in 1942. He relies very strongly on the stringing together of isolated quotations, arguing not so much that Marx presents an underconsumptionist theory as that it "would have been of primary importance" in his analysis had he lived to complete his work. He says:

> On this ground it could be maintained that Marx regarded underconsumption as one aspect, but on the whole not a very important aspect, of the crisis problem. This appears to be the opinion of Dobb, and there is no doubt much to back it up. Another view is possible, however, namely, that in these scattered passages Marx was giving advance notice of a line of reasoning which, if he had lived to complete his theoretical work, would have been of primary importance in the overall picture of the capitalist economy. Many of his followers have evidently been of this opinion, and, on the whole, it seems to me the more reasonable of the two alternatives.[4]

This admits the weakness of his own case; but the basic fault is that he does not go into the question of precisely what an underconsumption theory is, and how it accords with the ensemble of Marx's work. He takes a number of longish passages from *Capital*, and to a lesser extent *Theories of Surplus Value*, in which he finds a suggestion of the idea that it is the poverty of the masses which is responsible for crises, but his interpretation of these passages is very questionable: on the whole, as I shall show, they do not live up to the demands he makes of them. Furthermore, it should be remembered that only the first Volume of *Capital* was published during Marx's lifetime, and that much of the rest — and especially the passages on which Sweezy relies — has remained in a rather rudimentary state, and the exact interpretation of it is difficult. It is not surprising, therefore, if a precise meaning cannot be put to some of these passages. I focus on Sweezy's argument in some detail, because his is really the definitive attempt to argue that Marx is an underconsumptionist.

Sweezy produces the following quote:

> The ultimate reason for all real crises always remains the poverty and restricted consumption of the masses as opposed to the drive of capitalist production to develop the productive forces as though only the absolute consuming power of society constituted their limit.[5]

This sentence is his best piece of evidence. It appears in the midst of a discussion on credit, and it appears to identify the poverty of the masses as the "ultimate" reason for crises. We can read this passage in an underconsumptionist fashion: if we identify the central contradiction of capitalist production as the problem of finding consumers for the output of Department II, this sentence seems clear evidence that Marx is in agreement. The problem is that (a) it is totally isolated within the book itself from the other discussions of crises, and (b) as Sweezy himself says, it has very much the character of a parenthetical remark, and it is unclear precisely what the phrase "the ultimate reason for all real crises" means. On the other hand, no alternative interpretation immediately presents itself. Leaving it aside for the moment, let us look at the main evidence.

Sweezy quotes another long passage from Volume III, from the Chapter "Exposition of the Internal Contradictions of the Law (of the Falling Rate of Profit)".[6] The relevant sections run:

> The conditions of direct exploitation, and those of realising it, are not identical. They diverge not only in place and time, but also logically. The first are only limited by the productive power of society, the latter by the proportional relation of the

various branches of production and the consumer power of society. But this last-named is not determined either by the absolute productive power, or by the absolute consumer power, but by the consumer power based on antagonistic conditions of distribution, which reduce the consumption of the bulk of society to a minimum varying within more or less narrow limits. It is furthermore restricted by the tendency to accumulate, the drive to expand capital and produce surplus value on an extended scale. This is law for capitalist production. . . . . . But the more productiveness develops, the more it finds itself at variance with the narrow basis on which the conditions of consumption rest. It is no contradiction at all on this self-contradictory basis that there should be an excess of capital simultaneously with a growing surplus of population. For while a combination of these two would, indeed, increase the mass of produced surplus value, it would at the same time intensify the contradiction between the conditions under which this surplus value is produced and those under which it is realised.

Sweezy claims that Marx here traces interruptions in production to a restricted volume of consumer demand — restricted by low wages and capitalists' "tendency to accumulate". But this passage is hardly as clear-cut as that. Firstly, if the consuming power is restricted by the drive to accumulate, this may restrict demand for consumption goods but this is compensated for by the demand for the output of Department I. Problems of realisation only arise if, as presumably Sweezy is assuming, the accumulation does not actually come about; but there is nothing in the passage to suggest this and if anything the opposite is suggested: that competition enforces incessant revolutions in the methods of production as a general law of capitalist production, that consumption is squeezed because of the demands of accumulation.

Coming to the second part of the quotation, "But the more productiveness develops etc", this can hardly be interpreted as meaning that "depression is pictured as a period in which expansion of production is held up by an insufficient demand for the final fruit of production, namely, consumption goods."[7] For what Sweezy means by this is that the threat of a lack of sufficient demand for consumption goods hangs like a pall over capitalist production, exerting a continual depressive force, pressing it down towards stagnation, and that the problem in studying the cycles of a capitalist economy is much more: why does it expand? than, why the periodic interruptions of expansion?[8] This contrasts quite markedly with Marx, who, even in the passage quoted above, always stressed the dynamic, revolutionary character of capitalist production. The one sentence on which Sweezy's interpretation of this passage rests is this: "But the more productiveness develops, the more it finds itself at variance with the narrow basis on which the conditions of consumption rest". But it is not possible to claim that this sentence expresses the logical conclusion of the rest of the passage; if anything it introduces new confusions.

Sweezy also produces a quote from Volume II:

> The epochs in which capitalist production exerts all its forces are always periods of overproduction, because the forces of production can never be utilised beyond the point at which surplus value can be not only produced but also realised; but the sale of commodities, the realisation of the commodity capital and hence also of the surplus value, is limited not only by the consumption requirements of society in general, but by the consumption requirements of a society in which the great majority are poor and must always remain poor.[9]

This passage is as ambiguous as the previous one. Sweezy's attempt to deduce from it that Marx means that the normal state of affairs in capitalist production is stagnation, because "it is only from this standpoint that periods of full utilisation can be rationally designated as 'periods of overproduction',"[10] obviously reads into it far more than there is in fact. Can one deduce anything from a statement of this level of generality, which amounts to saying that commodities once produced do not automatically sell themselves, and that the demand for them is limited "by the consumption requirements of society in general"? This statement does not treat seriously any of the important questions which would have to be answered before it could be held up as an underconsumptionist argument: it ignores the demand for investment goods, although Marx elsewhere puts a lot of stress on this, as we have seen, and in contrast to the discussion in Volume I it makes no attempt whatsoever to look at the mechanism of the precipitation of a crisis. Like the passage quoted above about "the ultimate reason for all crises", this sentence does not bear to be treated as a serious discussion of the problem of crises.

It is obvious that Sweezy's arguments are founded on the most ambiguous and obscure quotations from *Capital.* As to the passage already quoted from Volume II specifically attacking the Sismondian type of underconsumption theories, Sweezy quotes it, but he passes it by without comment. It is worth noting, too, that In Volume III of *Capital,* just a few pages after one of the passages on which Sweezy relies so heavily, Marx reiterates the theory of the cycle that we have already described. He says:

> As soon as capital would, therefore, have grown in such a ratio to the labouring population that neither the absolute working time supplied by this population, nor the relative surplus working time, could be expanded any further (. . .); at a point, therefore, when the increased capital produced just as much, or even less, surplus value than it did before its increase, there would be absolute over-production of capital; i.e., the increased capital C + △C would produce no more, or even less, profit than capital C before its expansion by △C. In both cases there would be a steep and sudden fall in the general rate of profit, but this time due to a change in the composition of capital not caused by the development of the productive forces, but rather by a rise in the money-value of the variable capital (because of increased wages) and the corresponding reduction in the proportion of surplus to necessary labour.[11]

This theory, which remains the only coherent account of the industrial cycle in Marx, has nothing whatsoever in common with underconsumption theories.

Sweezy, apart from arguing that Marx inclines towards an underconsumptionist theory of crisis, himself produces a sketch of such a theory. It is worth analysing precisely what his argument is, for it shows once again some of the characteristic ideas of underconsumptionism — although it goes without saying that it is more sophisticated than and free of the elementary errors of the theories we have examined so far. He sets out to show that there is an inherent tendency in a capitalist

economy for the output of consumption goods to outrun the
demand for them, a tendency which will manifest itself either in
a sudden crisis and collapse as the excess supply reveals itself, or
in a general stagnation of the economy as capitalists realise that
there are no grounds for an increase in production. The analysis
of the trends in the demand for consumption goods is based on
two factors: the capitalists' drive to accumulate, emphasised so
much by Marx, and the rising "organic composition of capital".
The drive to accumulate means that capitalists will consume a
decreasing proportion of the total surplus value as the economy
develops, and that investment will take a correspondingly larger
portion, while the rising organic composition of capital means
that a smaller and smaller proportion of this investment goes as
wages to workers and an increasingly large share goes to buy
plant and machinery. The result of this is that "the rate of
growth of consumption (i.e. the ratio of the increment of
consumption to total consumption) declines relative to the rate
of growth of means of production (i.e. the ratio of investment to
total means of production)".[12]

Now Sweezy looks at the relationship of the growth of
consumption goods to the growth of means of production from
another viewpoint: that of production. In a given technical
situation, he says, there must be a definite relation between
changes in the stock of means of production (investment) and
changes in the output of consumption goods, and what statistical
evidence we have confirms the impression that in an industrial
capitalist economy the incremental capital-consumption ratio
stays constant for a very long period of time. Thus there is a
technically determined relation between the increase in means
of production and in the output of consumption goods, and this
relation implies that "the ratio of the rate of growth in the
output of consumption goods to the rate of growth of means of
production remains constant".[13] This last in fact only follows if
the marginal capital-consumption ratio is equal to the overall
capital-consumption ratio, in which case the constant is 1; but
this is a minor point.

The result of this is that while the technical conditions of
production require a rate of growth of consumption goods
output which stands in a constant relation to the increase of the
means of production, the drive to accumulate and the rising
organic composition of capital indicate a fall in this ratio, with

the result that the output of consumption goods tends to exceed the demand for them. In Sweezy's view, this is the fundamental cause of depressions. In this argument we can see clearly the essential underconsumptionist thesis that crises are more than just a stage in the trade cycle, for Sweezy affirms that the depressive tendency to underconsumption is the dominant characteristic of capitalist production, and that even in its apparently most vital, dynamic periods — its period of youth, of Industrial Revolution — this tendency exists but is merely obscured by offsetting factors.[14]

Secondly, like all other underconsumptionists — except in so far as they neglect to mention the problem altogether — Sweezy has to explain why investment cannot fill the gap in effective demand left by consumption. Sweezy's way of doing this is by postulating a strict technical relation between investment and the increment in consumption resulting from it, so that the demand for investment goods is always strictly tied to a planned increase in the output of consumption goods. Now of course Sweezy is quite aware that machines can be used to produce machines, rather than consumption goods, but the assumptions of his model are such that the problem of the disproportion, or the potential disproportion, of the demand to the supply of consumption goods steadily increases in intensity, so that a gradually larger and larger proportion of total investment would have to be devoted to producing means of production in order for the collapse to be avoided. The rate of growth of national income would have to increase steadily. Sweezy clearly imagines this to be an impossible solution, although he does not say so in so many words, because at some point the "irrationality" of investment just in order to provide the ingredients of more investment must show itself, and precipitate a collapse.

But the question is: does this "irrationality" exist for a capitalist economy, or is it an illusion created by the idea that investment must, in any form of economy, justify itself by ending up with an increase in the material welfare of human beings? Why, in a capitalist economy where investment is based exclusively on expectation of profit, should a high rate of growth not be able to sustain itself? Even more to the point, is not a steadily increasing rate of growth, which Sweezy dismisses as a solution to his problem, precisely what we observe in the history of the advanced industrial capitalist countries of the world in the long run? These are questions which raise doubts about the very foundations of Sweezy's argument.

The fundamental mistake which Sweezy has made, in fact, is to assume that because in the logic of human welfare investment is unjustifiable if it does not lead to increased consumption, so also must it be true for capitalist production, which cannot for long persist with a rate of investment "out of line" with its consumption demand. In the last instance, this false analogy is the reason why he cannot accept investment as a substitute for consumption demand, but it is not a reason which can be justified by a scientific analysis of the characteristics of capitalist production. Sweezy seems to assume that the problem can only be temporarily solved by a high rate of investment, and that if any interruption of the growth should occur, the economy will be faced with an immediate collapse back into stagnation. The possibility of oscillation around a consistently high rate of growth is dismissed as impossible, although a little reflection shows that such a possibility is perfectly feasible.

So Sweezy's attempt to build an underconsumption theory on the basis of Marx's work brings out some of the fundamental ideas behind underconsumptionism. But although the assumptions of Sweezy's model are based on Marx's ideas, the underlying conceptions do not accord with Marx's own. In particular, Marx always emphasised the dynamic, revolutionary nature of capitalist production as compared with previous epochs, and never suggested that there was a fundamental tendency towards stagnation within it. Equally, there is no trace of underconsumptionism in his theory of the trade cycle, which emphasises fluctuations in the rate of investment.

The fact that Marx fundamentally rejected underconsumption theories has obviously had a profound impact on their later history. Had he given them more support, there is no doubt that many more Marxists would have pursued the idea. As it is, however, even in the days of the Second International when theories of the impending "economic breakdown" of capitalism were particularly in vogue, underconsumption theories never managed to establish an ascendancy in the Marxist camp. They have generally been treated with a considerable degree of scepticism, and the term 'underconsumptionist' has tended to be an uncomplimentary label to apply to a fellow theorist. In fact, as will be shown in Chapter Twelve, the influence of underconsumptionism amongst Marxists has been greater than is commonly imagined — but the influence has been surreptitious, unadmitted and often unrecognised. Underconsumption theories have never found a secure base in the world Communist movement.

NOTES

1 D.Ricardo, *On the Principles of Political Economy and Taxation*, p.80.
2 K.Marx, *Capital*, Vol 2, pp.475–6.
3 K.Marx, *Capital*, Vol 1, pp.113–4.
4 P.M.Sweezy, *The Theory of Capitalist Development*, p.178.
5 K.Marx, *Capital*, Vol 3, p.484.
6 ibid, pp.244–5.
7 Sweezy, op.cit., p.176.
8 ibid, p.177.
9 quoted in Sweezy, op.cit., pp.176–7.
10 ibid, p.177.
11 K.Marx, *Capital*, Vol 3, pp.251–2.
12 Sweezy, op.cit., pp.181–2.
13 ibid, p.182.
14 ibid, Ch 12.

7

THE RUSSIAN POPULISTS

INTRODUCTION

The Russian Populists, or Narodniks, are almost completely unknown to Western bourgeois economists, whilst Western Marxists are usually only familiar with the polemics directed against them by Lenin and Plekhanov and rarely read the original texts. Only historians of Russian economic development have paid much attention to them. The reasons for the lack of interest amongst economists are manifold, but a list of the factors involved would definitely include the following: firstly, the fact that Narodism was very much a Russian movement with little influence elsewhere, at least in the Western part of Europe; secondly, the specific economic situation with which they were concerned and which they were trying to analyse, which was that of a backward agrarian and not an advanced industrial economy; and thirdly, the theoretical tradition from which their views were drawn, which did not accord with the mainstream of European economic thought at that time, or subsequently. The combined effect of these things was that Western economists knew little or nothing of the debate about the development of capitalism in Russia. Of the two main economic theorists of Narodism on whose work this chapter will concentrate, Vorontsov was never translated into any West European language, although Nikolai-on's book appeared in French and German.

Nowadays, however, with the liberation of the ex-colonial countries and the aspirations of their peoples to a higher standard of living, and with the explosive growth in the money and effort put into the study of economic development in Western universities stimulated by the ideological and political struggles being fought out in those countries, the questions raised by the Narodniks would appear to have more contemporary relevance than before. It would be surprising if echos of their ideas were not to be found in present-day debates. For this reason I have devoted a few pages at the end of the chapter to discussing a modern line of thought which does have some connections with Narodnik views.

The two authors whom I shall study in detail are V.Vorontsov and N.F.Danielson (Nikolai-on or, in French, Nicolas-on), who were active in the 1880's and 1890's. These authors must be understood within the wider context of Narodism, for they are steeped in a tradition without an understanding of which some of the salient features of their thought could not be explained.

There has been some disagreement in the literature over the definition of Russian Populism,[1] which has essentially centred around the issue of whether or not to accept Lenin's characterisation of it. It is obviously not the place here to enter into such a dispute, and I shall confine myself to saying that, like Walicki, I fundamentally accept Lenin's approach. The following summary is based on his work.

Narodism is an ideology, an anti-capitalist ideology which made its appearance in Russia in the late 1860's and quickly gained support in intellectual circles, out of which grew a political movement of various strands and varying degrees of radicalism, some of them extremely revolutionary, and others extremely tame and conservative. The basis of this ideology was a belief in the specific historical destiny of Russia, due to the character of its institutions, in finding a path of development different from that of the West. It combined unremitting hostility to the development of capitalism in Russia, and to attempts by the State to support that development, with a belief in the peasant commune, or *obshchina*, as the basis for a non-capitalist development which would avoid all the horrors of industrialisation in the West. "Our communal ownership presents a far greater threat to the states of Europe than our army," said Flerovsky.[2]

Not far below the surface lay the idea that capitalism was fundamentally alien to all the principles of Russian social life, that it was a grave threat to it, and that its infiltration into Russia (its increasing influence was never denied) was the result of a subterfuge or a mistake: the complaint of Flerovsky's about the educated community being "contaminated with West European prejudices of the last century"[3] was entirely typical, for to the Narodniks it was indeed contamination. To this the Narodniks opposed the *obshchina*. But all was not well with the *obshchina*, because the Reform of 1861 had not provided the foundations for the flourishing of peasant agriculture, but had crushed the peasantry with new burdens which kept it as poor, and its cultivation as technically backward, as before. The *obshchina* was cramped, trodden down, and discriminated against, and as long as it stayed that way, it could not withstand the assault of capitalism against it. This unblinkered vision of the realities of the 1861 Reform was the essence of the radicalism in Narodism. To quote Lenin:

> The essence of Narodism: it is protest against serfdom (the old-nobility stratum) and bourgeoisdom (the new middle-class stratum) in Russia from the peasant's, the small producer's, point of view. Secondly, it shows at the same time that this protest is based on fantasy, that it turns its back on the facts.[4]

Politically, Narodism divided itself into two broad trends: "revolutionary" and "liberal" (i.e. non-revolutionary) Narodism.[5] Roughly, in the 70's the former predominated, and after 1880 the latter. Revolutionary Narodism was characterised by attempts to rouse the peasant masses to fight for their interests, either in the form of the "Go to the People" movement — dressing up in peasant clothes and preaching socialism in the villages — or by terroristic attempts to assassinate high State officials, which it was hoped would spark off a general peasant uprising. By 1881 (when the Tsar himself was assassinated) both these methods had proved themselves conspicuous failures — which was one of the main reasons for the demise of revolutionary Narodism and the growing influence of Marxism in radical circles. Liberal Narodism, on the other hand, concentrated on trying to persuade the intelligentsia and the government that giving the peasants enough land for a comfortable existence was — together with the communal spirit engendered by the *obshchina* — the best guarantee of successful economic development to catch up with the West. Most of the theoretical statements about the development of capitalism in Russia came out of this trend and not the other, since its political conception required elaboration of arguments for official consumption, rather than simple appeals to the masses to recognise their oppression.

As for the economic ideas of the Narodniks, it is worth

quoting the following passage, written by Lenin at the start of a pamphlet which aimed to criticise the Narodnik economists, to show that their theories had nothing to do with the ideas of Marx, and that they made the same theoretical mistakes as Sismondi half a century before:

> The title of Sismondi's chief work is ... *New Principles of Political Economy, or Wealth in Relation to Population.* This subject is almost identical with the problem known in Russian Narodnik literature as the "problem of the home market for capitalism". Sismondi asserted that as a result of the development of large-scale enterprise and wage-labour in industry and agriculture, production inevitably outruns consumption and is faced with the insoluble task of finding consumers; that it cannot find consumers within the country because it converts the bulk of the population into day labourers, plain workers, and creates unemployment, while the search for a foreign market becomes increasingly difficult owing to the entry of new capitalist countries into the world arena. The reader will see that these are the very same problems that occupy the minds of the Narodnik economists.[6]

It is entirely correct, as we shall see, to identify Sismondi as the theoretical ancestor of Vorontsov and Nikolai-on. At the same time, however, it is necessary to see the differences which arise from the different historical situations. Sismondi was writing at the time of the first rise of industrial capitalism, when its durability was still in doubt, and when it could still be claimed with some plausibility that the periodic crises heralded the imminent collapse of the whole system for lack of consumers. The Narodniks, on the other hand, while contesting that capitalist development was not possible in Russia, had at the same time to explain why this development had been possible elsewhere. Thus they put a lot of emphasis on the specificities of Russia, and on the impossibility for a backward country of competing effectively with the advanced industrial countries of the West. It is this new feature which gives them, and the criticism of them by their Marxist opponents, a contemporary interest in connection with the backward countries of today.

LARGE-SCALE AND SMALL-SCALE PRODUCTION

Initially, in the 1860's and early 1870's, Narodnik publicists denounced capitalism and asserted their faith in communal landownership and the virtues of peasant cultivation without developing a theory of the direction or the ultimate fate of capitalist development in Russia. For instance, Flerovsky's book, *The Condition of the Working Class in Russia,* first published in 1869, points out how capitalism had developed in the years since the Reform and argues very eloquently against it, but it contains nothing that could be described as a theory as opposed to a programme for action. This is Vorontsov's originality. He tries to prove not just that capitalism is undesirable but that its demise is inevitable under Russian conditions.

Vorontsov's most important work is his book *The Fate of Capitalism in Russia* (1882) — actually a collection of articles, most of which had been published elsewhere in the previous few years. This book presents the main Narodnik arguments as to why capitalist development is impossible in Russia, and incidentally it also reveals their big theoretical stumbling-block: the absence of a concept of mode of production.

Vorontsov starts by contrasting Russia with Western Europe. In the West, he says, the "established laws of political economy" work. Production is organised in large-scale capitalist units; the product is distributed amongst three groups of people (landowners, capitalists, workers) who are usually sharply differentiated from one another. If we find handicraft industry in England, it is usually the last remnants of a dying form of production, or it has managed to perpetuate itself for some special reason. Even such phenomena of economic life as periodically recurring crises, pauperism and emigration, which contradict the generally healthy state of the economy, are easily explainable by the laws of capitalist production, and this is why a few basic principles are sufficient for an understanding of the economy.[7]

In Russia, however, he says, this is not the case. The established laws of political economy do not apply, and the situation is so complicated that no one has yet elaborated the principles underlying the movement of the Russian economy. This is an authentically Narodnik idea, for it implies that Russia is so different from the West that a completely new economic and social theory must be developed in order to analyse it. It seems clear from the reference to crises, pauperism and emigration that Vorontsov is thinking not of the dominant schools of economic theory in the West but of their opponents — and probably of Marx's *Capital*. This reflects the Narodniks' high appreciation of Marxism as a forceful analysis of the evils of capitalism and their contempt for writers who tried to justify it.[8] But the Narodniks' appreciation of Marxism always stopped at the borders of the already industrialised capitalist countries, and they did not feel it was adequate for analysing their own societies. This is the basic idea behind Vorontsov's statement that a new theory must be developed for Russian conditions.

In Vorontsov's opinion, the main feature of Russian society is undoubtedly the struggle between large- and small-scale production.[9] In some areas, as in the processing industry, he says, large-scale production has already vanquished its opponent; in others, especially in agriculture, there is an intense battle and it is not always easy to work out which way it is going. All the Narodniks' conceptual problems and confusions are essentially condensed into this formulation of the struggle as one between large- and small-scale production, and, in fact, Vorontsov in places seems to recognise its inadequacy. At the very beginning of the book he states that even if peasant (i.e. small-scale) agriculture wins in the countryside, this does not determine what path of development it will take: it could be divided up into small, self-supporting units as in France, or a German type of peasant-aristocrat system could develop in which there is differentiation of "more competent" from "less competent" individuals, or finally a new form could arise with substantially the same features as the present *obshchina*.[10] Vorontsov recognises that the second possibility implies that the majority of peasants will be hiring themselves out as labourers to a minority of kulaks, and he does not appear to miss the point that this would be a form of capitalist development of agrarian relations. But this recognition does not seem to lead him to question the adequacy of the opposition large-scale/small-scale production on which his analysis is largely based. For example, in discussing the development of capitalism in Russian agriculture he asks at one point:

Has capital accomplished everything which is characteristic of the socialisation of labour, and if it has can we see in reality the inevitable results of the development of large-scale capitalist industry — the reduction of small units as a result of not being able to compete with the large ones, the elimination of independent peasant agriculture, and consequently the transformation of peasants into hired labourers?[11]

The large units referred to here are the landowners' farms, and the small units are the peasants' farms. Having posed this question, Vorontsov presents the results of a study of developments in some black-soil gubernias of White Russia, and the tendency to identify large-scale production with capitalism while small-scale production is seen as essentially non- and even anti-capitalist comes out clearly. He explicitly states at one point[12] that letting land out to tenants is for the landlord a system of getting an income outside the capitalist form of production, and it is clear that he regards the increased leasing of land to peasants as an index of the demise of capitalist production in an area, even though other studies have shown that the rented land was heavily concentrated in the hands of the richer peasants.[13] In Saratov Gubernia, Vorontsov says, commercial economy has developed only to a very small extent, while landowners for the most part "return the land to the peasants, for money or for work". Sowing on peasant land has increased while sowing on landlord land has fallen. In sum, he concludes, there is little evidence here of "the serious development of capitalist production or of its vanquishing of peasant production".[14] The opposition of 'capitalist' to 'peasant' production is symptomatic of his theoretical confusion.

Examples could be multiplied. In a later chapter, discussing the question of grain exports, Vorontsov points out that Russian agriculture will prove itself increasingly unprofitable on the basis of competition with the United States in the world market and landowners will be increasingly forced to abandon the fight and let their land out to tenants.[15] He says that the State has been confronted with two forms of production in the countryside, small-scale and large-scale, represented by two classes with conflicting interests — the peasants and the landowners.[16] The 1861 Reform did not come down whole-heartedly on one side or the other in this struggle, and it combines within it measures for the support of both small- and large-scale production.[17]

The industrial equivalent to the struggle between large-scale private landownership and independent peasant agriculture, as Vorontsov sees it, is the struggle between large-scale, mechanised factory production and domestic handicrafts carried on by independent artisans. Just as Vorontsov makes no attempt to examine trends in peasant economy or to ask whether the *obshchina* really is the bulwark against capitalist development which the Narodniks always claim it is, so now he professes a complete ignorance of any earlier or more primitive stages of the development of capitalist production relations in industry than fully fledged machine production. He never examines the statistics to find out whether, in fact, the bulk of domestic industry is carried on by fully independent producers or whether these producers are not, in the majority of cases, reduced to some sort of capitalist dependence. So we can see that Vorontsov's definition of capitalism is very restrictive: he defines it as *large-scale, mechanised* production, carried on under a system of private ownership of the means of production and with hired labour, and he lumps together all other forms of production as 'non-capitalist'. This point is of central importance since without this restricted concept (which is common to all Narodniks) it would be very difficult for Vorontsov to argue that capitalism in Russia is merely a 'hot-house plant' introduced by artificial government measures, and by no means a 'natural' development.

One of the characteristics of Narodnik writing is that survivals of feudal production relations, which played such an important part in the Russian countryside at this time, never really figure in the analysis. It is not that the Narodniks are unaware of these factors; on the contrary, as Lenin says,

> The point that the labour-service system is simply a survival of corvée economy is not denied even by the Narodniks.[18]

The point is that feudal relations are encompassed by the Narodniks' definition of capitalism. Since the basis of feudalism is the large landed estate, if capitalism in agriculture is essentially identified with these landed estates, feudalism is merely an aspect of capitalism, another form of oppression of independent peasant agriculture. This leads the Narodniks to

some rather peculiar interpretations of the intention of the 1861
Reform, which some of them (including Nikolai-on[19]) idealise as
an attempt to establish independent peasant farming in Russia.
But it should also be pointed out that the Narodniks could
hardly introduce feudalism into their analysis without
undermining their whole position. To quote Lenin again:

> The Narodniks do their utmost to avoid admitting the clear
> and simple fact that the present system of private-landowner
> farming is a combination of the labour-service and the
> capitalist systems, and that, consequently, the more devel-
> oped the former, the weaker the latter, and vice versa. They
> avoid analysing the relation of each of these systems to the
> productivity of labour, to the payment of the worker's labour,
> to the basic features of the post-Reform economy of Russia,
> etc. To put the question on this basis, on the basis of
> recognising the "*change*" *actually taking place*, meant to admit
> the inevitability of the progressive elimination of labour-
> service by capitalism.[20]

The above discussion on the Narodniks' concept of capitalist
production does not link in directly with the underconsumptionist aspects of their theories, but it does shed light on their
general position. It also prepares the way for the discussion of
Baran later in the chapter, since I shall argue that this is where
his similarity to them is most evident.

THE MARKET PROBLEM

In *The Fate of Capitalism in Russia* Vorontsov takes it as a
premise that Russian capitalism has a problem of markets that
inhibits its development. Only some years later did he publish
his thoughts on the general question of crises and the attitude of
earlier writers to this question. At this stage he proclaims himself
a disciple of Marx and adopts his terminology. In his book
Outlines of Economic Theory (1895) he argues as follows: the
workers consume products to the value of the wages that they
have been paid. Therefore the capitalists themselves must
consume in some way the rest of the product, "excepting that
part of it which the market requires for expansion". If they
succeed in this, there are no crises, no surplus of commodities.
So far so good. But the part of the product which "the market

requires for its expansion" (a peculiar phrase) is quietly forgotten from here on. The real problem, says Vorontsov, is that capitalists have to consume so much more, as surplus value is increasing so rapidly, that they find increasing difficulties in doing so:

> The Achilles heel of capitalist industrial organisation thus lies in the incapacity of the entrepreneurs to consume the whole of their income.[21]

Rodbertus had argued that it was the falling share of wages as a part of the total product that was the problem, but Vorontsov disagrees; the problem is that whatever is happening to the share of wages, the capitalists are unable to consume the whole of their share. This is the real source of the surplus of commodities on the market, and the crises that we observe in practice.

The difficulty is that Vorontsov has not examined the implications of investment in his theory. It is a part of the surplus value which is not personally consumed by the capitalists, so his problem could be solved by a sufficient increase of it. A discussion of the possibility of this is necessary, but not forthcoming.

Vorontsov has one interesting idea here: he is the first person to suggest arms expenditure as an outlet for this chronic surplus of commodities. This depends, of course, on the taxation to finance the expenditure being levied on the capitalists and not on the workers, as Vorontsov himself realises. Nowadays this conception of the role of arms expenditure is a very popular one in radical circles and it is interesting to see Vorontsov suggesting it. His mention of the possibility, however, in no way obscures the big hole in his argument: that he does not discuss the question of investment.

At the end of *The Fate of Capitalism in Russia*, Vorontsov says:

> My conclusions are that this form (of production), which was the vehicle of industrial progress in the west — capitalist production — has no firm foundation on Russian soil; this is shown, by the way, in the fact that the number of hired labourers in large-scale commercial industry has remained unchanged for the last 30–40 years, and in the agricultural sphere, the former large landowners, the nobility, are little by

little letting the land pass out of their control, and no other
class has appeared which is willing to tackle the problems of
organising production in large units.[22]

Of course, quite apart from problems of changing statistical
definitions (which may or may not operate here), the number of
workers employed is not the only measure of the significance of
factory production over a period of time, because rises in
productivity may allow a large rise in output with an unchanged
labour force. In fact Plekhanov points out that the output of
Russian industry grew considerably during this period.[23] Vorontsov's argument is that it is only due to the support which it
receives from the Treasury that capitalism has any significance
in Russia at all. Firstly, because Russia is so backward, and
Russian capitalism so young, it is effectively shut out from the
vast external world market since it is not competitive enough
there. Therefore it is confined to the home market. But in the
home market also it finds difficulties. In order to grow it
requires a growing market. But it itself undermines this market
by impoverishing the peasantry, eliminating their domestic
handicrafts, forcing them off the land and reducing them to
mere proletarians without property, living from hand to mouth.
Thus Russian capitalism is caught in a vicious circle: it cannot
grow, so its technical progress takes the form of reducing the
number of workers employed — thus impoverishing still more a
section of the mass of the people.[24] Thus capitalism, which in the
West has played such a glorious progressive role, in Russia is
merely a mechanism of the exploitation of the people, which will
never be able to develop the country. A new, non-capitalist path
is needed.

Vorontsov also finds arguments against Russian capitalism in
the degree of concentration to be observed in it. The development of industry in the West, he says, is the result of competitive
struggle between individual firms. But in the Russian machine
industry, for example, this competition is largely absent and will
stay absent for a long time, to judge by the extent of the market.
Thus capitalism in Russia lacks the motor of competition which
makes it a progressive force in the West.[25] In Russia it is only a
device for the enrichment of a small group of people, and acts as
a brake on the development of economic life.

Putting this argument beside the previous one, we get the

following: capitalism in Russia is highly monopolistic and therefore not at all dynamic; but in so far as it is progressive and does introduce new techniques of production, in the context of a limited market these result mainly in a reduction in the labour force rather than in an expansion in production, and thus serve to limit still further the market for the goods produced. So capitalist production in Russia finds itself in a cul-de-sac, in which after every step in advance it only gets stuck more deeply in the mud than before.

Vorontsov's interpretation of the history of capitalist development in Russia is quite consistent with this analysis. His main point is that capitalism did not arrive naturally on Russian soil, but has been artificially introduced by the State. He says:

> Our large-scale production came into being according to the wishes of the government, and some of its branches are still half under its direct management, while others it supports with subsidies and with orders.[26]

Furthermore, since Russian capitalism is so weak, and undermines its own market, this is not just a question of temporary State support to enable it to get off the ground; on the contrary, it will require more and more assistance as time goes on. For Vorontsov, the two alternatives facing Russia are not capitalist and non-capitalist development, but non-capitalist development or stagnation and decline.

One cannot but be impressed by the ingenuity of Vorontsov's position. He has a penetrating insight into the weaknesses of Russian industry (and agriculture) by comparison with the West, and he does not inveigh against capitalism in general but argues only that it is not suitable for Russia (or other backward countries). Here he draws on the traditional Narodnik emphasis on the difference between Russia and the West. His main point of attack is its need for government support, which in his view proves the necessity of its demise. But his theory is very dubious: in arguing that capitalism undermines its own market he neglects the very important question of the integration of the peasantry into the money economy. For on the feudal estate the peasant had very little contact with the market, producing almost entirely for his own consumption, and as such would constitute no outlet at all for the capitalist producer. It is precisely the extension of commodity production that accelerates

the differentiation of the peasantry and the impoverishment of
the majority, but it is also precisely the extension of commodity
production which turns the countryside into a market for
capitalist industry. Of all these phenomena Vorontsov notes only
the impoverishment of the masses and builds a theory on that,
without understanding that this impoverishment is nothing more
than one side of the development of capitalism *within peasant
economy itself.* This is where Vorontsov's restrictive concept of
capitalism leads him astray.

Nikolai-on (N.F.Danielson) is in some ways quite different
from Vorontsov in his intellectual formation (although his
arguments are very much the same in substance). He definitely
regarded himself as a Marxist, corresponded with Marx from
1868 onwards, and actually translated the first volume of *Capital*
into Russian. Moreover, the influence of Marx can readily be
seen, for example, in his discussion of the determination of the
value of a commodity, and of the separation of industry from
agriculture and its connection with the development of capitalist
production. His book, *Outlines of our Social Economy since the
Reform* (1894), is sprinkled throughout with quotations from
Capital.

It is this book with which we shall be concerned. It could
hardly be described as a comprehensive history (although this is
what the title of the French translation suggests[27]); it is more an
elaboration of an argument with extensive historical digressions
and references to support it. Some of the reasoning is very similar
to Vorontsov's; but there are some differences, and these
differences quite definitely reflect the different intellectual
influences to which Nikolai-on was subject. For instance,
Nikolai-on has no truck with the position that "the laws of
political economy" established for the West do not apply to
Russia — which for Vorontsov signifies the abandonment of
Marx's theory for the purpose of the discussion in hand; on the
contrary he is at pains to use that theory to the full. He shifts the
emphasis from the struggle between large- and small-scale
production (the centre of Vorontsov's argument) to the effects of
the separation of industry from agriculture and the destruction
of peasant handicraft industries by the development of capitalist
industrial production. Likewise, Nikolai-on does not argue that
capitalism is actually declining in Russia — he shows that the
number of workers it employs has risen somewhat over a period

of 25 years, and its output has risen a lot more — nor does he claim that its presence is merely due to the frenzied support of the government. Instead he seems to accept its development as more or less inevitable but claims that its progress is always limited by retarding factors, the chief of which is the poverty of the masses on whom it relies as consumers of its products. At this point he rejoins Vorontsov, and Rosa Luxemburg gives a largely correct summary of the position when she says that in spite of his quite different theoretical premises, Nikolai-on comes to much the same conclusion as Vorontsov as to the basic analysis of capitalism. He interprets Russian history and analyses the main forces at work in the same way as Narodnik authors do.

Following Marx, Nikolai-on regards the continuous revolution in productive techniques, the continuous reduction in the quantity of labour-time socially necessary for the production of a commodity, as one of the characteristics of capitalism. The most important result of this is that labour is continually being freed for re-employment on new projects, and in particular, with the pushing out of domestic handicraft industries unable to compete with the factories, large numbers of people in the countryside who work the land during the summer find themselves unemployed during the winter. In England, the removal of the source of supplementary income forced many people to move to the towns, or to emigrate. In Russia, however, an overwhelmingly agricultural country, it merely pushes the peasant to a more intense exploitation of his plot of land.

> All the statistical surveys report the extension of cultivated fields, even at the expense of other economic requirements, of the reclamation of grazing land etc. And they do that in order to get from the land what was formerly given them by their small domestic handicrafts.[28]

Now, in order to clothe themselves, the peasants have to sell more of their corn on the market than they did formerly. The exchange value of this corn is determined by the quantity of labour socially necessary for its production. But unfortunately for our poor Russian peasant, the market for corn is a world market and the relevant labour time is not his own, but an average of that of all the producers all over the world, which includes some (e.g. in the United States) far more efficient than himself, and getting more efficient every day. The combination of these two forces — the elimination of handicrafts and the competition in the world grain market — has reduced the income of the peasant considerably. From 1881 to 1887, for example, the price of barley (the main product of peasant agriculture) fell by more than 50 per cent.[29]

The argument here requires some more precision. While it is absolutely true that grain prices fell in the years prior to when Nikolai-on was writing, his argument about the freeing of winter labour-time raises some questions. Why should cottage industry be eliminated? This could only happen if it came directly into competition with larger-scale, more efficient production, i.e. if it was already commodity production. The peasant household which provides its own clothing is not necessarily affected by this at all. Only the peasant household a substantial part of whose income is derived from production of textiles etc. for the market suffers as the price of these goods falls and the hours of labour required to maintain a given income from domestic handicrafts steadily increase. And of course this is precisely the point at which this household has difficulty in finding the money to purchase raw materials and starts to borrow them from the buyer-up. Nikolai-on, who at the beginning of the book had demonstrated quite clearly that he knew the difference between commodity and non-commodity production, falls back in practice into the Narodnik habit of presenting capitalism as something entirely outside the peasant community and treating that community as a collection of independent households with no stratification or differentiation within it. It is true that the fall in the world price of grain is likely to affect the majority of peasants adversely; but what effect does this have on the already existing tendencies within peasant economy itself? This is the real question.

Here is Nikolai-on's analysis of capitalist production: the product divides itself into two parts, the wages of the labourers and the income of the capitalists. The first part can buy only a quantity of products equal in value to the sum total of wages paid out, but as society "tends always to limit wages to a minimum", in spite of their importance for the market the role of workers as buyers is becoming less and less. The contraction of wages is accomplished by all sorts of devices such as the lengthening of the working day, the intensification of work and the perfectioning of productive techniques which allows the replacement of adult male by female or child labour. Together with the elimination of domestic handicrafts amongst the agricultural population, this amounts to a reduction in the purchasing power of the vast mass of the population.

But the capitalist class is unable to absorb the whole of its share of the product. This is partly because one portion must be set aside for investment, and partly because with the development of production there develops also the manufacture of means of production, machines and so on, which cannot enter into personal consumption and must be consumed productively; they can never enter into revenue, but must always act as capital. In addition, the increasing productivity of labour means that the product is sold more cheaply, and more people are able to buy it.[30]

"But how does this prove that the capitalists cannot absorb the whole of their profits?" one might legitimately ask. Well, apparently, the point is that all of these products are intended for a huge market, and therefore they are too much for the entrepreneur himself to consume.[31] So after all we come back to Vorontsov's point: that the capitalists do not have a big enough personal consumption. Nikolai-on's argument is merely a garbled version of Vorontsov's, with the addition of one inspired thought: the impoverishment caused by the elimination of peasant handicraft industries.*

Nikolai-on aims to prove by this that after it has attained a certain degree of development, a capitalist nation finds its own internal market insufficient and is forced to seek outlets abroad (Russian capitalism, however, is so backward that it is bound to fail in this, and can be competitive inside the country only if it is protected by a high tariff wall[32]). In a survey of the recent economic history of the United States, he tries to show that the fortunes of manufacturing industry have fluctuated according to the prosperity of the farming community,[33] a fact which he claims to be true of all capitalist nations.

The long chronic crisis, sometimes more acute, sometimes less, from which the world economy has suffered for the last 10 to 15 years, is due to the relative impoverishment of the

*And even this is mentioned by Vorontsov although he does not discuss it from a theoretical viewpoint.

most numerous class of the population, the agricultural class.[34]

And his conclusion is this:

> In every country which has set out on the path of capitalist production, it is only an isolated comparatively small class, and not the whole population, which benefits from more productive, socialised labour. . . . The result is that the limits of the development of capital are fixed by the growing poverty that depends in its turn on this development of capital, on the growing number of workers unemployed and unemployable by capital, unable to satisfy their most basic needs.[35]

We can note that unlike Vorontsov, Nikolai-on seems to be aware of the gradual differentiation of the peasantry, of the power which the richer ones acquire over their poorer neighbours, and he is under no illusions that this is anything but the first primitive development of capitalism in the peasant community.[36] In his view, under present economic conditions, the death of the *obshchina* is merely a question of time. (He explicitly rejects the view, prominent in Narodnik circles and reflected in Flerovsky's book, that its decline is merely due to the prevalence of mistaken ideas in high positions.) But he believes that in principle it represents the germs of a higher form of social development than capitalism, and he quotes Marx and Engels to the effect that in the wake of a socialist transformation of the West the *obshchina* might form the basis of a non-capitalist path of development in Russia.[37] Nikolai-on sees socialism as the only alternative to capitalism, and thus rejects Vorontsov's solution; but his theory is the same in all important respects, and much less coherently argued.

What can we say by way of conclusion about the Narodniks? First of all, they are very much immersed in the situation of Russia at the end of the nineteenth century, which gives their ideas a very specific quality. The idea that capitalism was a western development which Russia was privileged enough to avoid by virtue of the institutions she had built up in the course of her history was an article of faith with them. Nikolai-on is really only a semi-Narodnik in this respect; in his view the specific advantages of Russia lie only in the possibility of the *obshchina* functioning as a basis for socialist development, and he does not subscribe to any of the effusions over "the noble character of our Russian muzhik" which lie barely beneath the surface of much Narodnik economic writing.

But in making the transition from saying merely that capitalism is undesirable to saying that it contains definite contradictions which prevent or limit its development in Russia (a transition first made by Vorontsov), they have to face new questions. For Russian capitalism must bear all the characteristics of capitalism in general, while at the same time being different — for it is only by this means that the simultaneous success of capitalism in the West and its projected failure in Russia can be explained. This demands that statements about the social undesirability of capitalism in Russia have to be transformed into economic arguments about its prospects.

The basis of the arguments of Vorontsov and Nikolai-on is an underconsumption theory of a Sismondian type, which attributes the lack of consumers to the poverty of the workers, for which the demand of the capitalists themselves is insufficient to compensate. Like Sismondi also, they see the elimination of the independent producer as the removal of precisely the source of demand which might have resolved the problem. What is not quite clear, however, is how the problem is resolved by capitalist production on a world scale; for although it is simple enough to say that unlike foreign countries Russian capitalism is so backward that it is unable to solve the problem by pushing into foreign markets, foreign markets can never be a solution for capitalist production as a whole. There is a gap in the Narodnik argument here. But the fundamental difficulty is that they ignore the fact that investment absorbs a significant part of the surplus product. Now it is quite true that Sismondi also ignores the demand generated by investment and the possibility that it may remove the surplus product from the market, but he is held back by the specific interpretation of investment which prevailed at the time, which tended to reduce it, in effect, to merely a transfer (as opposed to an addition) of demand from capitalists to workers, followed by a more or less immediate increase in the production of consumption goods. Sixty or seventy years later, however, this excuse is no longer a valid one, since by then the idea that investment took time and was a matter of buying fixed capital was well established, and it is difficult to see how the creation of demand aspect of investment could be overlooked. This is all the more true in view of the Narodniks' acquaintance with the work of Marx, who emphasised this a great deal and made explicit criticisms of his predecessors on this point. Effectively, the Narodniks take over the whole of Sismondi's theory, including its mistakes, which they should have been wise enough to notice.

In fact, both Vorontsov and Nikolai-on recognise that capitalists set aside money for investment purposes, but neither of them discusses the significance of this as regards crises. Vorontsov argues that after wages have been paid, capitalists have to consume what remains of the product themselves, "excepting that part of it which the market requires for expansion". He never discusses what determines the volume of this latter. Nikolai-on is simply confused, for he even appears to argue that the act of investment, by producing goods which cannot be consumed, actually aggravates the problem! The criticism levelled by Lenin at the Narodniks, that they ignore the demand for consumer goods represented by workers and capitalists in the investment goods industries, is thus fundamentally correct — for they only pay lip-service to it. Their underconsumptionism, when they try to give it an abstract theoretical expression, is relatively unsophisticated, and their work acquires its effectiveness more from an acute description of the weaknesses and difficulties of Russian capital (or capital in any backward country) than from any theoretical justification of their positions.

MODERN PARALLELS

Marxist critics of Narodism did not just confine themselves to abstract theoretical objection to Narodnik theorising; in fact they were more concerned about its overall interpretation of the development of capitalism in Russia. The Narodnik view, as we have seen, was that Russian life and conditions were such that capitalism could never flourish there and could never develop the country. It was dependent on State support for its existence, and would always remain so. Marxists took a diametrically opposed position on the fate of capitalism in Russia. They argued that in spite of the preponderance of feudal relations in the countryside and in the State apparatus, capitalism was developing and becoming stronger in Russia with every day that passed. It was developing even within the *obshchina*, which the Narodniks portrayed as an unbreachable obstacle to the advance of capitalism. All the main lines of a Marxist critique of Narodism were laid down by Plekhanov in his book *Our Differences* (1884), which was written while Marxism in Russia was still only a very recent development.

However, it is not the place here to discuss in detail the debate between Marxists and Narodniks. What is interesting is to see whether any echos of Narodnik theories can be discerned in present-day debates on underdevelopment. And here I want to look particularly at the growth in radical circles of the idea that the problems of the modern underdeveloped countries in their struggle for industrialisation can never be solved within a capitalist framework, and that only a socialist revolution can save them from permanent stagnation. This idea grew out of awareness of the support given by the Western industrial powers, and above all the U.S., to the most reactionary political forces in these countries, and the knowledge that these forces represented classes and strata which had no significant interest in the industrial development of their countries. Western support was based on their willingness to turn a blind eye to the activities of foreign capital, to allow it the free run of the natural resources of the country and to impose the minimum conditions on the generation and export of profits. This alliance of the Western capitalist states with the most backward social forces in the underdeveloped world was, and is, the starting-point for the theory that only socialism can save these countries from their backward condition.

The book which launched this theory, and which remains its finest and most comprehensive statement, is Paul Baran's *The Political Economy of Growth* (1957). *The basic thesis of the book is that capitalist industrialisation in the West has had repercussions on the underdeveloped world which have prevented any independent national economic development of these countries,

*Baran's theory is a little crude and although it has been very influential in left-wing circles, it probably would not nowadays be accepted in quite the same form (for a more recent discussion of these issues see Owen & Sutcliffe, 1972); nevertheless it is one of those important books which establish a whole line of thought, and in a short discussion such as this it is legitimate to confine our attention to it alone.

even in the cases where at one point they looked as if they might be working towards such development (e.g. India) before they were hit by colonial plunder. The argument runs as follows: the development of factory production in the West had the effect of giving the Western powers the military superiority required to overcome the resistance of native rulers in other parts of the globe. It also gave Western products the cheapness required to eliminate the competition of handicraft producers in the now unprotected colonised areas, and the laborious development of handicraft industries which had been part of the build-up to industrialisation in the West was now undermined almost overnight. The best example of this was the Bengal cotton industry. At the same time the stocks of gold and other precious objects which might have played an important role in the industrialisation of these countries were systematically plundered and taken back to Europe as adventurers' booty. Gradually, the colonies were integrated into the world market as exporters of two or three primary products for whose production they were particularly fitted, and imported what industrial goods they consumed from abroad. Hence the peculiar economic structure of the underdeveloped countries today, which is not at all like that of Western Europe on the eve of its industrialisation.

Baran's argument continues as follows: nowadays Western politicians profess great interest in and concern for the development problems of these countries. The truth, however, is that the interests of Western capital in these countries, which politicians in the West are always keen to defend in the name of "freedom", are diametrically opposed to those of the developing country. These business interests take out more from the underdeveloped countries each year in the form of profit, interest and dividends than they put back in new capital investments. Furthermore, the typical mineral or agricultural investment has very little effect on the host economy, and in many ways is just an outpost of a foreign economy. Only a small percentage of the price of the product goes to increase demand in the host country. This is due to high profit rates, low tax rates, the importation of skilled workers from abroad who spend their money on U.S. products, and the low pay of local unskilled labour. So this — the predominant — type of foreign investment makes very little contribution to the development of the country.

The chief political interest of these foreign investors is to keep tax rates low, and to prevent expropriation by a nationalist government. This means in practice alliance with the powerful landowning interests, for these are the class of people who will resist most strongly any radical pressures. It is a myth that the underdeveloped countries are too poor to liberate the resources required for investment. In reality, a tremendous surplus exists over and above the consumption of the direct producers — but it is consumed by rich landowners and middlemen who have no interest in putting their money into productive investment projects, and spend it on foreign luxuries, hoard it in Swiss banks, indulge in property speculation etc. Meanwhile agriculture remains in a state of backwardness and no funds are provided for industrial development.

> What results is a political and social coalition of wealthy compradors, powerful monopolists, and large landowners dedicated to the defence of the existing feudal-mercantile order. Ruling the realm by no matter what political means . . . this coalition has nothing to hope for from the rise of industrial capitalism which would dislodge it from its positions of privilege and power. Blocking all economic and social progress in its country, this regime has no real political basis in city or village, lives in continual fear of the starving and restive popular masses, and relies for its stability on Praetorian guards of relatively well-kept mercenaries.[38]

So Baran has this to say about capitalism in these countries:

> Far from serving as an engine of economic expansion, of technological progress, and of social change, the capitalist order in these countries has represented a framework for economic stagnation, for archaic technology, and for social backwardness.[39]

This is essentially the same as what Vorontsov said about capitalism in nineteenth century Russia. The theory is more sophisticated, relying especially on an assessment of the political forces at work, but the theme of the impossibility of capitalist development remains. It is interesting to note that in spite of the apparent differences Baran makes the same primary mistake as the Narodniks. The kernel of the Marxist critique of the Narodniks was that they had no concept of mode of production, that they therefore were incapable of a scientific analysis of the trends of the Russian economy and of peasant agriculture in particular, and that they substituted for the concept of the capitalist mode of production a mere image — the image of the Western model of capitalist development. Since Russian conditions dictated that local capitalist development could not follow this model exactly — in particular it relied heavily on State support — the Narodniks concluded that capitalism was destined to fail in Russia. Baran's conception too is dominated by this image of the Western model. For him the relevant features are not lack of State support but a balanced economy, industrialisation, and control over the economy by domestic rather than foreign capitalists. This image is summed up in the idea of "independent national economic development".[40] In the interests of this image unsuitable examples such as Ireland or Brazil (i.e. industrialisation on the basis of heavy foreign investment) are glossed over or left out of account. The average underdeveloped country, with its lopsided economy and dominated by foreign capital, is presented as incapable of attaining the desired form of development under capitalist conditions. In Baran as in the Narodniks this image takes the place of a serious analysis of the development of capitalism in these countries based on a concept of mode of production.

The main concept with which he operates is that of the "economic surplus"; but the distinguishing feature of this concept is that it over-rides any distinction of modes of production in calculating the total absolute quantity of resources which might be available for investment if the economy was organised for development purposes. As Baran himself points out, what lies beneath this concept is the idea of an ideal rationally organised society against which existing ones can be judged. But this pushes into the background the question of the mode of production which predominates, and of whether capitalist production is extending its influence or not, because a surplus product is a feature of feudal as well as of capitalist production. Thus while superficially Baran's economic surplus resembles Marx's surplus value, in fact it obscures what has been the central concern of Marxist analyses of the transition from feudalism to capitalism (e.g. Lenin's *Development of Capitalism in Russia*) — the study of the extension and development of the capitalist mode of production. It is a concept geared to the schemes of the development economist rather than to an analysis of current trends in capitalist development in the economies concerned, and the result is that such an analysis is not provided in the book, and the possibility that, for instance, integration into the world market, however lopsided it may have been, might actually have promoted capitalist development is not seriously considered. Thus the real historical truth, as opposed to Baran's thesis, about capitalist development in these countries never comes out. And this is exactly the reproach which Plekhanov and Lenin levelled at the Narodniks.

There is no doubt that Baran, like the Narodniks before him, is very perceptive about all the factors which are retarding capitalist development, but the issue is whether, as Baran claims, this development is ultimately impossible, or just slower than it might be. For instance, national liberation movements may achieve power in these countries and use the state machinery to smash the remnants of feudalism and to promote significant industrial development, without the working class being strong enough to push the movement beyond the limits of bourgeois nationalism. This kind of thing has already happened, and it implies that considerable progress can be achieved short of socialism. Baran does not recognise these possibilities.

So the Narodnik ideas on capitalist development have more contemporary relevance than appears at first sight. But the enduring feature is the idea of the impossibility of a capitalist path of development, and not the particular form of underconsumption theory which they espoused.

NOTES

1 For a discussion of these questions see A.Walicki, *The Controversy over Capitalism.*
2 N.Karataev, *Narodnicheskaya Ekonomicheskaya Literatura,* p.207. This book is a collection of Narodnik economic literature, including the last chapter of Flerovsky's book *The Condition of the Working Class in Russia* and sixty pages of extracts from Vorontsov.
3 ibid, p.203.
4 V.I.Lenin, *Collected Works* Vol 1, pp.340–1.
5 For a full discussion of these issues see Walicki, op.cit., or F.Venturi, *Roots of Revolution.*

6 Lenin, *Collected Works* Vol 2, p.134.
7 Karataev, op.cit., p.417.
8 It is not too far-fetched to suggest that Flerovsky took the title of his book from Engels's study of the Manchester working class.
9 Karataev, op.cit., p.418.
10 ibid, p.418.
11 ibid, pp.433–4.
12 ibid, p.434.
13 eg Lenin, *The Development of Capitalism in Russia* (DCR), pp.83–4.
14 Karataev, op.cit., p.435.
15 ibid, pp.455–6.
16 ibid, p.457.
17 ibid, p.467.
18 Lenin, DCR, p.213.
19 Nikolai-on says: "The Principle of the 1861 Manifesto was: to give the instruments of labour to the producers themselves, in order to increase productivity and to create the conditions which would guarantee the economic development of the population as a whole." (*Histoire du Développement de la Russie depuis l'Affranchissement des Serfs*, p.3)
20 Lenin, DCR, p.213.
21 Quoted in R.Luxemburg, *The Accumulation of Capital*, p.281.
22 Karataev, op.cit., pp.479–80.
23 G.V.Plekhanov, *Selected Philosophical Works*, Vol 1, p.242.
24 Karataev, op.cit., p.464.
25 ibid, p.427.
26 ibid, p.427.
27 Nicolas-on, *Histoire du Développement de la Russie depuis l'Affranchissement des Serfs*. All references are to this volume.
28 ibid, p.150.
29 ibid, Part 2 Ch 6.
30 ibid, pp.250–1.
31 ibid, p.252.
32 ibid, p.483.
33 ibid, Ch 28.
34 ibid, p.440.
35 ibid, pp.483–4.
36 ibid, p.486.
37 ibid, pp.495–6.
38 P.Baran, *The Political Economy of Growth*, p.338.
39 ibid, p.300.
40 The intrinsic vagueness of this idea is pointed out by Bill Warren in an article in New Left Review no 81.

8

J.A.HOBSON

INTRODUCTION

J.A.Hobson's published writings span a period of half a century (1889–1938) and include 37 books, mainly on contemporary economic and political questions. Only a few of these books will concern us here: chiefly *The Physiology of Industry* (1889), *The Problem of The Unemployed* (1896), *The Economics of Distribution* (1900), *Imperialism* (1902), and *The Industrial System* (1909).

First a few general remarks about the man. He came from a Liberal middle-class background, and was himself for a long time a member of the Liberal Party. At school he apparently read widely, and went on to Oxford University, where he read classics. To get an idea of the young Hobson, one can do no better than to quote Brailsford:

> In the Oxford of his day, as his contemporary Nevinson described it, the chief influences were Ruskin, Jowett, and T.H.Green. Ruskin as yet meant nothing to Hobson, who was never interested in the visual arts. Wide as his interests were, they centred chiefly in the social sciences. . . . The contemporary Socialism of this period, with Morris, Hyndman, Edward Carpenter, and the Christian school as its spokesmen, made no appeal to him: he found them 'either too inflammatory or too sentimental'. I doubt whether T.H.Green or any of the Neo-Kantians influenced him greatly: the cast of his mind was traditionally English. Marx repelled him, and though he made an early study of *Capital,* he never discussed it at any length. He criticised Marx chiefly for his one-sidedness in concentrating his attack on capitalism upon a single aspect, the exploitation of the wage-earners, and he dismissed the dialectical method as frivolous pedantry.[1]

At this time he was no socialist, and it was only later, after coming into contact with Ruskin, that he moved in that direction. It was the humanistic indictment of the degradations of contemporary society that Ruskin provided that captured his imagination. Ruskin attacked the classical economists for identifying value with marketable goods and services, and his doctrine that "there is no wealth but life" had a powerful influence on Hobson. As Hobson himself puts it:[2]

> Though Ruskin in no single book set out his economic "science" in its full strength, a reading of his several writings yields a sufficient basis for a human political economy, which should take account of the related processes of production and consumption, and should evaluate both processes in terms of human worth. From him I drew the basic thought for my subsequent economic writings, viz. the necessity of going behind the current monetary estimates of wealth, cost, and utility, to reach the body of human benefits and satisfactions which gave them a real meaning.

This shows the ethical, humanistic standpoint from which Hobson criticised the world around him. Although Hobson himself was a radical, anti-Establishment, anti-Church, this kind of critique was not so different from the backward-looking aristocratic condemnations of industrial society which were quite common in the nineteenth century. Both abhorred the predominance of "the values of the market-place", and both maintained a mild detachment which allowed them not to sully their hands by meddling in the real world. Lenin described Hobson as a "social-liberal", and this is quite apt, for while he supported the trade union movement and ended up in the Labour Party, he always retained the liberal passion to be rational through detachment, to be untainted by commitment to any class, and to represent the interest of all. He was a socialist convinced on intellectual grounds of the need for radical change, but ultimately frightened by the working-class movement. To him it was not the rhetoric and language of class struggle that was needed, but the possibility of escape from the all-pervasive influences of class and personal interest that were the great obstacle inhibiting the search for rational solutions to the social questions of the time; the intellectual must strive to be above class.[3]

This determined his attitude to Marxism: he was always repelled by it. For a thinker who strove to rise above all prejudice, the idea that the world should be revolutionised by the uneducated masses was unlikely to be of much appeal. Brailsford sums this up very well:

> The fact is, of course, that Hobson, a rationalist and humanist to the core, was repelled not merely by the lack of scientific objectivity in the proletarian economics of the Marxists, but even more by their reliance on force. When he himself adopted a socialist programme which called for a fundamental change in the structure of our society, he rejected the class war as a right or possible way of reaching it. He had no belief that an organised party of workers could ever achieve it unaided, and relied on rational persuasion to win over a part of the middle class. He disliked the 'envy, hatred and all uncharitableness' which he found too often in the Labour Party. ... It was natural, therefore, that the Russian Revolution, which meant so much to his younger contemporaries, ... meant much less to him.[4]

In sum, his was a radicalism very much in the tradition of John Stuart Mill: a profound rationalism, a belief that reason would ultimately triumph by the force of its own logic against the weight of prejudice, combined with a sympathy for the sufferings of human beings and a clinical recognition of the more corrupting aspects of capitalist society to convince him that socialism was the only possible solution; but like that of J.S.Mill it was socialism built on the foundations of liberalism, which abhorred Marxism or anything which smacked of a division of the world in class terms.

His economic ideas show the same characteristics. His conclusions are highly unorthodox, but the theoretical framework is not. He takes over the basic ideas of Malthus, but the quite sophisticated elaboration which he gives to them is centred very much around the concepts of neoclassical economics, above all the notion of "factors of production". He does not try, like Marx, to challenge the entire theoretical basis of orthodoxy, but rather to take it over and draw new conclusions out of it.

The most obvious development in economic theory between the time of Malthus and the time of Hobson is the rise of marginalism. Both Hobson and Keynes are very clear that this did not make any fundamental difference to the orthodox position on the general glut question: Keynes includes what is nowadays often referred to as neoclassical economics in classical economics, because it did not fundamentally question Say's Law. This is obviously true in the sense that the major emphasis in the explanation of crises and depressions was still put on maladjustments and delays in the functioning of the process of competition, as it was by James Mill and Ricardo; few people wanted to ascribe crises to more basic causes, or to suggest, as Marx did, that considerable fluctuations creating periodic overproduction of capital and labour were an inherent feature of an industrial capitalist economy. A whole host of theories of the trade cycle grew up which attributed them to the phenomena of credit and banking (the credit cycle), to sunspots, to harvest fluctuations etc, but there was always a gap between these attempts to account for an unavoidable reality and the pure theory established by theoreticians, since the theory did not really admit a coherent explanation of the phenomenon.

Actually, within this apparent continuity, things had changed somewhat. James Mill and his supporters seemed to assume that planned saving and planned investment would balance each other automatically, unless for some freakish reason there was considerable hoarding; and from this it was a simple logical deduction that general gluts were impossible. Marginalism introduced the idea that supply and demand were related to price, so that excess supply could not be said to exist in the abstract: all that could be said was that the supply exceeded the demand at such and such a price. It therefore only required a fall in price to remove the excess. From this it followed that an excess supply of any commodity or factor could always be attributed, in the end, to an obstacle in the functioning of the price mechanism. For example, if there was large-scale unemployment, this was probably due to the monopoly power of trade unions keeping wages "artificially" high. Capitalists did not find it profitable to take more workers on. So fundamentally, marginalist writers dismissed the general glut theory as forcefully as their predecessors had and demanded the removal of the inadequacies in the functioning of the competitive mechanism. In essence, a shift in theoretical approach led to the same conclusions as before in the explanation of depressions. Hobson could complain that in spite of all the attacks on J.S.Mill's ideas towards the end of the nineteenth century, no one seemed inclined to question his dogma about overproduction.[5]

THE PHYSIOLOGY OF INDUSTRY

Hobson's first book was written in conjunction with a businessman, A.F.Mummery, who had eventually convinced him, after much argument, that excessive saving was the fundamental cause of the trade depressions with which everyone was so familiar.

This man entangled me in a controversy about excessive saving, which he regarded as responsible for the under-employment of capital and labour in periods of bad trade. For a long time I sought to counter his arguments by the use of the orthodox economic weapons. But at length he convinced me and I went in with him to elaborate the over-saving argument in a book entitled "The Physiology of Industry", which was published in 1889. This was the first open step in my heretical career, and I did not in the least realise its momentous consequences.[6]

It is clear from this that Mummery was the real inspiration behind the book. However, his only other published work is on climbing in the Alps and the Caucasus, and he never made any other contribution to economics; it was Hobson who went on to progressively develop the arguments of *The Physiology of Industry* over the next twenty years.

The book is directed towards an exposure of the fallacy that "saving enriches and spending impoverishes the community along with the individual", as J.S.Mill put it, and to proving that an excessive level of saving will in fact impoverish the community. The outline of the argument is presented briefly in the Preface. It runs as follows: the object of production is to provide consumers with 'utilities and conveniences', and the function of capital is to serve as an aid to the production of these, at every stage from the first extraction of the raw materials to the final sale. Since this is the *only* function of capital, it is clear that the total used must vary with the volume of goods and services consumed within any given period of time. How does saving affect this? An increase in the rate of saving will reduce the rate of consumption, at the same time as it increases the existing aggregate of capital; therefore, if saving is carried too far, there is an accumulation of capital beyond what is required for current use, and the excess will manifest itself in the form of general overproduction.[7]

This leads the authors to reject the orthodox notion, dating back to Adam Smith, that saving does not reduce aggregate consumption, but only varies the consumers. They attribute this fallacy to the wages fund theory, which provided it with a logical basis; the fact that it has managed to persist beyond the collapse of that doctrine can only be due to the "commanding authority of the great men who asserted it".[8] In its place, the authors set up the equation: 'Production – Saving = Consumption'.

This equation means quite simply that with a given level of production, an increase in saving will diminish by exactly the same quantity the aggregate consumed. What it amounts to, therefore, is that the output of the community is equal to its income — which was in fact the main argument used by James Mill in defence of his position. Hobson and Mummery express the identity in this form, however, in order to concentrate attention on the level of consumption.

The thesis is that the revenue of the various factors of production — natural agents, capital, and labour — which depends on the level of demand for them, is determined by the quantity of utilities and conveniences consumed. Since undue saving by individuals necessarily cuts back the rate of current consumption, it cannot but reduce the remuneration of factors and hence the revenue of the community. Thus

> We contradict the generally accepted dogmas that the saving of the individual must always and necessarily enrich the Community, and that wages can only rise at the expense of profit, or profit at the expense of wages, or both at the expense of rent.[9]

Here income is made to be dependent on consumption, since consumption determines the level of employment and remuneration of factors of production. The importance of saving, therefore, is in its influence on the level of consumption.

> Saving, while it increases the existing aggregate of Capital, simultaneously reduces the quantity of utilities and conveniences consumed; any undue exercise of this habit must, therefore, cause an accumulation of Capital in excess of that

which is required for use, and this excess will exist in the form of general overproduction.[10]

It is worth stopping a moment to consider this Preface, since it sets out the bare bones of an argument which is characteristic of all Hobson's later work.

First of all, it is apparent that it is an underconsumptionist argument, since the demand which is important is the quantity of utilities and conveniences *consumed*. From the passage just quoted, it can be seen that the demand for means of production created by investment is not included in this category, for when the authors talk about an accumulation of capital they undoubtedly mean that the savings are invested and not just retained as money (this is clear from other parts of the book), and yet savings are still treated as a pure subtraction from the quantity of utilities and conveniences consumed.

Secondly, we can see that the justification for this singling out of consumption demand is the idea that the object of production is to provide consumers with 'utilities and conveniences'. This is a point of some importance, because it seems to me that this is an idea which is subconciously active in the heads of most underconsumptionists, inducing them to believe that the demand provided by immediate consumers as opposed to other purchasers occupies some special role in the economy, although there is no reason why this should be so in a capitalist society in which production depends on the expectation of private profit. To say this is of course no substitute for an examination of the theoretical merits and defects of underconsumption theories as such, but I feel certain that the prevalence of this idea is highly significant as an explanation of the peculiar history of underconsumption theories, in which they manage to carry on a tenacious subterranean existence in spite of being denounced time and time again by orthodox economists. I shall discuss this fully in Chapter Eleven.

The third point is that Hobson's theory is very much a Malthusian rather than a Sismondian type of underconsumption theory, since it emphasises the level of saving as opposed to the distribution of income between capitalists and workers. The fact that in later books Hobson goes on to explain a tendency to over-saving as a consequence of the inability of workers to force their wages up further does not fundamentally alter this, since this distributive factor only operates via its effect on savings, which remain the crucial variable.

The central thesis of *The Physiology of Industry* is the law of the quantitative relation between consumption and production, which must work in such a way that it is final consumption which is the determinant of production, and not vice versa, as usually contended, in the wake of J.S.Mill. The authors establish this law by an examination of the technical processes through which any product must pass before it emerges in a consumable form; hence the title: "The Physiology of Industry". Take any product, say, a piano. Although at the final stage of production a complete, workable piano may emerge, there are any number of stages of working up raw materials, assembling the various parts etc., which come before this. Thus the authors represent the whole of commercial life as follows:

R.M.	(Natural Agents	— Plant —	Labour)
R.M.1	,,	,,	,,
R.M.2	,,	,,	,,
Goods	,,	,,	,,
Goods 1	,,	,,	,,
Goods 2	,,	,,	,,
Shop goods	,,	,,	,,
Commodities	,,	,,	,,

(Note: R.M. = raw materials; the authors define commodities as "valuable articles in the possession of consumers", and goods as "valuable articles in the various stages of production between raw material and commodity". Shop-goods are goods in the hands of retailers).

In the first stage, the natural agents, plant and labour engaged in that line of production will take the input R.M., and in the process of production will transform it into R.M.1, and so on up the scale.

At each step in the process there will be a portion of the raw material on its way to become a commodity, a portion of natural agents in the shape of land, &c. (important in production of agricultural commodities, less important in other cases), a portion of plant in the shape of factories, storehouses, and machinery, and a portion of human labour.

In a well-organised industrial society it is evident that these three agents in production (natural agents, plant, labour) will have a definite relation to the work they are to do at each stage in the process of production; that is to say, they will bear, both as a whole and singly, a definite proportion to the quantity of raw material in its various stages which it is their business to assist. Given the amount of R.M.1 or R.M.2 on its way to become commodities, a certain definite amount of each of the agents in production will be required to assist in furthering the work.[11]

At this stage the argument is a purely technical one: it is of no consequence, for instance, whether the whole process of piano-making, from beginning to end, takes place under the auspices of a single firm, or whether there are myriad purchases and sales of the unfinished products in the course of manufacture. And provided there is no alteration in technical conditions, there must be a fixed and exact relation between the amount of capital required at each stage, and the amount of consumption of finished commodities.[12] This is true of the other factors of production also. The authors admit that in the real world this exact relationship between the agents in production and the raw material is seldom reached and never long maintained, but, they say, "in so far as the actual state errs from this ideal there is a loss of economic energy."[13] In other words this exact relation represents an optimum situation.

The argument continues as follows: not only, at any given stage of production, must the quantity of the various productive agents bear a fixed relation to the volume of production, but also, the volume of production at each stage must bear a fixed relation to the volume of production at other stages, and in particular, to the rate of consumption of finished goods.

If we were to assume that all raw material on its way to become commodities were obliged to pass through all the stages we have named, R.M., R.M.1, &c., it is clear that in order to supply a definite quantity of commodities there must have been a certain definite and precise amount of R.M., which afterwards assumed the form R.M.1, then R.M.2, and so on right through the series.[14]

Thus we reach the conclusion that a given quantity of finished commodities of a known nature determines absolutely the amount of raw material, plus agents in production, previously existent at each stage in production. According to Hobson and Mummery's definition of wealth, wealth consists of all stocks of finished and unfinished goods, raw materials, plus all agents in production, both material and non-material (i.e. including labour-power and skill of workers), so this conclusion can be restated in the following way:

> A given quantity of commodities of a known nature determines the amount of wealth previously existent at each stage so far as the production of these commodities is concerned.[15]

Hence a fixed quantitative relation exists between the present rate of consumption and the aggregate of wealth "which has had an economic existence in the immediate past". It is also apparent, say the authors, that there must be a similar relation between consumption and production. Since every product must either be consumed or added to accumulated wealth, the relation between consumption and wealth must mean a more or less definite relation between consumption and production.[16]

At this point the reader could justifiably complain about the imprecision of the formulation. It is important to bear in mind that the authors were talking of the relation between present consumption and *past* wealth (i.e. the wealth in existence at the time when the commodities now being consumed were being produced). Thus, when they say: "every product must either be consumed or added to accumulated wealth", if they are referring to present consumption, they must also be referring to production in the present period and wealth accumulated up to the beginning of the present period (which is not necessarily the same as the wealth involved in their quantitative relation). More important, the relation they quote is between production, consumption, and *the change in wealth*, so that it cannot be deduced from this that the relation between consumption and *the absolute value of wealth* implies "a more or less definite relation between consumption and production." The argument, which has been carefully built up so far, is riddled with holes at this point. This is very serious, because the whole object of this laborious discussion of piano-making and the techniques of production is to show the necessity of this definite relation between consumption and production, and this relation is essential for proving that the level of consumer demand is the driving force behind economic development — which is ultimately what the authors are trying to prove.

The rest of the chapter is taken up with a long polemic against J.S.Mill on the question of saving. The polemic runs very much on traditional lines, even down to the conception that savings are not just saved but are also more or less automatically invested.[17] The authors' main point is that if people wish to save and invest now, this will only be effective if they spend more in the immediate future.[18]

This is a very Malthusian position, making the level of accumulation dependent upon the extension of demand for the product, while simultaneously giving no indication as to what influences the extent of this demand and treating it almost as an external variable. The function of the examination of the technical process of production discussed above is to show that an exact quantitative relation must exist between the amount of "useful capital" and the rate of consumption, and the authors now proceed to prove that, because of this relation, the rate of consumption is the crucial variable in determining the amount of "useful capital" that can be employed in a time of trade depression.[19] In other words they go beyond Malthus in trying to show, by means of technical relations, that the level of production must be dependent on the demand for consumption goods.

At each stage in the production of a good, they claim, it is obvious that the demand for the product depends essentially on the demand for the final product — i.e. consumer demand. On this basis they establish definitions of supply and demand "from the point of view of the community" as respectively "the aggregate of all shop-goods available to consumers", and "the quantity of purchasing power applied to purchasing the aggregate of shop-goods bought by consumers".[20] It is not explicitly stated that shop-goods refers only to consumer goods, but if this were not so, then accumulation, by increasing the demand for means of production, would not lead to a reduction in the rate of consumption because these also would qualify in

the definitions of 'demand' and 'supply'. This would undermine
the whole argument that saving cuts off demand; so it is safe to
assume that in fact only consumer goods are indicated. This is
confirmed by the definition of consumers given on p.xv of the
book.

The final consumer demand determines not only the rate of
production but also the quantities of requisites of production in
use at each stage. This leads to two conclusions:

> First, that in a condition of steady consumption the conti-
> nuous existence of capital, and of the same number of forms
> of capital, is maintained by a force which owes its impetus to a
> constant demand for commodities. Second, that the profits
> which form the money incomes of all capitalists concerned in
> production, the wages of all labourers concerned, and the
> rent of all natural agents required, are, in a regular condition
> of commerce, paid out of the prices paid by consumers, that
> is, out of retail prices.[21]

Thus everything depends on the demand for and supply of final
products. If the demand falls relative to the supply, the retailer
will find his profits falling and cut back his supply, and so on all
down the chain of production. But the price of all commodities
resolves itself into payment of incomes to the owners of the
various factors of production. Thus this fall in demand must
inevitably, by its effect on prices, cause a fall in the general
incomes of the community, because of the dependence of these
incomes on the strength of final demand.[22] Thus a fall in the
rate of consumption is to be identified as the cause of
depression, and a fall in the rate of consumption comes only
from undue saving.

The argument can be summarised as follows:

> 1. Depression in trade is a general fall in the rate of incomes
> (i.e. a given total of a requisite of production yields its owner a
> lesser income).
> 2. A general fall in the rate of incomes proves that the
> quantity of the use of the requisites of production demanded
> has decreased relatively to the supply.
> 3. The quantity of the use of the requisites of production
> demanded is determined by the quantity of commodities
> demanded (consumption).

4. Consumption would always equal the maximum possible, were it not for the habit of saving and thrift.
Whence we conclude depression in trade and excessive thrift are terms describing different phases of the same phenomenon.[23]

What is striking about this whole argument is that the production of investment goods has disappeared off the scene altogether. Most people would accept that the demand for raw materials is more or less dependent upon the demand for finished goods, but not all finished goods are consumption goods, as Hobson and Mummery seem to imply. Once we accept the importance of the investment goods industries, however, their argument falls to the ground. The demand for investment goods has nothing to do with the expenditure of consumers, but depends upon the profitability expectations of capitalists in their particular programmes for expansion. Hobson and Mummery do not investigate what determines the level of investment, but they appear to assume that it is effectively determined by final consumer demand. By failing to discuss this question, they effectively treat accumulation merely as a subtraction from present consumption, and completely. ignore the other side of the coin — the increased demand for means of production. This is precisely the same mistake as that made by Malthus.
However we have to take into account the development of economic thought between 1820 and 1890. Malthus's mistake was due mainly to the fact that investment was habitually conceived as taking on more labourers for an expansion of production, so that the expansion of production appears to come almost simultaneously with the reduction in demand. Part of the confusion here is simply one of different time-periods not being adequately distinguished. By 1890 investment was conceived much more in terms of factory and machine installation, and was therefore obviously a time-consuming process, and one in which, one would have thought, the demand-producing effects for at least some lines of industry could not be ignored. In other words, as in the case of the Narodniks, it is not so easy to explain the mistake of Hobson and Mummery as that of Malthus. This is where the law of the quantitative relation between consumption and production is important. For while it might appear to mean simply that a given demand for finished

goods generates a particular level of demand for unfinished goods and factors of production, it seems to me that its real intention is to do what Sweezy tries to do in the model in *The Theory of Capitalist Development*: to show that investment is limited by the demand for consumption goods, on the basis that investment in the production of machinery is intrinsically unsound except where it is accompanied by a healthy boost in consumption demand sufficient to justify it. This comes out more clearly in *The Industrial System*.

THE EVOLUTION OF THE CONCEPT OF SURPLUS

By the turn of the century, Hobson's ideas had developed somewhat further along the same lines. In *The Economics of Distribution*, for example, published first in 1900, we encounter for the first time in fully worked-out form the idea of a surplus, a concept which will assume considerable importance in his later work. And in *Imperialism*, published two years later, he attempts an explanation of the phenomenon of imperialism on the basis of the need to find outlets for this surplus. But first, *The Economics of Distribution*.

There was in fact a chapter devoted to the question of distribution in *The Physiology of Industry*, but this confined itself to stating what was called "The Law of the Limiting Requisite". If there is an increase in consumption, this will increase the demand for all three requisites (or factors) of production: labour, capital, and natural agents. Since there is no reason to suppose any change in supply, all three are likely to rise in price, but not necessarily to the same extent. The "Law of the Limiting Requisite" simply stated that the bulk of the rise in the prices of commodities that resulted from the increase in demand would be swallowed up by that factor of production which could be least easily increased in supply.[24]

Then in 1894 we find a reference to the tendency to save 'surplus elements of income'; but, as far as can be made out, this surplus does not bear much relation to the concept as Hobson later developed it, but refers only to a surplus above "a customary class standard of consumption".[25] It is only in *The Problem of the Unemployed* (1896) that we first meet the idea of class distribution of income as the source of a tendency to over-saving, and this is the starting point of the development of his later concept of economic surplus. When it is first introduced this tendency appears to be based on an appreciation of human psychology: if people have earned their living by work, they will enjoy spending the money more than if they had performed no physical exercise in order to get it, so that people who live off 'unearned' incomes have a high propensity to save.[26] This seems to be an attack on property income as such. Later, however, when Hobson talks about "the top portion of large incomes, drawn from economic rents of land, profits of speculation, high interest of capital derived from monopolies"[27] and when, in discussing how to counteract the tendency to over-saving, he picks out these same elements of income as suitable targets for taxation while also insisting on the necessity to pay private investors a suitable price for their savings in order to furnish capital,[28] it seems that 'unearned' income is not synonymous with property income but merely represents something over and above the price in a perfectly competitive market. This is something much closer to his later concept of surplus.

The Economics of Distribution, as its title implies, is a study of the distribution of income from a theoretical point of view. It shows how deeply immersed Hobson is in the marginalist approach, in trying to establish a general law of price for all factors of production, or indeed for any sort of exchange transaction, and to deduce the distribution of income from that. It is therefore very much based on Marshallian analysis, but Hobson introduces an idea of his own — the concept of 'forced gain'. This is the foundation of his concept of surplus.

Hobson takes a close look at the formation of price. Although Marshall and other writers say that the price is such as to equate supply and demand, the question is whether this equalisation gives a single price point, or merely a limited range within which the price must fall. If it gives only a range, then some other rule must be invoked to establish the price within this range. This problem was first seriously discussed by Böhm-Bawerk in his *Positive Theory of Capital,* and he seems to conclude that the outcome will depend on the two sides' relative skill at bargaining.[29] Hobson illustrates the problem as follows: suppose that A,B, . . . H are sellers of horses, and the minimum prices which they are prepared to accept vary from £10 in the case of A to £26 in the case of H. Similarly, I,J, . . . R are buyers in the market, with maximum prices that they are willing to pay varying from £15 (I) to £30 (R). Hobson specifies the maximum/minimum price of each buyer/seller. It comes out that supply and demand are equal at any price between £21 and £21. 10s, for at any price in this range there are five sellers and five buyers. The limits are set by buyer M dropping out as soon as the price rises above £21, and seller F dropping out as soon as it drops below £21. 10s.[31]

The fact that we have only established the price to within £21. 5s ± 5s is the result of the smallness of the market. However, accepting for the moment that this may be a more accurate view of the world than the price-point theory, we must look at the determination of price within this range. Hobson basically accepts the idea that it is the result of bargaining, but he picks out the power and strength of the bargainers rather than their skill at bargaining as the operative factor. The last buyer (N) and the last seller (E) will each try to cajole the other into thinking that his limit price is much lower or higher (whichever the case may be), so that he can get the best bargain for himself, but anything which gives one an advantage over the other will obviously exert a significant influence over the result. Thus, within the price limits established by supply and demand, a price-point is fixed "by the bargaining power of a single buyer or seller."[31]

For each buyer (seller) we can now look at the maximum (minimum) price he would have been prepared to accept, and compare it with what each actually got. The difference between these Hobson refers to as their gain. From our analysis, it appears that this gain accruing to buyers and sellers can be divided into two elements: the 'forced gain' represented (in the case of sellers) by the degree to which the final price has been raised above the lower limit of £21, and which is common to all sellers; and the 'specific gain' due to the difference between the individual seller's minimum price and the limit price of £21. The differential gains are entirely familiar from previous economic literature, under the heading of producers' and consumers' rents, but, says Hobson,

> the existence and nature of the other element, viz. forced gain, which clearly emerges from the analysis of market-price, has not received the attention it deserves.[32]

Now, of course, whether this element really deserves attention depends upon its importance in practice, and Hobson readily admits that for some markets it may not be significant. He himself chose the horse market, whereas Marshall took the corn market as his example, and Hobson points out two major differences between them: (1) the indivisibility of horses, so that producers cannot vary the proportion of their total output that they are willing to sell according to fine variations in the price, as in Marshall's example; and (2) the local corn market is very closely linked to the world market, so that it is effectively just a small element of a very large market. In these conditions it appears that the price limits established by supply and demand would be so close together as to constitute effectively one unique price point. But Hobson insists that this depends on a divisibility of the product, and a depth of the market in both space and time, that is absent in the vast majority of cases, and that 'forced gains' are a significant feature of the markets for most commodities.[33]

The essential point of this is that 'forced gains', like differential rents, are elements of income which exist over and above the price necessary to bring the present supply of the factor onto the market. Thus, in Hobson's view, these two together represent the proper subject of taxation, since such taxation would not in any way reduce the productive powers of the community. The chief problem, of course, is to find a system of taxation which hits particularly these elements of income. In the last chapter of the book Hobson goes into this in some detail; to us, however, it is not of great importance, and we shall confine our attention to the last few pages of the chapter.

Here Hobson advances the thesis that an increasing proportion of these 'forced gains' is adhering to entrepreneurs and is appearing under the name of profits. This is due, firstly, to the fact that the labourer, pressed by the necessity to eat, drink and house himself, is in a very weak bargaining position vis-à-vis his employer and in practice "is selling his labour-power under the conditions of a forced sale."[34] The weakness of the labourer's bargaining position may have been alleviated by the development of trade unionism and collective bargaining, but it has been matched by an if anything greater degree of combination on the part of the employers.[35] Thus, in the market for labour-power, most of the 'forced gains' go to the employers.

Secondly, the businessman by "arranging price lists by agreement with competitors, entering into closer agreements with
these competitors, and eventually organising alliances, syn-
dicates, or trusts"[36] strives continuously to strengthen his
bargaining power at the expense of middlemen or consumers.

> His success in achieving these results is the dominant feature
> of modern industry so far as the distribution of wealth is
> concerned. There is good reason to believe that an increasing
> proportion of 'forced gains' or 'unearned income' continually
> assumes the form of the business profits of undertakers.[37]

It is therefore entirely correct, in Hobson's view, to talk about
surplus value, as Marxists do, but Marx goes completely wrong
in focussing exclusively on the relation between capital and
labour as the source of it. Hobson makes the classical marginalist
criticism of Marx in asking why it is that labour should be the
source of all value, and how capital is judged to be exploiting
labour. He summarises his own views on the subject as follows:

> Surplus value, then, is not something which emerges in the
> dealings of capital with labour or of land with labour; it
> emerges in every competitive bargain and adheres to the
> stronger bargainer; it is only because in modern industry the
> owner of capital, land, or business capacity is normally found
> to be the stronger bargainer, that he obtains most of the
> surplus.[38]

In this world the function of organisation and association of
labour and capital is simply to establish a strong bargaining
position in a definite field of industry and so get hold of part of
this surplus.[39] One of the implications of this theory is that
Hobson, unlike many marginalist writers, is quite in favour of
trade unions, for these forced gains have no effect on the supply
and demand of factors of production and are just there to be
grabbed by someone, and it is as well that the poorer sections of
the community should organise to get them for themselves.

Hobson does not discuss the question of savings at all in *The
Economics of Distribution*, and makes no explicit connection
between the concentration of the surplus in the hands of the rich
and the tendency to over-saving. But he had already made a
suggestion to this effect in *The Problem of the Unemployed*, as we
have seen, and in *The Industrial System*, which synthesises most of

his previous work, this idea receives a full development. The importance of *The Economics of Distribution* lies in the theoretical development of this concept of surplus. What it amounts to is a critique of the monopoly power of businesses, on the one hand vis-à-vis the working class in the market for labour-power, and on the other hand vis-à-vis the consumer in the market for finished products. Hobson's awareness of and emphasis on concentration and increasing monopolisation in the business world plays a big part here, and it is a quite consistent feature of his thought throughout his life. It receives considerable attention in *The Evolution of Modern Capitalism*, and plays a big role in his explanation of overseas investment and imperialism. Hobson's defence of trade unionism is that it is the only effective defence that workers have against Big Business, and that within the framework of capitalism it can potentially reduce the economic inequalities in society, and help to solve the problems created by the tendency to over-saving.

IMPERIALISM

Hobson's book, *Imperialism,* first appeared in 1902. The only part of it which is of real importance to us is Chapter 6, entitled 'The Economic Taproot of Imperialism'.

The book aims to torpedo the notion that the subjugation of vast areas of the world by a few colonialist powers is merely the expression of the civilizing mission of the white man, Christianity, Europe, or of any other idealistic notion, by establishing that the true motives behind the actions of the imperialist countries are economic ones, and that the state of the economies of the advanced countries is such that they have to resort to this expansionist strategy in order to save their home economics from collapse.

The economic force underlying imperialism is the need to find outlets for surplus savings and markets for surplus manufactures produced at home. Hobson sets out the development of British imperialism as he sees it in the mouth of an imaginary apologist:

So long as England held a virtual monopoly of the world markets for certain important classes of manufactured goods, Imperialism was unnecessary. After 1870 this manufacturing and trading supremacy was greatly impaired: other nations, especially Germany, the United States, and Belgium, advanced with great rapidity, and while they have not crushed or even stayed the increase of our external trade, their competition made it more and more difficult to dispose of the full surplus of our manufactures at a profit. The encroachments made by these nations upon our old markets, even in our own possessions, made it most urgent that we should take energetic means to secure new markets. These new markets had to lie in hitherto undeveloped countries, chiefly in the tropics, where vast populations lived capable of growing economic needs which our manufacturers and merchants could supply. Our rivals were seizing and annexing territories for similar purposes, and when they had annexed them closed them to our trade. The diplomacy and arms of Great Britain had to be used in order to compel the owners of the new markets to deal with us: and experience showed that the safest means of securing and developing such markets is by establishing protectorates or by annexation. . . . The new markets might not be large, but they formed serviceable outlets for the overflow of our great textile and metal industries, and, when the vast Asiatic and African populations of the interior were reached, a rapid expansion of trade was expected to result.[40]

This is very reminiscent of Sismondi's idea that the problem of surplus manufactures at home would lead to ferocious competition in foreign markets — and indeed, if one thinks of underconsumption as taking the form of a surplus product in manufacturing industry, then it is quite logical to see the fight for colonial markets as an attempt to overcome the difficulty. But Hobson attaches even more importance to the demands for external fields of investment. The point is that in Britain large savings are made which can find no profitable investment at home, and so they are forced to look for outlets abroad. But while the trader may be content with a mere show of force in the background to assist in his transactions, the investor demands a greater commitment, up to and including political annexation. Thus, Hobson's apologist concludes, however costly imperialism may appear to be, it is necessary to the economic life of the nation.[41]

Why is imperialism a feature of the modern world particularly? It is clear that Hobson sees the concentration of industry as the major single factor, because trusts and combines manage to increase the profitability of an industry while at the same time, through regulation, reducing the outlets for the investment of these profits. This analysis is based on the well-known features of profit-maximisation for a monopoly: the trust restricts its output and closes down its most inefficient plants, while being able to keep its prices substantially above the cost of production in the rest. Isolation from competition yields a higher rate of profit. It is doubtful, however, whether all of this extra profit can find an outlet inside the same industry:

> New inventions and other economies of production or distribution within the trade may absorb some of the new capital, but there are rigid limits to this absorption. The trustmaker in oil or sugar must find other investments for his savings.[42]

The growth of concentration, then, makes it increasingly difficult to absorb savings at home. Hobson also expresses the idea in another way: the problem is that the increase in consuming power is failing to keep pace with the increase in productive power. Saving is justified, from the social standpoint, so long as the capital in which it takes material shape can be fully employed in producing commodities which will be able to find a market. Saving in excess of this limit, however, can only accumulate as surplus capital not needed to assist current consumption, and "either lies idle, or tries to oust existing capital from its employment, or else seeks speculative use abroad under the protection of the Government."[43]

The reason for the persistent tendency for saving to exceed this limit lies in the distribution of wealth. Workers consume more or less all of their income, whereas the rich save a fair percentage of theirs. Thus if, for the same total national income, its distribution could be made more equal, this would decrease the rate of saving.

> The over-saving which is the economic root of imperialism is found by analysis to consist of rents, monopoly profits, and other unearned or excessive elements of income, which, not being earned by labour of head or hand, have no legitimate

raison d'être. Having no natural relation to effort of production, they impel their recipients to no corresponding satisfaction of consumption: they form a surplus wealth, which, having no proper place in the normal economy of production and consumption, tends to accumulate as excessive savings. Let any turn in the tide of politico-economic forces divert from these owners their excess of income and make it flow, either to the workers in higher wages, or to the community in taxes, so that it will be spent instead of being saved, serving in either of these ways to swell the tide of consumption — there will be no need to fight for foreign markets or foreign areas of investment.[44]

Here we have the ideas of *The Economics of Distribution* coming out again. It is not clear, however, why saving out of these "excessive elements of income" should be higher than out of others even in the hands of the same individuals, as it seems unlikely that the recipients are as discerning as Hobson in deciding which parts of their income have a "natural relation to the effort of production". Maybe he is harking back here to his earlier opinion that the psychological satisfaction of having worked for your income creates a greater satisfaction in consuming it.

Hobson concludes from all this that social reform and redistribution of income can remove the economic necessity of imperialism. Although today it appears necessary to open up new foreign markets, in fact home markets are capable of indefinite expansion. Whatever is produced in England could be consumed in England, provided that the income is properly distributed.

> This only appears untrue because of the unnatural and unwholesome specialisation to which this country has been subjected, based upon a bad distribution of economic resources, which has induced an overgrowth of certain manufacturing trades for the express purpose of effecting foreign sales.[45]

The natural enemies of imperialism are therefore trade unionism and socialism, striving to remove the surplus incomes of the "imperialist" classes.

There are considerable similarities between Hobson's ideas here and Baran and Sweezy's book *Monopoly Capital.* Baran and

Sweezy start from the idea that twentieth-century monopoly capitalism is very different from nineteenth-century competitive capitalism, and they identify a problem of 'absorption of the surplus' above the necessary cost of production of commodities. This surplus originates in the ability of oligopolistic firms to reduce costs while maintaining price levels, thus at least potentially raising the share of profits, except in so far as they are absorbed by advertising, depreciation, taxes and so on. The authors identify a tendency for the share of this surplus in the economy to increase, and unless full outlets can be found for the expenditure of it, the economy will be depressed.

The basic idea behind this argument — the power of firms in the market — is important also in Hobson, and in *Imperialism* he is effectively identifying a problem of absorption of the profits resulting from it. His theory of imperialism is that it is the solution to this problem generated by the concentration of industry, although he never explains how the poor countries that receive the investment have the consumer demand to justify it which the richer countries do not. The fundamentals of *Monopoly Capital* are already prefigured in *Imperialism*: even Sweezy's capital-consumption ratio is nothing other than Hobson and Mummery's quantitative relation between consumption and production. This will be discussed further in Chapter Twelve.

THE INDUSTRIAL SYSTEM

The Industrial System, first published in 1909, recapitulates on and systematises the ideas already worked out elsewhere. In Chapter 3, Hobson reproduces a diagram of the production of a commodity, from raw material to finished product, very similar to that of *The Physiology of Industry* (see above), and says:

> If now we regard the entrance of raw materials into the industrial system as the first stage in production, we shall come to the conclusion that, pooling together all the productive processes, there must be a definite quantitative relation between the rate of production and the rate of consumption, or, in other words, between the quantity of employment of capital and labour and the quantity of commodities withdrawn from the productive stream within any given time.[46]

This is a bolder statement than in *The Physiology of Industry*, which was careful to elaborate in detail the logical steps in the proof of this relation. As we saw, the main result of this attempt was only to show how difficult it was to prove it, and it looks as if twenty years later Hobson feels that its own intuitive plausibility is sufficient to support the statement. As before, it is now necessary to give this quantitative relation a flow of causality, to show that it is consumption that determines production and not vice versa. The argument is as follows: every worker, capitalist or landlord receives his income ultimately from the consumer of finished products; so the total money-income of an industrial community is equivalent to the total money expenditure of consumers, distributed to individuals as payments for the use of factors of production. The real income of the community consists of the aggregate of goods passing into the hands of consumers.[47]

What happens if people save? If we label the various stages in the process of production of a commodity A,B,C,D,E, then consumption means the application of money at the final stage E. Saving, however, means the application of money at some earlier point in the process, such as B or C, for the setting up of new means of production.

> As we have recognised, saving (as distinct from hoarding) does not mean a refusal to apply the money stimulus, but only a refusal to apply it at the retail stage in 'demand' for commodities. The 'saving' persons who reduce the 'demand' for commodities apply the same quantity of 'demand' at various interim points in the industrial process. They pay more money for developing new mines, they place contracts for putting up more mills and workshops, they give more orders for machinery. In other words, instead of applying all their money at E, they apply some of it directly at A, B, or C, so as to set-up more forms of plant, &c., at these points in production.[48]

So the immediate effect is to slacken "even circulation of money and stimulation of industrial energy", and to substitute for this an encouragement of the growth of certain parts of the industrial system, in the expectation of "a general increased flow of productive energy towards commodities".

Hobson's mistakes come out even more clearly here than in

his earlier writings. In the Preface to *The Physiology of Industry* Hobson had stated that "the object of production is to provide 'utilities and conveniences' for consumers", and of course from this point of view investment can only be regarded as provision for future consumption. Hobson's mistake, however, is to imagine that because investment is provision for consumption at some time in the future, it must necessarily be strictly proportioned to *current* consumption. The object of the discussion of the technical aspects of the production process, which is a constant feature of Hobson's work, is to prove the necessity of this proportion, but the omission in the argument is the fact that the goods which come out at the end of the process A-B-C-D-E are not all consumption goods; *they may also be investment goods.* Investment is not an application of demand at point A or B but at E, just as consumption is. Therefore, although technical conditions may determine a given capital-output ratio, they do *not* determine a given capital-consumption ratio as Hobson claims, because not all of the output need be consumption goods. As it is, however, Hobson accepts a very Malthusian line of reasoning, which asserts the necessity of a definite level of expenditure on consumption goods.

Hobson says that it is not correct to assume that just any proportion of the income of the community can be advantageously saved. This is so because in a stable community a fixed proportion is maintained between the amount of productive energy employed at the various processes, and only a given aggregate of capital could be employed in forwarding the work of turning out the fixed output of commodities.

> Of course, this limitation of useful capital no longer holds in a progressive community; a larger amount of saving is continually wanted to supply capital to meet not only the current but the prospective increase in consumption. But though the limits of saving are made more elastic, they are not entirely cancelled.[49]

In a primitive community, however fast it may be growing in population, these limits are actually quite narrow, for the simple techniques of production restrict them. But in a modern capitalist society, the possibilities of socially useful saving are enormously extended. Nevertheless the limits exist even here:

The great bulk of capital fructifies in an early increase in commodities, and so the saving embodied in it is only socially useful on condition that an early increase of consumption proportionate to the increased saving takes place.

A little reflection will make it evident that this implies the maintenance of a definite proportion between the aggregate of saving and spending over a term of years. An individual may, of course, continue to save any proportion of his income: a class of persons, or even a whole nation, may do the same provided they can find other classes or other nations ready to borrow and to spend what they are saving. But the industrial community as a whole cannot save at any given time more than a certain proportion of its income: that proportion is never accurately known, and it is always shifting with changes in the arts of production and consumption, but it imposes as real a limit on the economy of saving for the industrial community to-day as there was for Robinson Crusoe on his island or for a primitive isolated tribe of men before the era of machine production.[50]

We are entirely familiar with this line of argument from *The Physiology of Industry*. The big hole in it — the inability to give a definition of the critical level of saving — comes out more clearly here than ever before. There is a definite hint of Lauderdale here, in the suggestion that technical possibilities limit the opportunities for saving, and that beyond such a point saving would not be 'socially useful' and so presumably there would be no demand for it. But the main question is: where does the demand come from even for the investment that can be justified as 'socially useful'? Judging by the argument as it has so far been built up, the total income of the community is absolutely dependent on the flow of consumer expenditure, so that presumably if this is reduced by any significant degree of saving at all, demand will go down and income will fall. So where is the increased consumption which justifies investment to come from? Hobson fails to give an economic definition of what the proper ratio of saving to spending should be, because he is caught in exactly the same trap as Malthus — that the logic of his analysis is that any saving at all precipitates a slump.

In the next two chapters, Hobson elaborates his ideas on the 'surplus'. The total income of a community can be divided into a section labelled by Hobson 'costs', defined as "that part of the product, or its equivalent in other goods, necessary as payments to maintain the current output of productive energy in a factor of production",[51] and 'surplus' (that part of the product which remains after costs have been defrayed). Within the surplus, we can make a distinction between the productive and unproductive portions. In a growing economy, not all of the surplus is superfluous, since while costs only enter for the maintenance of production at its present level, some part of the product must be allocated for the increase of the supply of the factors of production in order that output may increase. This part is the 'productive surplus'. So the total product may be divided into:

A. Maintenance (costs of subsistence)
B. Productive Surplus (costs of growth)
C. Unproductive Surplus (unearned increments)

A. Maintenance includes (1) minimum wages for various sorts of labour and ability necessary to support and evoke their continuous output at the present standard of efficiency; (2) depreciation for wear and tear of plant and other fixed capital; (3) a 'wear-and-tear' provision for land.
B. The productive surplus includes (1) minimum wage of progressive efficiency in quantity and quality of labour and ability of various grades; (2) such amount of interest as is required to evoke the saving needed to supply the requisite amount of new capital for industrial progress.
C. The unproductive surplus consists of (1) economic rent of land and other natural resources; (2) all interest beyond the rate involved in B; (3) all profits, salaries, or other payments for ability or labour in excess of what is economically necessary to evoke the sufficient use of such factor of production.[52]

It is a feature of modern industry, says Hobson, that it tends continually to increase the size of the surplus, and

the principal problem of modern industrial civilization consists in devising measures to secure that the whole of the industrial surplus shall be economically applied to the purposes of industrial and social progress, instead of passing in the shape of unearned income to the owners of factors of production, whose activities are depressed, not stimulated, by such payments.[53]

All rent of land and other natural resources is defined as unproductive surplus because it is always a 'scarcity' price,[54] due to the monopoly of landownership. No genuine human effort has to be made in order to bring marginal land into cultivation, according to Hobson, so that there are no genuine costs of growth in increasing the supply of it. This contrasts with his analysis of capital, in which he accepts the 'reward for waiting' argument as a legitimate reason why in a growing economy interest rates should be higher than in a stationary one.

The new element here is the distinction between the productive and unproductive surplus. It is specifically the unproductive surplus which Hobson now picks on as responsible for the problems which he had formerly attributed to the element of 'forced gain' in its entirety.[55] As before, he thinks that the bulk of it will build up in the hands of landlords and capitalists, because of their superior bargaining positions, that it should be the main target of taxation, and that the function of trade unions is to try to appropriate some of this unproductive surplus for labour.[56]

In sum, *The Industrial System* pulls together the various strands of Hobson's writings over the previous twenty years, and includes his most sophisticated development of the idea of the surplus. As such, it must be regarded as the highest statement of his thought.

THE TRADE CYCLE

In the early nineteenth century no one conceived of what has now become known as the trade cycle. This was not just the result of the predominant acceptance of 'Say's Law', for even those who rejected this theory never thought of the phenomena of general overproduction as a cyclically recurring set of events; they tended to treat them as evidence of something fundamentally inadequate or wrong about the new society that grew out of the Industrial Revolution, which could be cured so long as the right measures were pursued, e.g. the equalisation of the distribution of income (Sismondi) or the maintenance of the unproductive consumption of the rich (Malthus). It was only some time later that the idea of industrial fluctuations as a regular feature of capitalist production came to predominate, and the shift can, I think, mainly be ascribed to the realisation that the new order of things had proved its durability in spite of its periodic cataclysms, so that a theory of these fluctuations had to be provided. In Britain this had been so much accepted by Hobson's time that Hobson himself, while ascribing the phenomena of general overproduction to similar causes as earlier writers, had also to attempt on top of this a theory of fluctuations, of when the tendencies to underconsumption manifested themselves, and how they were temporarily overcome, and then manifested themselves overtly once more, and how this up and down process repeated itself in a relatively regular way.

In *The Physiology of Industry* we find two chapters, one on 'Overproduction and Economic Checks', and the next one on 'Expansion and Contraction of Trade', which are relevant here. The first of these amounts to a critique of the prevailing theory that crises are impossible. Hobson and Mummery point out against Mill and Ricardo that since the power to purchase and consume in a money economy need not necessarily be employed, there is the possibility of overproduction in such an economy in a way that there is not in a barter economy.[57] Then, having recapitulated their reasons for thinking there to exist a continual tendency to over-supply in the modern economy, Hobson and Mummery proceed to discuss the more modern ideas about why over-supply is impossible. The main arguments given by modern economists are: (a) that any incipient over-supply will cause a general fall in the price-level, thus stimulating demand and depressing supply; and (b) that there will be a fall in the rate of interest such as to act as a check on saving and keep consumption at a high level.[58]

On the first argument, the authors complain that it leaves out the question: what is the effect of the general fall in prices on the income of the community?[59] Hobson and Mummery have argued that the money income of each individual in an industrial community, whether received in the form of wage, profit or rent, is ultimately paid out of the money received from retailers for the sale of commodities.[60] Thus any fall in prices must mean a corresponding fall in the money income of the community; and how can a general decline in retail prices act as an effective stimulus to increased demand for commodities, when the income of consumers has fallen correspondingly? For demand to increase, consumers would have to increase their real consumption even though their real incomes had not changed at all;[61] this, although possible and desirable, is not very likely.

As to the second check, it is alleged that a fall in the rate of profit (and hence also of interest) will lead to a fall in the rate of saving, consumption will increase, and the problem of over-supply will disappear. But will a fall in profits raise consumption? the authors ask. If we look at the capitalist who actually suffers from this fall, it is clear, they argue, that his consumption is likely to fall because his income has fallen. And since in a condition of slump there is no reason why this fall in profits should be accompanied by a rise in any other class of income, the argument that falling profits raise consumption seems fallacious.[62] And in so far as the balance of production and consumption is recreated by a fall in the rate of production rather than a rise in consumption, this is precisely the condition of a depression in trade and under-utilisation of resources whose possibility is denied.

Anyone familiar with Keynesian arguments must be sympathetic to Mummery and Hobson's objections here, for they focus on the big gap in the arguments of General Equilibrium theorists: the effect on the level of incomes. At this point Hobson appears quite Keynesian, because the basic difference between them — whether it is the relation of saving to investment or merely the absolute level of saving that is the important variable — does not enter into the discussion here.

The next chapter analyses the boom of 1873 and the depression immediately afterwards. The authors ascribe this boom to the immense demand for commodities by the belligerent governments in the Franco-Prussian War.

This increased demand for commodities was not merely a demand that a larger amount of raw material should be turned into food, guns, saddles, clothes, &c., for consumption; it was also a demand which was effective in calling into existence new and immense quantities of machinery and plant required to assist in the work of increased production of commodities. This latter fact has an important significance, for it serves to explain how it was that the wonderful activity in trade did not collapse as soon as the abnormal demand for commodities was remitted, that is at the close of the war. A large part of the increased saving stimulated by the increased war demand found a natural investment in the construction of machinery and plant to assist production and in other machinery and plant to assist production of the first machinery, and so forth. The enormous quantity of new plant which stood in France and other European countries at the close of 1873 represented actual savings that had been effected during the years immediately subsequent to this great war. The huge war debt incurred by France, and paid in the next few years, extended her war expenditure considerably beyond the actual period of the war, and provided a combined use for the saving and the mass of forms of capital in which it had been stored.[63]

Furthermore, after the end of war expenditure, the full effects of the saving that had been going on did not appear until all the investment projects were completed a little while later. But now that consumer demand had fallen off, capitalists found their stocks of unsold goods building up, and although they might be able to stave off liquidity problems for a while by borrowing, sooner or later the crisis was bound to break out.[64] Once bankers refused to increase their loans, stocks had to be sold fast and at any price in order to avoid bankruptcy, and wholesale prices plummeted. Thus a boom is transformed into a slump, in the face of a cutback in the demand for consumption goods. There is no discussion in the book, however, of the reverse process.

The essential point of this chapter of *The Physiology of Industry* is to show that fluctuation in the level of consumption is the primary determinant of fluctuation in economic activity. In the example the authors give, it is the rise in government expenditure, through its effects on the demand for commodities and then on the level of investment, which causes the boom, and the slump comes about through the high level of saving and investment thus stimulated being continued into a period where the demand for consumption goods is no longer as great, resulting in overproduction. This is precisely the kind of theory we would expect on the basis of the ideas contained in the rest of the book.

Hobson's theory of the trade cycle is best elaborated in *The*

Industrial System and *The Economics of Unemployment* (1922). A really detailed analysis of it would require much more space than is available here, and I shall confine myself to a bare outline. A consistent feature is that he rejects all explanations which give the primary role to monetary factors — the fluctuation of credit, the behaviour of the banking system, etc. The financial factors play a part, but it is a secondary part which serves only to exacerbate the consequences of the underlying industrial fluctuations. These underlying fluctuations would exist even if they were not supplemented by the periodic swelling and collapse of credit, and derive from the maladjustment between production and consumption.

> It is the ultimately futile and mischievous endeavour to apply to production an excessive proportion of income derived from it that stimulates trade to a period of feverish activity followed by a period of depression and collapse. The rapid expansibility of purchasing power through the creation of bank credit serves, as we have seen, to facilitate both the boom and the collapse, and by its reactions upon prices and expectations to carry both processes farther and faster than they could go under a system of cash payments or of properly restricted credit.[65]

In a depression, Hobson says, all factors of production exist in excess of actual industrial requirements. This occurs only because capitalists believe they cannot set them to work and sell the products at a price that will cover the costs of production. Thus a condition of underproduction is directly connected with a condition of underconsumption.[66]

> Take the case of an economic community of a progressive type with an income of twenty units, spending seventeen, and saving three for regular investment in new productive capital, which finds full regular employment in meeting the growing demand for commodities. Now suppose, owing to some change in distribution of incomes, some return to simplicity of living or some increased appreciation of future as compared with present satisfactions, spending is reduced to sixteen, saving raised to four, what must happen? The increased savings cannot take shape in productive capital, for as the increase of current and prospective consumption of

commodities is reduced, a smaller amount of new productive capital can be put into operation, and any attempt to put into operation as much as before must speedily be checked by the obvious glut. Instead of three units of saving taking shape in productive capital, there is now only room for two and a half. But owing to increased saving four are available. What happens to the extra one and a half?[67]

We may expect some of it to be hoarded, but this is unlikely to account for more than half a unit. And some of it may be used in buying property from people impoverished by the depression who then go and spend it — but then it would not necessarily be saved at all.

Directly a shrinkage in demand for commodities and new productive capital occurs, the lessened rate of production begins to reduce all incomes, including those of the saving class. Aggregate income no longer stands at twenty, but falls to eighteen, or even seventeen. The saving class who were trying to save four out of a total twenty, leaving sixteen for spending, are not willing to save four or even three out of an aggregate income reduced to eighteen or seventeen. Their permanent standard of comfort stands in the way. When the shrinkage of production and of income has gone far enough, not merely is the actual amount of saving reduced, but the *proportion* of saving to spending is brought back towards the normal rate which preceded this attempt to oversave, or even below that rate. When the depression has reached its lowest, there is for a time a state of actual under-saving, i.e. an insufficient provision of new productive capital to meet the reasonable calculations of future demand for commodities. This condition even checks the recovery of trade.[68]

Thus the crucial variable is the proportion of saving to spending. As soon as this proportion rises above the limit level, the economy falls back into depression. But the account of the recovery process is never very satisfactory. Hobson almost seems to imply that it is sufficient for the excess saving to be removed, for the proportion to be brought back to its 'normal' or 'correct' level, for full employment to be restored. Hobson does not have a Keynes-like concept of "under-employment equilibrium", which would occur when the proportion of saving to spending reaches its correct level at a time of depression but does not fall below it, analogously to a balance of planned investment and planned saving in the Keynesian system. Thus, for the modern economist, his account of the recovery is not very satisfactory, since it seems to imply that once the problem of over-saving has been cured by the fall of income, everything springs back to normal semi-automatically. At one point Hobson says this:

> Before the turn in the commercial tide, current production even falls below the level of current consumption, thus allowing for the gradual passage into consumption of the glut of goods which had congested the machine. After the congestion which had kept prices low is removed, prices begin to rise, demand is more active at each point of industry, and we see the usual symptoms of reviving trade.[69]

This more or less implies that escape from depression involves a temporary under-saving, equivalent to the over-saving which created it; but Hobson really paid very little attention to the problem of explaining the recovery. Nevertheless, it is easy to imagine from his suggestions a kind of underconsumption theory of the trade cycle analogous to the multiplier-accelerator theory: just as in the latter the level of investment relative to saving acts on the level of income which then reacts back on the level of saving and investment so as to produce a regular oscillation, so in Hobson's theory the relation of saving to consumption acts on the level of income which reacts back on the relation of consumption and saving in such a way as to generate fluctuations. Such a theory would be quite consistent with his ideas on over-saving. In fact, though, Hobson did not present the trade cycle in this way, and this is clearly because he thought that the cycle itself was unnecessary and could be removed. It was not, to his mind, an oscillation which could not be avoided but was precipitated by over-saving due to inequalities in the distribution of income. This over-saving induced a depression, and a "trade cycle" was merely the struggle to return to the full employment situation. If, however, the disease of over-saving could be rooted out, there would be no reason why full employment could not be continuously maintained. Like other underconsumptionists, Hobson does not regard fluctuations in economic activity as an oscillation about a mean, but as periodic collapses due to a structural fault in the economic system followed by periods of recovery.

CONCLUSIONS

The skeleton of Hobson's economic ideas can be expressed as follows:

1) The demand for consumption goods is the motor of production — the expenditure of consumers is the source of all incomes gained by the factors in production, and falls in the rate of production below the capacity of the resources available can be traced to an inadequate level of consumption, or what is the same thing, an excessive level of saving. The proof of this lies in the Law of the Quantitative Relation between Consumption and Production, which shows the necessity of a fixed relation between the current rate of consumption and the rate of production. Since production without consumption would be useless and in any case would not find a market for the products, this law must be interpreted to mean that the rate of consumption *determines* the rate of production.

2) The fluctuations in the fortunes of commerce result from changes in the ratio of saving to spending, or more precisely, a depression results from the rise in this ratio above the 'right' level, and is only eliminated by the readjustment of this ratio back to 'normal' brought about by the processes of the depression itself. But if the ratio of saving to spending could be prevented from rising too high, then there would be no reasons for depressions to occur, since their cause — a too slow growth in consumption relative to production — would have been removed. Depressions are the expression of the tendency in modern society for saving to rise to too high a level. The remedy lies in a redistribution of income from the rich to the poor, who save a lower proportion of their income; and trade unions perform a valuable function in this respect.

3) The source of the excess saving is to be found in the surplus accruing to the various factors. The existence of differential rents is generally acknowledged in the case of land, but in fact they exist also for other factors. So the actual level of remuneration received by factors at present engaged in production is in excess of the minimum required to bring that volume of each factor onto the market, and the difference

between these two quantities Hobson calls the surplus. The surplus can in fact be further subdivided into 'productive' and 'unproductive' portions. For in a growing economy, more of each factor must continually be drawn into operation, so that the remuneration must be greater than that required just to satisfy the quantity currently at work. So one portion of the surplus, the productive part, is necessary for growth. The rest, however, is pure waste from the social point of view. Most of it ends up in the hands of the capitalists, by virtue of their superior bargaining power, and they may even encroach upon the productive surplus of labour. This unproductive surplus is the cause of all the economic evils of today.

The main difficulty with Hobson's position is that he has set up the idea of a 'right' ratio of saving to spending, but he is never able to give an economic definition of it. In this he is like Malthus and his followers at the beginning of the nineteenth century. The root of the difficulty lies in that he conceives investment only as a means to the production of consumption goods, and never as a department of production, and even more importantly, of *expenditure*, in its own right. Thus he treats saving, even when the money is entirely invested and not hoarded, as a subtraction from demand in the way that hoarding is, because it is a subtraction from the demand that he regards as crucial: consumption demand.

Hobson's underconsumption theory is more developed that Malthus's because whereas Malthus only invoked the consumption of the rich as a protection against over-saving, Hobson tries to show that there is a persistent tendency towards underconsumption. The concept of surplus, based on marginalist theory, is supposed to show precisely what sections of the total income of society are responsible for this. He also tries to account for the phenomena of the trade cycle; but since like his predecessors he does not attempt to distinguish between planned and actual saving and investment, but more or less assumes that savings will be automatically invested, unless for some reason or other they are hoarded, he makes no progress towards the Keynesian solution to the problem.

The fundamental mistakes in Hobson's theory are exactly the same as in Malthus's: both of them fail to understand the basic relations between the main sectors of the economy in one time-period, and to separate clearly one time-period from another. So they mix up the increased future output from present investment with the immediate reduction in consumption, and draw the conclusion that there is a major contradiction here.

A NOTE ON LENIN'S IMPERIALISM

Lenin, in his famous pamphlet *Imperialism, The Highest Stage of Capitalism*, pays tribute to the work of Hobson on the subject. All other writers, he says, have scarcely gone beyond the ideas expressed by Hobson and Hilferding.[70]

The theme of Lenin's pamphlet is that imperialism constitutes a special stage of capitalism which evolved in the course of the second half of the nineteenth century and had by the time of writing (1916) reached full maturity. The main features of this stage, according to Lenin, were: the concentration of production and capital into monopolies which dominate economic life, the merging of bank capital with industrial capital, the export of capital, the creation of international monopoly combines and the completion of the territorial division of the world by the largest capitalist powers.

It is not in the documentation of these tendencies — a task already performed by Hilferding and Hobson — so much as in the knitting together of them into the concept of a new stage of capitalism that the originality of Lenin's pamphlet lies. The modern use of the terms 'monopoly capitalism' and 'state monopoly capitalism' is due to Lenin's *Imperialism* and his later observations on the growing economic role of the state, for it was he who introduced these terms to describe these phenomena.

The difficulty with *Imperialism* is that it is only, in the words of its subtitle, 'A Popular Outline', and yet the full-scale theoretical work whose outline it would be does not exist. This means that the argument is not always clear. The implication throughout is that the idea that imperialism represents a qualitatively new stage of capitalism is derived from the fact that all its five main features can be interpreted as the result of the increased centralisation of capital. This tendency would then be the underlying tendency which explains all the others. But this is not explicitly stated, and sometimes the case is very loosely argued: for instance, Lenin's contention that the centralisation of capital was the main force behind the rush for colonies is based simply on the chronological coincidence of these events.* Neither Hobson nor Hilferding, although mentioning that the desire to export capital might stimulate annexations, had presented monopoly as the single cause of the burst of colonisation, and Hobson's apologist for imperialism, quoted above, emphasises a quite different factor — the loss of Britain's industrial monopoly and the developing strength of her competitors. This example is symptomatic of the pamphlet's shortcomings if taken as a theoretical text.

It is not the place here for an overall discussion of the pamphlet or of the concept of a new stage of capitalism. It is relevant, however, to examine the argument by which Lenin connects the increased centralisation of capital to the export of capital. Hobson, it will be remembered, had argued that capital was forced to look for outlets abroad because more savings were accumulated at home than could be invested there. He attributed this to the concentration of industry, which allowed the big trusts to increase their profitability by restricting their output. Lenin appears to argue along very similar lines. He says:

> On the threshold of the twentieth century, we see a new type of monopoly being formed. First, monopolist combines of capitalists in all advanced capitalist countries; second, a few very rich countries, in which the accumulation of capital has reached gigantic proportions, occupy a monopolist position. An enormous "surplus of capital" accumulated in the advanced countries. . . .
> . . . The necessity of exporting capital arises from the fact that in a few countries capitalism has become "over-ripe", and, owing to the backward stage of agriculture and the im-

*"For Britain, the period of vast increase in colonial conquests falls between 1860 and 1880; and the last twenty years of the nineteenth century are also of great importance. For France and Germany it falls precisely during those last twenty years. We saw above that the apex of pre-monopoly capitalist development, of capitalism in which free competition was predominant, was reached in the period between 1860 and 1880. We now see that it is *precisely after that period* that the tremendous "boom" in colonial annexations begins, and that the struggle for a territorial division of the world becomes extraordinarily keen. It is beyond doubt, therefore, that the transition of capitalism to the stage of monopoly capitalism, to finance capital, is *connected* with the intensification of the struggle for the partition of the world." Lenin, ibid, p.71 (italics in original).

poverishment of the masses, capital lacks opportunities for "profitable" investment.[71]

The emphasis on the impoverishment of the masses as a reason for the lack of investment outlets lends to the passage a definite underconsumptionist tinge. There is nothing in Lenin's explanation that Hobson could disagree with, and indeed the whole theory is very similar to his own.

It is interesting to note that a similar idea was produced independently by Hilferding. Hilferding argues that while there is still pressure to innovate in a cartel because of the fear of being undercut by outsiders, a specific feature of cartels is that cost-reducing technical innovations do not necessarily lead to a reduction in price. This raises the rate of profit, while at the same time the rate of investment of capital is slowed down because in the cartellised industries the first rule is limitation of production and not its extension, while in the uncartellised industries the rate of profit is so depressed by competition with the cartels that not much investment can be financed. So on the one hand the mass of capital allocated for accumulation grows, while on the other the possibilities of advancing it contract. This contradiction finds its solution in the export of capital.[72]

There is no evidence that Hilferding had read Hobson, and yet the argument is very similar. The basic idea is that the changed relations within the capitalist class reduce price competition and so allow a rise in the rate of surplus value to occur. Cost reductions are not followed by price reductions. This theory is implicitly accepted by Lenin in his *Imperialism*, along with the conclusion that this generates the export of capital in search of investment outlets, although why there should exist outlets in the less developed parts of the globe which do not exist in the more developed parts is not explained by him any more than it is by Hobson. The underconsumptionist element arises, of course, in the emphasis on the increasing rate of surplus value as the source of growing difficulties of realisation.

NOTES

1 H.N.Brailsford, *The Lifework of J.A.Hobson*, pp.5–6.

2 J.A.Hobson, *Confessions of an Economic Heretic* (CEH), p.42.
3 ibid, p.14.
4 Brailsford, op.cit., pp.6–7.
5 J.A.Hobson & A.F.Mummery, *The Physiology of Industry* (PI), pp.iii–iv.
6 CEH, p.30.
7 PI, p.v.
8 PI, p.iv.
9 PI, p.viii.
10 PI, p.v.
11 PI, pp.23–4.
12 PI, p.25.
13 PI, p.25.
14 PI, p.25.
15 PI, pp.26–7.
16 PI, p.31.
17 See, for instance, p.47 of the book.
18 PI, p.37.
19 PI, pp.54–5.
20 PI, p.58.
21 PI, p.71.
22 PI, p.88.
23 PI, p.98.
24 PI, p.172.
25 J.A.Hobson, *The Evoluton of Modern Capitalism* (EMC), p.307.
26 J.A.Hobson, *The Problem of the Unemployed* (PU), pp.88–9.
27 PU, p.91.
28 PU, pp.102–3.
29 J.A.Hobson, *The Economics of Distribution* (ED), p.16.
30 ED, p.19.
31 ED, p.19.
32 ED, pp.21–2.
33 ED, p.32.
34 ED, p.219.
35 ED, p.221.
36 ED, p.351.
37 ED, p.351.
38 ED, p.357.
39 ED, p.354.
40 J.A.Hobson, *Imperialism* (I), pp.77–8.
41 I, p.78.
42 I, p.81.
43 I, p.88.
44 I, p.91.

45 I, pp.93–4.
46 J.A.Hobson, *The Industrial System* (IS), p.28.
47 IS, p.45.
48 IS, p.49.
49 IS, p.52.
50 IS, p.53.
51 IS, p.xii.
52 IS, p.80.
53 IS, p.81.
54 IS, p.100.
55 IS, p.viii.
56 IS, Ch 13.
57 PI, p.102.
58 PI, p.117.
59 PI, p.120.
60 PI, p.121.
61 PI, p.124.
62 PI, p.139.
63 PI, p.139.
64 PI, pp.142–3.
65 J.A.Hobson, *The Economics of Unemployment*, pp.77–8.
66 IS, p.298.
67 IS, p.302.
68 IS, p.303.
69 EMC, p.288.
70 V.I.Lenin, *Imperialism, the Highest Stage of Capitalism*, p.15.
71 ibid, pp.57–8.
72 R.Hilferding, *Das Finanzkapital*, Ch 15.

9

ROSA LUXEMBURG

It is undoubtedly the common view that Rosa Luxemburg is an underconsumptionist. Paul Sweezy refers to her as "the queen of underconsumptionists";[1] Ernest Mandel classifies her theory of crisis as an underconsumptionist one;[2] and Oskar Lange also regards her as an underconsumptionist.[3] However, both Sweezy and Mandel follow the old tradition in Marxist literature of classifying all theories of crisis as either "underconsumption theories" or "disproportionality theories", and this restrictive approach leaves us with a somewhat broad and loose interpretation of the phrase "underconsumption". For example, Mandel's definition of an underconsumption theory is:

> In order to explain the periodical crises, the supporters of underconsumption theories start from the contradiction between the tendency to unlimited development of production and the tendency to limitation in consumption by the broad masses, a contradiction which is indeed characteristic of the capitalist mode of production. The periodical crises thus appear as crises of the realisation of surplus-value.[4]

This is obviously vague, and based more on the repetition of certain phrases in Marx than on a rigorous analysis of the various types of theories of crisis. It is not surprising, therefore, that neither Mandel nor Sweezy produce a convincing explanation of the underconsumptionism in Rosa Luxemburg.

Another line of argument is that of Joan Robinson. She identifies the point that Luxemburg is trying to get at in her discussion of the realisation question — the question of how the surplus product can be sold and realised as money — as the problem of the absorption of the surplus as it is conceived in Baran and Sweezy's *Monopoly Capital*. This form of underconsumptionist interpretation focusses on armaments expenditure:

The analysis of militarism in the last chapter over-reaches itself by trying to prove too much. The argument is that armaments are built up out of taxes which fall entirely on wages. . . . The analysis which best fits Rosa Luxemburg's own argument, and the facts, is that armaments provide an outlet for the investment of surplus (over and above any contribution there may be from forced saving out of wages), which, unlike other kinds of investment, creates no further problem by increasing productive capacity.[5]

A similar view is displayed by Kalecki.[6]

I shall argue that it is wrong to regard Rosa Luxemburg as an underconsumptionist. Her problem is a different one. Her persistent inquiries about where are the consumers to come from to justify accumulation and her insistence that some pre-existing extra demand must be found somewhere before investment can take place are, it is true, very reminiscent of the Malthusian type of underconsumption theory. But her problem does not have the characteristics of underconsumptionism as I have defined it. I attribute the fact that so many people should have thought of her as an underconsumptionist partly to the difficulty of understanding what she is trying to say, and partly to vagueness in the definition of underconsumption theories, the combined effect of which is a confusion of superficial resemblances with the deeper divergences.

Rosa Luxemburg regards the central problem of economics as that of the accumulation or reproduction of the total social capital.

Karl Marx made a contribution of lasting service to the theory of economics when he drew attention to the problem of the reproduction of the entire social capital. It is significant that in the history of economics we find only two attempts at an exact exposition of this problem: one by Quesnay, the father of the Physiocrats, at its very inception; and in its final stage this attempt by Marx. In the interim, the problem was ever with bourgeois economics. Yet bourgeois economists have never been fully aware of this problem in its pure aspects, detached from related and intersecting minor problems; they have never been able to formulate it precisely, let alone solve it.[7]

However, we have to wait until we reach the chapter on 'Expanded Reproduction' before we get an inkling of what this problem consists of. Luxemburg reproduces Marx's diagrammatic examples of expanded reproduction:

I. $4,000c + 1000v + 1000s = 6,000$
II. $1,500c + 750v + 750s = 3,000$
Total $9,000$

Suppose that half the surplus value in department I is accumulated. Thus $500s_1$ goes to buy luxury goods from department II. The rest, to be accumulated, divides itself into $400s_{1c} + 100s_{1v}$,* because the organic composition of capital in department I is $4:1$. Now department I has produced commodities to the value of $6,000$. This must equal c_1 $(4,000) + c_2$ $(1,500) + s_{1c}$ $(400) + s_{2c}$ $(?)$. So $s_{2c} = 100$. Since the organic composition of capital in department II is $2:1$, $s_{2v} = 50$, and a total of $150s_2$ is accumulated rather than consumed. What is the position with respect to department II? Its output is 3000. Demand for its output is:

$v_1 (1,000) + v_2 (750) + s_{1v} (100) + s_{2v} (50) + b_1 (500) + b_2 (600)$
$= 3,000$

So there are no problems. Luxemburg follows it through as far as the fifth year just to prove the point.[8]

It is easy to draw mathematical pictures of the accumulation process — that is not where the difficulty lies. The question is whether these fine mathematical schemes can be realised in practice:

> There are no limits to the continuation of this diagrammatic development of accumulation in accordance with the few easy rules we have demonstrated. But now it is time to take care lest we should only have achieved these surprisingly smooth results through simply working out certain fool-proof mathematical exercises in addition and subtraction, and we must further inquire whether it is not merely because mathematical equations are easily put on paper that accumulation can continue ad infinitum without any friction.

*I use the following notation: for dept I, the constant and variable capital laid out are respectively c_1 and v_1, surplus value consumed is b_1, and those portions of surplus value accumulated for the purchase of respectively means of production and labour-power are s_1, s_{1v}.

In other words: the time has come to look for the concrete social conditions of accumulation.[9]

The first objection Luxemburg makes is that accumulation in department II is always "subordinated" to that in department I. In each of the five years in Marx's example, it is assumed that exactly half of the surplus value in department I is capitalised. This determines a somewhat erratic course for accumulation in department II. In sum, Luxemburg says, it is always department I that takes the initiative, while department II is reduced to the role of a passive appendage.[10]

This argument seems to rest on an elementary confusion. Under the assumptions of the expanded reproduction schemes, it is sufficient to assume a given rate of accumulation in either department for all the other parameters of the system to be uniquely determined. Marx chooses to assume a steady rate of accumulation of 50 per cent in department I: each year half the surplus value in that department is accumulated. But the result does not reflect the "domination" of department I over department II, but merely the fact that Marx has started by assuming a given rate of accumulation *in that department.* It would of course be perfectly possible to assume a steady rate of accumulation in department II, in which case no doubt accumulation in department I would follow a zig-zag course from year to year.

But this quibble is of little importance to the basic problem — which turns out to be one of effective demand. Where is the demand to come from that is to justify all this accumulation that looks so good on paper? This is the point at which the "concrete social conditions" come into consideration. Rosa Luxemburg expresses it as follows:

We must ask first of all: what is the starting point of accumulation? That is the approach on which we have to investigate the mutual dependence of the accumulative process in the two departments of production. There can be no doubt that under capitalist conditions department II is dependent upon department I in so far as its accumulation is determined by the additional means of production available. Conversely, the accumulation in department I depends upon a corresponding quantity of additional consumer goods being available for its additional labour-power. It does not follow, however, that so long as both these conditions are observed, accumulation in both departments is bound, as Marx's diagram makes it appear, to go on automatically year after year. The conditions of accumulation we have enumerated are no more than those without which there can be no accumulation. There may even be a desire to accumulate in both departments, yet the desire to accumulate plus the technical prerequisites of accumulation is not enough in a capitalist economy of commodity production. A further condition is required to ensure that accumulation can in fact proceed and production expand: the effective demand for commodities must also increase. Where is this continually increasing demand to come from, which in Marx's diagram forms the basis of reproduction on an ever rising scale?

It cannot possibly come from the capitalists of departments I and II themselves — so much is certain right away — it cannot arise out of their personal consumption. On the contrary, it is the very essence of accumulation that the capitalists refrain from consuming a part of their surplus value which must be ever increasing — at least as far as absolute figures are concerned — that they use it instead to make goods for the use of other people.[11]

So the capitalists cannot provide the demand, because they have deliberately refrained from consuming in order to accumulate. It is precisely the part of the surplus value that they capitalise, that their personal consumption will be unable to realise. The consumption of the workers will of course be able to realise no more than is equivalent to the variable capital advanced. Nor can we accept the solution, in the manner of Malthus, that sees some kind of 'third force' in society — the clergy, landowners, State officials, etc. — as the source of the necessary demand, for their incomes are either entirely derived from workers' wages, or they form a portion of the total surplus value. Either way, their demand has already been accounted for either in 's' or in 'v'.[12] Equally, nothing is solved by foreign trade since, if we look at the question from the point of view of the *world* market, there can be no foreign trade.[13]

So the problem can be solved only by going outside the two departments, outside the capitalist mode of production.

The surplus value must therefore shed its form as surplus

product before it can re-assume it for the purpose of accumulation; by some means or other it must first pass through the money stage. So the surplus product of departments I and II must be bought — by whom? On the above showing, there will have to be an effective demand outside I and II, merely in order to realise the surplus value of the two departments, just so that the surplus product can be turned into cash.[14]

But if effective demand is a real difficulty for the process of accumulation, why does this not reflect itself in the reproduction schemes? Luxemburg concedes that the schemes appear to provide a solution. They show that the capitalised surplus value is realised partly by the capitalists themselves, who need new means of production for expanding production — this accounts for the 'constant capital' portion — and partly by the newly employed workers, who have to consume in order to live — this accounts for the 'variable capital' portion. But, says Rosa Luxemburg:

> That implies a previous capitalist incentive to enlarge production; if new workers are set to work with new means of production, there must have been a new demand for the products which are to be turned out.[15]

In other words, the solution given by the reproduction schemes is not wrong, but it ignores the preliminary question of incentives to accumulation. However, if the reproduction schemes are right, then the only incentive which should be needed by an individual capitalist is the expectation that other capitalists will be accumulating, and will provide him with a demand for his own additional product. Thus the question of incentives would appear simply to be one of expectations on the part of the individual capitalists. But if that is so, then the difficulty arises: why should there be a distinction between simple and expanded reproduction? For from the point of view of an individual capitalist, the problem of a wrong forecast of the demand for his product will exist whether he expects his demand to rise or fall by a given amount, or to stay exactly the same. There is nothing special about a zero rate of growth. Thus if the problem Rosa Luxemburg is thinking of is really one of expectations, then she seems to have made a definite mistake in presenting it solely in terms of expanded reproduction, as if it did not assert itself with equal force in simple reproduction. So we are still not clear why this demand from outside the capitalist mode of production is so necessary.

In Rosa Luxemburg's view, Marx posed the problem of accumulation more accurately than anyone else; but he did not solve it. Indeed, in so far as he grasped that there really was a problem, he conceived it only as finding the additional money necessary to lubricate the increased circulation of commodities, and not as finding an additional demand.[16] Thus he could not come up with a correct answer. But Luxemburg is not very good at explaining what precisely is the difficulty in expanded reproduction, which does not show up in the reproduction schemes, which Marx could not explain, but which nevertheless necessitates the intervention of a non-capitalist stratum of buyers to secure the smooth progress of accumulation. It appears that the real difficulty is to find out who are the *beneficiaries* of capitalist accumulation. She says at one point:

> In the first section we ascertained that Marx's diagram of accumulation does not solve the question of who is to benefit in the end by enlarged reproduction. If we take the diagram literally as it is set out at the end of Volume II, it appears that capitalist production would itself realise its entire surplus value, and that it would use the capitalised surplus value exclusively for its own needs.[17]

Yes indeed: it is precisely the capitalists themselves who benefit from their own expansion of production. But Luxemburg cannot accept this as an explanation:

> Accumulation here takes its course, but it is not in the least indicated who is to benefit by it, who are the new consumers for whose sake production is ever more enlarged. The diagram assumes, say, the following course of events: the coal industry is expanded in order to expand the iron industry in order to expand the machine industry in order to expand the production of consumer goods. This last, in turn, is expanded to maintain both its own workers and the growing army of coal, iron and machine operatives. And so on ad infinitum.[18]

And again:

> Who, then, realises the permanently increasing surplus

value? The diagram answers: the capitalists themselves and they alone. — And what do they do with this increasing surplus value? — The diagram replies: They use it for an ever greater expansion of their production. These capitalists are thus fanatical supporters of an expansion of production for production's sake. They see to it that ever more machines are built for the sake of building — with their help — ever more new machines. Yet the upshot of all this is not accumulation of capital but an increasing production of producer goods to no purpose whatever.[19]

It is simply inconceivable to Rosa Luxemburg that this process can go on by itself, without some external prop. In this particular example she takes the expansion of investment goods alone, but this is merely for rhetorical effect. For her objection is not at all the underconsumptionist one that the production of means of production is outrunning what is justified by the demand for consumption goods, but that a general expansion of production in all departments is not fundamentally justified by any demand: it is production for production's sake. We should note that she defines this as "not accumulation of capital" — this is an important key to her difficulty, as will be seen later.

Luxemburg likens Marx's diagrams of reproduction to the theories of Tugan Baranovsky. Tugan Baranovsky notices that in the reproduction schemes as they are set out by Marx there is no problem of a lack of demand, and he concludes that therefore capitalists will always find a market for as much as they want to produce. He is aware of the existence of crises and depressions but attributes them to disproportions between the level of production in various branches of industry and the distribution of consumption. In fact Tugan Baranovsky's position seems to be very close to that of the proponents of "Say's Law" much earlier in the century, since it precludes the possibility of general overproduction. Luxemburg objects that the reproduction schemes lead naturally to this kind of interpretation and are antipathetic to her own. In particular, the only explanation of crises that the diagram permits is a disproportionality theory and there is a contradiction between it and certain passages in Volume III of *Capital* where Marx explicitly mentions the level of consumption in its relation to the level of production as *a* (if not *the*) cause of crises.

Here Rosa Luxemburg brings out an undoubted truth about the reproduction schemes, under the assumptions which Marx inserted into them, but it shows also her peculiar vision of their role. Marx clearly treated them as an illustrative device, firstly (in the case of simple reproduction) to show how the class relations and the technical basis of society are reproduced, and secondly (with expanded reproduction) to show how accumulation of capital is possible on this basis. He did not imagine that they were an accurate picture of the interrupted, anarchic process of development of a capitalist economy. Rosa Luxemburg, on the other hand, treats them as just such a picture; hence her accusations of Tugan-Baranovskyism. This odd attitude reflects the threat which they pose to her own thesis, for even if the capitalist economy does not run smoothly as in the reproduction schemes, they do imply that it can develop of its own accord, without the help of the surrounding non-capitalist world.

Luxemburg thinks that these problems do not exist in simple reproduction, for so long as there is no accumulation, the capitalists and workers between them easily consume the total product. It is as soon as a part of the surplus value is not consumed, but accumulated, that the problem arises, and we have to find buyers outside the capitalist mode of production:

> Realisation of the surplus value is doubtless a vital question of capitalist accumulation. It requires as its prime condition — ignoring, for simplicity's sake, the capitalists' fund of consumption altogether — that there should be strata of buyers outside capitalist society. Buyers, it would be noted, not consumers, since the material form of the surplus value is quite irrelevant to its realisation. The decisive fact is that the surplus value cannot be realised by sale either to workers or to capitalists, but only if it is sold to such social organisations or strata whose own mode of production is not capitalistic.[20]

The fact that buyers of means of production will do just as well as buyers of consumption goods shows once again the non-underconsumptionist character of Rosa Luxemburg's ideas. What is necessary is an injection of demand, into any line of industry, so that some capitalists can realise their product, and they will then, by completing their purchases with other capitalists, be able to realise gradually the whole product. Thus the external demand does not have to cover the entire accumulated surplus value.[21]

But the relations of the capitalist mode of production to its surroundings are not merely ones of buying commodities on one side and selling them on the other, with money always flowing in one and the same direction. It is definitely a matter of exchange. The capitalist mode of production has a great need of the raw materials provided by these other modes.

> From the aspect both of realising the surplus value and of procuring the material elements of constant capital, international trade is a prime necessity for the historical existence of capitalism — an international trade which under actual conditions is essentially an exchange between capitalistic and non-capitalistic modes of production.[22]

Luxemburg also stresses the importance of these other modes as a source of additional labour-power for the capitalist mode as they are gradually broken down by it. Thus the capitalist mode derives not only the economic conditions but also the material elements of its own expansion from these older modes. It is the struggle for the exclusive domination by capitalist nation-states over the non-capitalist areas of the world that is the phenomenon known as imperialism, a struggle made necessary by the needs of the accumulation of capital itself.

But there is a problem here: if the relationship between the capitalist and the non-capitalist world is one of exchange, then the non-capitalist buyers who take off the surplus product of the capitalist sector are exactly compensated by the non-capitalist sellers putting it back again. There can only be a consistent excess of imports from over exports to the capitalist sector if there is a continuous drain of money out of the non-capitalist sector, and this presupposes either (a) a very large stock of it to start with, or (b) that there is significant gold production in that sector. But Rosa Luxemburg has already ridiculed the invocation of gold producers to solve her problem, and there is no indication that she thought that the exports out of the capitalist sector should consistently exceed the imports into it. So where is the solution?

At one point she says this:

Between the production of surplus value, then, and the subsequent period of accumulation, two separate transactions take place — that of realising surplus value, i.e. of converting it into pure value, and that of transforming this pure value into productive capital. They are both dealings between capitalist production and the surrounding non-capitalist world.[23]

This is based on Marx's analysis of the circuit of an individual capital: $M\text{-}C..P..C'\text{-}M'$.[24] For each individual capital the sale of the finished product $(C'\text{-}M')$ is a necessary precondition for a new transformation of money into productive capital $(M\text{-}C)$. Now in a capitalist economy as a whole all the various individual capitals are at any one point of time all at various different stages of the circulation process, so that the circuit does not appear to have any particular starting-point or end-point but goes on continuously. But we could imagine things differently. Suppose we thought that at the beginning of each time-period all the capitalists get out their money, buy the elements of productive capital, produce, and at the end of the period all reappear on the market with their products. Then it would indeed appear, as Rosa Luxemburg suggests, that for the economy as a whole the conversion of surplus value into money is a necessary precondition of the beginning of production in the next period, and that it is not sufficient just to assume the satisfactory realisation of this surplus value in the natural course of things, as the reproduction schemes do. And it could then be claimed that the act of buying by the non-capitalist sector overcomes this hitch, while the act of selling is just part of the rest of the circuit, in which there are no particular difficulties. In this way one could suggest the necessity of non-capitalist buyers, even where their purchases are matched in value by sales from the non-capitalist to the capitalist sector.

But while conceiving things in this way explains Rosa Luxemburg's formulation of the problem, it does not explain why the problem exists at all. For why is the demand of the workers (consumption) and of the capitalists (consumption plus investment) not sufficient to realise the whole product, whether there is accumulation or not? This is the difficulty we have been up against all along.

THE ANTICRITIQUE

We have now been through the whole of *The Accumulation of Capital* without being able to decipher the difficulty. Rosa Luxemburg was shocked by the critics' hostile response to her book, and a couple of years later she fired back at them with an *Antikritik*.[25] It is easier to deduce from this what her problem is. In it she starts off as follows: products cannot be sold unless they fulfil some social need; so the expansion of capitalist production, the continual accumulation of capital, is bound up with the continual expansion of social need. But in capitalist production the market for the product of each individual producer is created by the activities of other producers. So:

> The 'social need' on which the accumulation of capital is dependent appears on closer inspection to be the accumulation of capital itself. The more capital accumulates, the more it accumulates — it is on this empty tautology or on this dizzy circle that the deeper analysis seems to run. One cannot make out where the beginning or where the impulsive force is. We are plainly turning round in circles and the problem eludes our grasp. But it does so only so long as we approach the thing from the stand-point of the superficialities of the market (Marktoberfläche), i.e. of the individual capital, that favourite platform of vulgar economy.[26]

Let us imagine all the commodities produced piled up in a great heap. This heap divides itself naturally into a number of portions:

1) Depreciation: money set aside by the capitalist class itself to pay for replacement of means of production used up.

2) The means of life of the population.

3) For accumulation.

Now what kinds of goods are there in this third portion, and who in society has need of them, and is willing to buy them off the capitalists? This is Rosa Luxemburg's question.[27] Obviously the workers cannot buy them, for they have not the money. Equally the capitalists cannot, for they have refrained from consuming in order to accumulate. But suppose there really is no problem, that the capitalists are mutual customers for this portion of the heap, in order to extend their production.

All right, but such a solution only pushes the problem from

this moment to the next. After we have assumed that accumulation has started and that the increased production throws an even bigger amount of commodities onto the market the following year, the same question arises again: where do we then find the consumers for this even greater amount of commodities? Will we answer: well, this growing amount of goods will again be exchanged among the capitalists to extend production again, and so forth, year after year? Then we have the roundabout that revolves around itself in empty space. That is not capitalist accumulation, i.e. the amassing of money capital, but its contrary: producing commodities for the sake of it; from the standpoint of capital an utter absurdity. If the capitalists as a class are the only customers for the total amount of commodities, apart from the share they have to part with to maintain the workers — if they must always buy the commodities with their own money and realise the surplus value, then amassing profit, accumulation for the capitalist class, cannot possibly take place.

They must find many other buyers who receive their means of purchase from an independent source, and do not get it out of the pocket of the capitalist like the labourers or the collaborators of capital, the government officials, officers, clergy and liberal professions. They have to be consumers who receive their means of purchase on the basis of commodity exchange, i.e. also production of goods but taking place outside capitalist commodity production.[28]

The imagery of heaps confirms the impression that she conceives the whole product as coming onto the market simultaneously at the end of the period. There are two problems in the argument here:

(a) What *is* the difficulty, which can be passed on from one period to another, but in the end results in 'production for production's sake'? If it is a difficulty why can it be solved for one period or two, but not for many?

(b) If Rosa Luxemburg is following Marx, then money capital is just *one* of the forms of capital — so it is meaningless to counterpose accumulation (= amassing of money capital) to expansion of production of commodities (= amassing of commodity capital), as one being the accumulation of capital, the other not. But if she does equate accumulation of capital only with accumulation of money capital, then this explains why the expanded reproduction schemes provide a false solution: for they can only resolve the question of realising the accumulated capital in money by postulating yet more production, yet more investment of this capital. And if you only accept accumulation of money capital as 'valid', this is indeed pushing the problem on to the next period and 'revolving in ever higher circles'.

Now we can understand Luxemburg's complaints about capitalists being "fanatics of production for production's sake". For since she is unwilling to accept accumulation of capital in its physical form as just as good as in its money form; and since, in the expanded reproduction schemes, if capitalists do not consume the whole surplus value then they can only avoid a crisis by investing in the expansion of productive facilities; this investment appears as just a temporary expedient to overcome a difficulty which will always be there and must some time be resolved. Thus it really does appear as if accumulation cannot go on without the intervention of outside consumers, as Luxemburg maintains, because otherwise it would just be "production for production's sake".

Bukharin, much the most perceptive critic of Luxemburg's ideas, says this by way of conclusion about her:

> Rosa Luxemburg's basic mistake is that she takes the total capitalist as an individual capitalist. She underestimates this total capitalist. Therefore, she does not understand that the process of realisation occurs gradually. For the same reason she portrays the accumulation of capital as an accumulation of money capital.
>
> From this — as we believe — results the manner in which she explains imperialism. Indeed, if the total capitalist is equated with the typical individual capitalist, the first of course cannot be his own consumer. Furthermore, if the amount of additional gold is equivalent to the value of the additional number of commodities, this gold can only come from abroad (obviously it is nonsense to assume a corresponding production of gold). Finally, if all capitalists have to realise their surplus value at once (without it wandering from one pocket to another, which is strictly forbidden), they need third persons etc.[29]

This is fundamentally correct. Luxemburg is incapable of

communicating precisely what her problem is because it is an imaginary one conjured up by the analysis of the form of circulation of an individual capital. In the circulation M-C-M', the starting- and the end-point is money, and so Luxemburg identifies accumulation with accumulation of money capital. I have already pointed out how that leads to the idea of expanded reproduction as production for production's sake. Because she imagines the whole capitalist class behaving as in the formula, like one 'total capitalist', she imagines the entire social capital being laid out as one lump, and that the whole of the surplus value has to be realised simultaneously, at the end of the period, rather than gradually throughout the course of it.* Hence the images of commodity heaps rather than a continuous flow of production, and the problems about who are the beneficiaries of the process of accumulation. For if she thinks of the whole class of capitalists as if they were one individual, continuous reinvestment and expansion of production must indeed appear senseless. This of course determines quite a different attitude to the question of accumulation from that of Marx: where Marx sees accumulation as the outcome of the struggle between individual capitals, Luxemburg has assumed this struggle away in *her* idea of the total capitalist, and so naturally the driving force behind accumulation becomes a problem.

Rosa Luxemburg's ideas have a superficial resemblance to a Malthusian type of underconsumption theory, firstly in differentiating sharply between a static and a growing economy, and secondly in invoking some third force of consumers to create the demand necessary for profitable accumulation. But ultimately Luxemburg cannot be classified as an underconsumptionist, because at no stage is it specifically consumption demand that is lacking, and indeed she quite explicitly states that demand for means of production is equally as good. Thus although she frequently phrases the question in terms of consumers, it would be more accurate to designate it as one of demand or of markets, words which do not have associations with a specific branch of production. In any case, the mistake which lies at the bottom of her analysis has nothing to do with a conception of the special importance of consumption goods production, but relates to her

*Rosa thinks that "the capitalists invest as a class rather than as individuals" (Kalecki).

understanding of the general process of the circulation of capital.

NOTES

1 P.M.Sweezy, *The Theory of Capitalist Development*, p.171.
2 E.Mandel, *Marxist Economic Theory*, p.361.
3 O.Lange, *The Rate of Interest and the Optimum Propensity to Consume*, in *Economica* Vol 5 No 17.
4 Mandel, op.cit., p.361.
5 R.Luxemburg, *The Accumulation of Capital*, pp.27–8.
6 M.Kalecki, *Selected Essays in the Dynamics of a Capitalist Economy*, pp.153–5.
7 R.Luxemburg, op.cit., p.31.
8 ibid, p.117.
9 ibid, p.119.
10 ibid, p.127.
11 ibid, pp.131–2.
12 ibid, pp.134–5.
13 ibid, p.136.
14 ibid, p.137.
15 ibid, p.133.
16 ibid, Chs 8 & 9.
17 ibid, p.155.
18 ibid, p.330.
19 ibid, pp.334–5.
20 ibid, pp.351–2.
21 ibid, pp.354–5.
22 ibid, p.359.
23 ibid, p.359.
24 K.Marx, *Capital*, Vol 2 Ch 1.
25 *Die Akkumulation des Kapitals, oder was die Epigonen aus der Marxschen Theorie gemacht haben. Eine Antikritik.* First published 1921.
26 "*Antikritik*", p.10.
27 ibid, p.17.
28 ibid, pp.19–21.
29 K.Tarbuck (ed.) — R.Luxemburg and N.Bukharin, *Imperialism and the Accumulation of Capital*, pp.201–2.

10

LESSER WRITERS OF THE INTER-WAR PERIOD

Hobson was the most influential underconsumptionist writer of the early twentieth century, not just because of the sheer volume of his writings, but also because he had the most sophisticated and plausible analysis of the ills of a capitalist economy. By the mid-20's he had had a considerable impact on Labour Party and I.L.P. thinking; although not officially a member of the I.L.P., he served on its Policy Committee which in 1925 drafted the programme embodying the idea of a living wage, and according to Brailsford he was probably the most respected intellectual influence in the Labour Movement at this stage.[1] But there were other underconsumptionists writing at this time who also deserve attention. The ones I shall discuss here are the American writers W.T.Foster and W.Catchings, and the Englishman Major C.H.Douglas.

Foster and Catchings published two substantial books in the mid-20's under the auspices of the Pollak Foundation for Economic Research, one called *Money* and the other called *Profits*. It is in the latter that they analyse what they call "the economic problem". This problem is that of periodic, and sometimes sustained, business depressions. The main cause of such depressions, as they see it, is the deficiency in the incomes of consumers. Consumers' incomes are insufficient to pay for output at final sales prices, so prices fall, profits fall, and producers cut back their output. The underlying premise of this argument is fundamentally the same as Hobsons's:

> Since the end of all economic activity is consumption, money spent by consumers is the force that keeps the wheels of industry moving. Current consumption is the chief incentive to current production; deficiency of current consumer buying is the chief cause of unemployment.[2]

Consumers justify themselves as the focus of attention because the satisfaction of their needs is the only logical basis for production. So long as they receive enough income to absorb all the output as it comes onto the market without any fall in the price level, business proceeds steadily. Now consumers' incomes are themselves dependent on the level of productive activity, so everything seems circular; but in fact it is incomes that play the determinant role, for an increase in productive activity without an increase in incomes would quickly induce a slump.[3]. The authors reject the idea that a high level of investment could sustain itself over a substantial period without a large rise in consumption on the basis that "business cannot run on optimism". In other words such a boom would be like a balloon which must burst sooner or later, because it is not based on continued increases in consumers' purchasing power.[4] Thus they dismiss the whole expectations approach to the trade cycle.

But how does the deficiency of purchasing power come about? The authors look at various forms of saving, starting with company saving. Undistributed profits in the form of building up of stocks or credit to consumers pose no problem, since in the former case the goods do not come on the market and in the latter the consumers borrow the money to buy them. If the money is just accumulated as cash balances, this is equivalent to hoarding and firms find themselves with a surplus product. But what happens if they invest the money in plant and equipment? Then the money is redistributed to consumers in the form of wages, but this does not necessarily recreate the balance between purchasing power and productive capacity. Indeed, paradoxically, this balance is only recreated so long as the investment is completely useless and results in no additional output whatsoever. For although in the current period there is no imbalance, in the next period when the increased output comes onto the market there is a surplus product, for total consumption is not increased.

At this rate, according to Foster and Catchings, the stocks of unsold goods will become larger and larger, since each year consumers can buy no more than the original output.[5] But in fact a simple mistake has been made in not treating period t + 1 in an analogous way to period t. It has been simply assumed that in period t + 1 the undistributed profits will appear in the form of unsold goods, whereas in fact capitalists have all the choices

Time Period		t	t + 1	
Output		100	110	units of goods
Sales		100	100	,,
Receipts		100	100	,,
Wages in consumption				
goods sector		90	100	pounds
Investment		10		,,
Unsold Goods			10	units of goods
(Price Index = 100)				

that were open to them in period t, and by reinvesting their profits can solve the problem in period t + 1 just as in period t. Like Rosa Luxemburg, Foster and Catchings imagine that accumulation only pushes the problem from one year to the next, without recognising that if you have solved it in one year you have solved it in every year.

Obviously this result is not dependent on the saving being done by firms, and investment matched by savings by individuals produces the same consequences. So, like Hobson and Malthus, Foster and Catchings come up against the "dilemma of thrift" — that saving is necessary to growth, but liable to precipitate a depression. But they are very critical of Hobson's argument, for they do not agree that the distribution of income is the source of the difficulty,[6] and they do not accept the idea of a right proportion between consumption and investment, since to them a very high level of wasteful investment is perfectly all right.[7] Their own argument, however, contains a much more elementary mistake than Hobson's.

Another writer of the 20's was Major Douglas, whose name is inextricably associated with the idea of Social Credit. Douglas's economic ideas are often difficult to understand, since, as one of his exasperated opponents wrote, "he possesses a remarkable gift for combining the false and the true in an ingenious mixture"[8] the exact meaning of which is obscure. But in spite of this, in some parts of the world Social Credit gained a significant number of supporters during the Depression years[9] — outside rather than within academic circles. This success was due to Douglas's ability at mobilising popular prejudices, his two chief targets being professional economists and big financiers. A pamphlet giving a précis of Douglas's proposals has this to say about financiers:

By far the strongest force in the world at present is the centralised power of finance. It is all the more powerful because it is not generally recognised. Probably nine out of ten bankers have no other motive than to retain the position of material advantage which their business ensures them, but it seems probable that there exists a small minority of men at the head of the international financial hierarchy to whom profit in the ordinary sense is a secondary consideration, who are actuated chiefly by the will to power. They aim quite definitely at a financial hegemony of the world, and their ideal is the servile state.

By their monopoly of credit they determine the size of national incomes, they control directly or indirectly all important organs of public information (the Press, the B.B.C., etc) and, as we have seen, the policy of political governments. . . . Such superficially opposite political movements as Fascism and Bolshevism obtain support from international finance because they are both examples of centralised control.[10]

This gives some idea of the quality of Douglas's work. Underconsumptionism comes into it at the point where he claims that the total national income is insufficient to buy the total national product. He tries to show this by means of what he calls the A + B theorem. Suppose we take one single firm. The prices of all the goods produced by this firm during a given period can be analysed under two headings:

(A) Personal Incomes i.e. wages, salaries and dividends drawn by the employees and shareholders of the firm.

(B) Payments to other firms for raw materials, machinery, plant etc. Now, say Douglas triumphantly, the price of the goods produced by this firm cannot be less than A + B; but only incomes A are available to buy these goods. The B incomes, representing the incomes of other workers in other factories, have already been spent in order to keep these workers alive. And since A is less than A + B, the joint incomes of employees and shareholders cannot buy all the goods they have produced; this must be true of all firms, and therefore of the whole nation.[11]

The mistake here is a simple one of double counting. The sum of the payments of all the firms in a closed economy is not equal to the sum of the A + B's but only to the sum of the A's, since the B payments of a firm include all the A payments for the goods bought of the firm from which it purchases. So the national income is adequate to the production after all.

The popularity of Major Douglas shows once again the potential appeal of underconsumptionist ideas at a time of depression and high unemployment, particularly when there exist working-class organisations which are looking for an explanation of the crisis which does not blame it on too high wages. Underconsumption theories neatly linked the poverty of the workers with the commercial depression, and at a time when academic economists and governments also were unable to produce convincing explanations, it is not surprising that the trade unions should take up the idea as a justification for public works programmes and for resisting wage-cuts. Opponents of underconsumption theories at this time frequently lamented the hold which they had acquired on the thinking of such institutions,[12] and for the first time in a century (in Western Europe at any rate) significant numbers of tracts and books attacking them were published.

There is no doubt that in the twentieth century the working-class movement has been, and remains, the centre of attraction for underconsumption theories, although the example of Major Douglas and his followers shows that they had their influence elsewhere also. In this context it should not be forgotten that however theoretically unsound they may be, underconsumption theories do contain an element of practical truth, since it *is* possible to stimulate the economy by stimulating consumption.

NOTES

1 H.N.Brailsford, *The Lifework of J.A.Hobson*, p.13.
2 W.T.Foster & W.Catchings, *Profits*, p.234.
3 ibid, p.236.
4 ibid, p.237.
5 ibid, p.279.
6 ibid, p.355.
7 ibid, p.278.
8 F.J.Docker, *Douglas Delusions*, p.2.

9 ibid, p.v.
10 C.G.M—, *The Nation's Credit*, pp.17–8.
11 ibid, p.20.
12 eg H.Gottschalk, *Die Kaufkraftlehre*, Preface.

11

AN ASSESSMENT OF
PRE-KEYNESIAN
UNDERCONSUMPTION THEORIES

As will be argued in the next chapter, the theoretical developments of the 1930's and the new intellectual atmosphere engendered by them had a powerful impact on the history of underconsumption theories — powerful enough, in fact, to justify making a sharp distinction between the pre- and the post-Keynesian situations. For this reason the usual practice of presenting all of one's conclusions in a final chapter is abandoned here, and this chapter is devoted to an assessment of pre-Keynesian underconsumptionism. The question of the modifications to be made in the light of more modern developments will be discussed in the next chapter.

Underconsumption theories up until the 1930's existed in an atmosphere in which it is quite fair to say that orthodox ideas could present no satisfactory explanation of crises. Because marginalism viewed macro-economic processes as the summation of micro-economic ones, and because of its emphasis on the notion of equilibrium, it inclined towards blaming obstacles to the functioning of competition as the source of fluctuations. A wide variety of practical explanations flourished, and many studies of the trade cycle appeared; but since they made no use of the concept of effective demand they tended to bear an air of superficiality. It is the enduring merit of underconsumptionists at this time that their theory of crisis was based on a concept of effective demand. Slumps, they argued, existed because the demand was not there to prevent them. Whatever the formal mistakes of their theories, their instincts had led them much closer to the truth than their orthodox opponents, and the policy measures which they recommended would almost certainly have been more effective in stimulating a recovery.

The difficulty, however, as the analyses of the preceding chapters have shown, is that all of these underconsumption theories have suffered from major theoretical defects. They consistently underestimate the role of investment expenditure, and although this is what lends them their specifically underconsumptionist quality, it is also a fundamental mistake. Their difficulty is that they are trying to prove the existence of a deficiency of effective demand while retaining the classical assumption that all savings are at all times automatically invested, which of course removes any possibility of such a deficiency. Only in a post-Keynesian work such as Sweezy's *The Theory of Capitalist Development* do we see an avoidance of this mistake and a more sophisticated analysis; but even here the basic error — the failure to recognise investment goods production as a truly independent and equal sector of the economy — remains. I shall argue later that underconsumption theories can be constructed without these mistakes, and that if they are it is still reasonable to describe them as underconsumptionist, — but that takes us a long way beyond the writers we have so far examined.

Underconsumption theories imply a pessimistic assessment of the prospects of capitalist production, at least so long as it remains unreformed, so that we must expect the forms in which the theory presents itself to be very sensitive to the actual achievements of capitalist industry. At the beginning, with the first rise of the Industrial Revolution, these theories undoubtedly questioned the viability of large scale industrial production (Sismondi) or the possibility of capitalist accumulation (Spence, Malthus, and above all Chalmers) in general. But if such ideas could seem plausible in the wake of the first industrial crises, they were bound to become increasingly less so as the economy continued to grow and develop in spite of these crises. An adjustment of approach was required. So we find Rodbertus who, instead of complaining only that wages are low, like Sismondi, makes the central point the fact that they are falling as a share of the total product. Both Hobson, and, later, Baran and Sweezy emphasise the concentration of industry, which is intended to explain why the difficulties identified for later stages of capitalist development have not made themselves apparent before. The emphasis is shifted to tendencies within capitalist development, as against the analysis of capitalist production in general. Only the Narodniks represent an exception to this general trend, since Russia was still an agrarian country with considerable vestiges of feudalism and only meagre capitalist development; but even they have to present some explanation of the great flourishing of capitalism in the West.

The social character of underconsumption theories also changes as time progresses. In the early period, they represented the protests of those social classes and strata whose position was most threatened by the rise of capitalism: the landlords, the Church and other non-capitalist rich (British writers), and the independent artisans and peasants being pressed down into the proletariat (Sismondi). The Narodniks play a similar role to that of Sismondi. If underconsumption theories had remained connected to these archaic social movements, there is no doubt that they would have suffered an early demise. Instead, however, they found a new lease of life in the developing working-class movement. Such a movement searching for an understanding consonant with its own experience of the world was a natural base for a theory which could make the poverty of the workers the main cause of the slumps which everyone detested so much. The fight for higher wages could then be justified as necessary to eliminate unemployment. Furthermore, since everyone was looking for ways to overcome the recession and put the economy back on its feet, higher wages could be argued to be in the interests of all classes, even if in the short run it might appear that they were not. Employers, it could be argued, were merely being short-sighted in opposing trade-union demands. This was a theory that was likely to obtain wide support in the working-class movement because it crossed many ideological barriers; it justified trade unionism without necessarily demanding a revolutionary theory of society, and so even the most right-wing trade unionists were likely to be sympathetic towards it. This is undoubtedly one of the main reasons why underconsumptionism has gained so much ground in the working-class movement in times of depression: when the ideological pressure to hold back was greatest, it justified struggle.

I have pointed out several times the sporadic history of underconsumption theories. It seems highly probable that their rise and fall is related to economic conditions. For if one of the main points of difference with orthodoxy is the assessment of the economy as inherently depressed rather than inherently dynamic, then it seems likely that the impressions gained by economists in their formative years will considerably affect their attitude to underconsumptionism. For instance, those post-war economists — such as Paul Baran, Paul Sweezy, Joan Robinson — who have argued that high expenditure on armaments was necessary in order to maintain full employment are obviously people who were profoundly influenced by the Great Depression, which they personally lived through in their youth. One could equally well point to the post-Napoleonic War depression, and the slump of 1873 — both of which had a big impact at the time and undoubtedly influenced Sismondi, Malthus and Hobson. Such experiences can form the basis of a general critical theory, and it is likely that these particular historical events have played a large part in the history of underconsumption theories.

I have divided underconsumption theories into Sismondian and Malthusian types. The essence of the Malthusian type is the idea of over-accumulation: too much is saved and also invested. This strand of underconsumptionism was bound to be killed off by the more sophisticated understanding of the relations of saving and investment heralded by 'the Keynesian revolution'. The Sismondian type, which is superficially more primitive, is actually more enduring. The essence of this type is the idea (a) that a very unequal distribution of income is inherent in capitalist production and (b) that capitalists cannot find ways to consume or invest all of their share and are 'forced' to save it. Baran and Sweezy's *Monopoly Capital,* the major post-Keynesian underconsumptionist work, essentially fits within this type, for their idea of the increasing surplus is precisely analogous to this. Their main advance over their predecessors is that they attempt a serious analysis of what determines the level of investment and how it affects aggregate demand — something which is notably absent in Sismondi and Rodbertus.

The rest of this chapter is devoted to the relationship of underconsumption theories to orthodox ideas, or more precisely, to the dominant ideology of capitalist society which has provided the foundation stones of orthodox theorising. This is crucial, amongst other things, to an understanding of their history and an appreciation of their historical significance. The basic thesis is that underconsumption theories in fact stand in a close relationship to the dominant ideology, although underconsumptionist writers generally see themselves as leading the field in theoretical radicalism. They do not at any stage provide a thorough critique of this ideology, or define their position in relation to it, and in practice they tend to take over some of its main elements and use them directly as a justification for their theoretical propositions. In spite of their obviously critical character in a political sense, and their challenge to some significant tenets of orthodoxy, the underlying theoretical conceptions do not represent a fundamental break with it. This is undoubtedly part of the reason why they are not consistently associated with any one political trend: they do not require a *consistent* radicalism.

The first aspect is the understanding of the macro-economics of a capitalist economy. A significant feature of orthodox writings on capitalism is the idea of an underlying harmony in the system, which holds it together and gives it strength, even though everyone appears to be striving to further his own particular interests. The function of the market, in this view, is to provide the stimuli to which the individual responds, and the theory is that the pressure of the market leads to steady innovation and increasing efficiency of production. The market is the 'invisible hand' which guides production. This is the standard argument that has been used in defence of private enterprise for the past two centuries. This view naturally emphasises the dynamic character of capitalist production, and it has always tended to minimise the significance of macro-economic fluctuations. It implicitly suggests that capitalism is naturally in a booming state and will always be so.

This orthodox conception was strongly attacked by the underconsumptionists. In arguing that consumption demand had a persistent tendency to be insufficient, they implied that a capitalist economy was naturally stagnant and unable to find a permanent solution to this problem, relying only on temporary reliefs which resulted in short periods of boom conditions. If orthodoxy could be said to conceive capitalism as a machine for economic growth, then the underconsumptionists were suggesting that there was a defective part which only occasionally allowed the machine to work at full speed, and usually meant that it could grind along at only a snail's pace. This analogy brings out well the relationship between the theories.

Because the underconsumptionists stress one single defect to which they then attribute all the major fluctuations of the economy, they must raise the possibility that if this defect could be cured, then the world really would operate as the orthodox writers imply. Trade cycles would be abolished. This seems to be the view of Hobson, for instance. Revolutionary underconsumptionists would of course deny that any cure was possible; but by stressing the underconsumptionist tendency as the major factor in all of the great depressions which capitalism has hitherto experienced, they inevitably reduce the historical, and hence also the theoretical, significance of other factors. Baran and Sweezy, for instance, are well aware that macro-economic fluctuations are inherent in a capitalist economy, but since their discussions of economic history minimise the importance of this fact and emphasise instead the development of the tendency to underconsumption, the point that the general 'anarchy' of capitalist production is itself capable of producing a 1930's situation — a fact which really undermines the orthodox conception — is obscured. This is a difficulty which, in my opinion, is inherent in the structure of underconsumption theories.

So because of their emphasis on a single factor, underconsumption theories tend to bypass a more profound critique of orthodox conceptions. The most valuable contribution of Sismondi is not his new version of underconsumptionism, but the vision of the economy expressed in his later articles, particularly the discussion of the Leipzig book trade, and rather less clearly in the *Nouveaux Principes*; this vision is radically different from that of the rest of classical political economy. Instead of suggesting that readjustment to a changed situation is a simple process, Sismondi suggests that the change can set off reactions throughout the economy which can have profound effects on aggregate demand. A vision of movement from equilibrium to equilibrium is replaced by one of what Marx termed the anarchy of a capitalist economy, and the possibility of large fluctuations immediately suggests itself. The development of this new conception is a profoundly revolutionary change, beside which the fact that neither Sismondi nor Marx was able to produce a theoretical demonstration of the possibility of crises is relatively unimportant. Their vision recognises the inadequacy of the orthodox conception, and can therefore grasp the importance of phenomena which other writers treated as superficial. Marx and Engels state that Sismondi "dissected with great acuteness the contradictions of capitalist production"; the most significant point is that he identified as serious contradictions what the rest of classical political economy interpreted as the gradual working out of an adjustment process.

What I am suggesting, then, is that underconsumption theories do not directly challenge the predominant conception of the inner harmony of capitalist production. The emphasis on the single defect operates very much as an alternative to the fundamental critique of the harmonious conception, and in practice tends to divert attention from it. Because of this, this conception can be retained in the writings of underconsumptionists themselves, and tends to reveal itself in their vision of how the economy would behave if the problem of underconsumption could be cured (assuming that they imagine this to be possible).

It has already been pointed out — in discussing Hobson, for instance — that underconsumptionists tend to justify the primacy which they accord to consumption demand by the idea that human consumption is the aim of all production. Hobson makes this explicit, but even those who do not make it explicit give the impression of having this idea at the back of their minds. In one sense this idea is just a truism: for even if machines are used to produce more machines the process ultimately has no point unless it serves to increase consumption at some stage. It becomes more than a truism, however, at the moment when it is used as a support for theoretical statements about the functioning of an economy, for then it itself acquires some theoretical status; and this is what happens to it in the hands of the underconsumptionists. Logically, the idea that the aim of all production is consumption need not have any of the implications given to it by underconsumptionists, because investment can always be justified as provision for future consumption, so that the issue is reduced to one of present versus future consumption. It need not mean that present consumption demand is the basic long-term determinant of investment. But in practice it helps to justify the importance of present consumption demand and bolsters the underconsumptionist case.

It is important to recognise that the idea of the primacy of consumption demand in this sense is not an innovation by the underconsumptionists. It is in fact quite prevalent amongst orthodox writers, although it is perhaps not so obvious since they do not often make direct deductions about macro-economics from it. To give just one example: in 1938 Oskar Lange wrote that

> It is a commonplace which can be read in any textbook that the demand for investment goods is *derived* from the demand for consumption goods.[1]

Whether or not Lange himself agrees with this is unimportant, although the implication is that he does; what is significant is that he can say that it is a commonplace and that it can be read in any textbook.

The prevalence of this idea obviously encourages the development of underconsumption theories. But why should this idea be so prevalent? It seems to me that it is an idea which is liable to be induced by the whole orthodox conception of the economic process in human society, which interprets it as a conscious co-operative exercise deliberately embarked upon in order to satisfy felt needs. From the very first moments consumption is set up on a pedestal as the justification of productive activity.

This conception is first clearly apparent in Adam Smith, and is an important aspect of the appreciation of his work by orthodox economists. Smith sees production as a response to necessity: men produce in order to consume and to live. Even though the productive process may create class divisions and therefore the division of the product may become a source of conflict — and classical political economy always recognised the existence of class struggle in the distributive sphere — the productive process itself is seen as free of conflict, as a simple struggle of Man against Nature. Men co-operate in production because such co-operation is more efficient. So in spite of social conflicts, the desire to consume is portrayed as the driving force behind economic activity.

In this conception, the necessity of consumption plays a fundamental theoretical role. But if, instead, we start not from production in general but from the idea of different forms of production, each involving different technical relationships and different relationships amongst the human beings playing different 'roles' in the process, and assume each form to have its own rules of functioning, then we do not allocate any special theoretical function to the subjective desire to consume. Consumption occurs, but our theory of production is not based on it. This is the essential point.

The orthodox conception leads to a difficulty in understanding capitalist production. We have assumed that production exists in order to satisfy human needs, and yet capitalist production is ruled by a different principle — the principle of maximum profit — which is not necessarily reconcilable with the first. If human needs are to rule in capitalist production, then they must rule via the profit principle; now what does this imply? It seems to me to imply that in spite of the apparent dominance of the profit criterion in capitalist production, really it is the decisions of consumers that determine the flow of capital. Consumers are the living representatives of human needs. Although investment can be justified as provision for future consumption, at no time do the future consumers appear on the stage to make the decisions for themselves; instead capitalists estimate their wants in order to further their own interests. So if, as this conception requires, it is consumers who must ultimately determine what it is profitable to produce, then it can only be the *present* consumers who do so. So this conception tends to induce an exaltation of present consumption over investment as the basic factor determining the course of the economy, because consumers must appear as the real rulers.* An atmosphere is created in which the idea of an essentially subordinate role for the investment goods sector can thrive.

Thus the effect of the classical conception of economic activity is to emphasise investment as a response to consumer demand,

*A good illustration of this is provided by the analogy between the market-place and the ballot-box which is sometimes used by defenders of capitalism. Consumers are pictured as being in possession of 'dollar votes' which they then distribute amongst the various goods and services on sale, while producers, as obedient agents of the collective will, set to work to satisfy these demands. If we forget about investment, this is a very pretty conception. But as soon as investment is included, it becomes clear that the dollar votes allocated for additional future consumption have all been accumulated in the hands of the producers. The stress on *present* consumer demand is therefore necessary if the example is to have its desired ideological impact.

and hence to think of investment as basically entirely induced, discounting the possibility of autonomous investment. In Chapter Five I discussed the early debates on the general glut question, where on the one hand, no reproduction scheme could be constructed because the investment goods sector was not set in its rightful place beside the consumption goods sector, and on the other hand, consumption took all the blame amongst those who saw a lack of effective demand. In that Chaper I explained this by conceptual mistakes, but the question still remains as to why Adam Smith made these mistakes in the first place and why they were reproduced by Ricardo and his followers. In my opinion, the effect of the classical conception of economic activity in discounting the possibility of autonomous investment was a powerful influence in this.

In Chapter Six, I showed that Marx was the first person to overcome these mistakes, and that his reproduction schemes of a capitalist economy were the result. This represents important circumstantial evidence of the significance of a conception of economic activity in this regard, for Marx is also the first person to break with classical ideas in this area. His introduction of the concept of mode of production has fundamental implications, because it means that instead of asking why production exists in general, he looks at each mode of production with a view to understanding its own rules of functioning. Here there is no operative role for the idea of consumption as the aim of all economic activity, and Marx fully recognises that in the capitalist mode of production it is capitalists themselves who make the basic economic decisions (indeed nothing comes out more clearly from the reproduction schemes than this), in response to expectations of profit. Once this point has been reached, the obstacle of a special economic role for consumption has been overcome, and there is no reason why investment should any longer be regarded as in some way tied to consumer demand.*

---

*This line of thought was stimulated by reading the work of Louis Althusser, particularly by his development of the concept of problematic and his attempt to distinguish between "humanist" and "anti-humanist" problematics. My analysis of the reasons for the continual and apparently spontaneous reappearance of underconsumption theories is based on the fact that they remain within the dominant "humanist" conception (in Althusser's sense of the word): they interpret production as the purposeful activity of human subjects, and

It has already been pointed out that the reproduction schemes show up very clearly the errors of underconsumption theories, and there is no doubt that had these schemes been generally accepted into economic literature, underconsumption theories would have had a much worse time of it. The fact that this did not happen, and that the classical conception of economic activity continued to hold sway, with all the attendant consequences, can of course be attributed to the way in which Marx's work was regarded by the orthodox economists of the time.

What I am arguing here is that the appeal of underconsumptionism is in large measure due to the fact that it reproduces the already existing and dominant conception of the economy and of the significance of consumer demand within it. The frequency with which underconsumptionists justify their position by stating that consumption is the aim of all production is indicative of this.

This is highly relevant to an understanding of the history of underconsumption theories. The chief characteristic of their history is the frequency of their appearance and disappearance. Like a desert seed which a shower of rain brings suddenly to life after years of inactivity, underconsumption theories seem to be an almost spontaneous response to a period of prolonged depression. But it is inadequate to have a purely mechanical view of this, arguing that depressions of themselves give rise to underconsumption theories. Rather it is depressions which stimulate the search for new ideas that eventually results in a burst of underconsumptionism, but the appearance of underconsumption theories as opposed to others must be attributed to their close relationship to the dominant ideology. Because, as explained above, the idea of the special significance of consumer demand is already widespread, the suggestion that periods of

so they tend to overestimate the economic role of consumption because this is the only conceivable purpose behind this activity. Correspondingly, the ability of Marx to overcome the mistakes of his predecessors may be interpreted as a consequence of his escape from this "humanist" conception, and his vision of the history of society as a "process of natural history" (as he once expressed it), in which human beings function as the bearers of social relations but not as the purposeful engineers of historical development — making history according to their will. This enabled him to avoid the errors of his predecessors and to attribute to the investment goods sector its true economic importance.

deficient effective demand are due to a tendency for consumer demand to be insufficient is almost a 'natural' response. The basic ingredient of an underconsumption theory is already to hand. In a period of abnormal economic depression, the ideological atmosphere of which the orthodox conceptions are a reflection will tend to generate this kind of critique.

This explains the apparently sporadic nature of their appearance and reappearance, and also why they have something of the character of an 'underground' theory. For while their radicalism has ensured their banishment from orthodox seats of learning, their relationship with the dominant ideology has equally ensured their continued reproduction in radical intellectual circles.

NOTES

1 O.Lange, *The Rate of Interest and the Optimum Propensity to Consume,* in *Economica* Vol 5 No 17, p.23 (emphasis in original).

12

THE MODERN SCENE

The publication of Keynes's *General Theory* marks a watershed in the history of underconsumption theories, mainly because it transformed the way in which orthodox economists thought about macro-economic questions. Up until the 1930's orthodox teaching had presented a solid front in opposition to the notion that the concept of aggregate demand was useful to economic understanding — a fact of which Keynes himself, who had been brought up to think in the old ways, was only too well aware. It is not surprising then that looking back over history he should be appreciative of the efforts of Malthus, as someone who at a much earlier date had had to fight similar battles to his own. In a biographical essay on Malthus, first published in 1933, he writes that he has long claimed him as the first of the Cambridge economists[1] because he subscribed to the good common-sense notion that

> prices and profits are primarily determined by something which he described, though none too clearly, as 'effective demand'.[2]

Keynes's overall assessment of the correspondence between Ricardo and Malthus is that:

> One cannot arise from a perusal of this correspondence without a feeling that the almost total obliteration of Malthus's line of approach and the complete domination of Ricardo's for a period of a hundred years has been a disaster to the progress of economics.[3]

These lines were written in the shadow of Keynes's own struggles; the question of to what degree Malthus can really be seen as having prefigured Keynes has already been discussed in Chapter Two.

Without going into the matter in detail, it should be clear that Keynes himself cannot be described as an underconsumptionist according to the definition adopted here. His theory is based on effective demand in general — consumption, investment, government expenditure, exports etc. — and no privileged place is allocated to consumers' expenditure. The only point in his work which could serve as a hook on which to hang an underconsumption theory is in his development of the idea of the propensity to consume. Since Keynes assumes that the marginal propensity to consume out of any given income is lower than the average propensity to consume out of that income, it would seem reasonable to conclude that as the population got richer its average propensity to consume would fall. It could then be argued that as capitalism developed, a larger and larger gap would open up between the productive capacity of society and its consumption. In fact no underconsumption theory has been based on this idea of Keynes's, and this is probably because empirical studies quickly showed that although at any given point in time the richer strata of the population saved a larger proportion of their income than the poorer strata, the average propensity to consume seemed to have remained fairly constant over decades, and no falling tendency could be discerned.

So Keynes was not an underconsumptionist; and yet he was appreciative of their ideas and made an effort to rehabilitate them. For him, their merit was that they attempted to develop a concept of effective demand and to use it in order to explain the movement of the economy as a whole. He felt that they were "on his side". For underconsumptionists, the publication of the *General Theory* from the pen of a prominent figure of the economic establishment must have seemed a dramatic vindication of their struggles. After decades of scorn and vilification, they awoke to find that the idea of curing the depression by public works programmes and other measures designed to boost workers' consumption had suddenly become respectable. In the flush of the discovery and of Keynes's own favourable remarks, perhaps some of the theoretical differences were missed. But the differences were there, and their consequences were unavoidable.

Up until the 1930's, underconsumption theories had established a certain role for themselves as the theories which explained depressions as due to a deficiency of effective demand. People who instinctively felt that this was the right sort of approach were likely to consider an underconsumption theory as the possible explanation. Within this category, they had a choice between a theory which emphasised the inequality of the distribution of income *per se* as the cause (the Sismondian type), and one which emphasised the aggregate level of saving (the Malthusian type). Both of these theories could be criticised on theoretical grounds: the Sismondian type because it could be redefined as a minor problem of adjustment of production to the distribution of demand, and the Malthusian type because the assumption that savings were automatically invested implied that the demand must be there to match the supply, however much saving is going on. The effect of Keynes's ideas was to displace the Malthusian type of underconsumption theory, and to force later underconsumptionists, because of the new theoretical atmosphere which resulted, to present a more sophisticated analysis of the role of investment than their predecessors.

Keynes transferred the emphasis from the absolute level of saving and investment, which is where Malthus and his followers had always placed it, to their relative level. He simultaneously made the necessary distinction between intended and actual saving and investment. In this way he allowed for the necessary identity of actual saving and investment, and thereby implicitly recognised the formal correctness of Malthus's critics, but he also demonstrated the erroneousness of the simplistic idea that 'supply creates its own demand'. In his theory savings automatically adjust themselves to the level of investment via the level of income, but whether this represents an expansion or a contraction of the economy depends on the relation of *intended* saving to *intended* investment. Macro-economic fluctuations can thus be explained. Since this theory achieved the objective of the Malthusian type of underconsumptionism, while avoiding and indeed showing up its rather elementary mistakes and developing a much higher degree of sophistication, its acceptance was bound to sound the death-knell of this strand of underconsumptionism.

The effect of Keynes's ideas on the Sismondian type of under-consumption theory was rather more subtle. The kernel of this type of underconsumptionism was not so much its theoretical explanation of how slumps developed as its appreciation of a deep contradiction in capitalist society, whereby the capitalist class found great difficulty in providing the demand for the surplus product which the working class was producing. It was implicitly much more concerned with the long-term prospects of capitalism than its short-term fluctuations. For this reason, the immediate impact of Keynes's ideas on the Sismondian type of underconsumptionism was small as compared with their impact on the Malthusian type. But the indirect influence, caused by the change in the general theoretical atmosphere as Keynes's ideas became more widely accepted, was quite marked. One of the characteristics of the Sismondian type was that it had tended to ignore the behaviour of investment and to concentrate mainly on capitalist consumption, and this was a serious weakness in the argument, since if capitalists are in fact quite happy to invest what they do not consume, the theory does not stand up. After Keynes, the omission became so glaring that a theory of the determinants of investment became necessary.

The omission became glaring because investment plays a central role in Keynesian theory. Apart from making investment, consumption, government expenditure and exports equal components of aggregate demand, Keynes says that it is intended savings which adjust to intended investment, rather than vice versa, or a compromise solution which the theory of adjustment by the rate of interest implied. This means that if we assume a closed economy in which the government budget is balanced, and we also assume a definite response of consumption to changes in disposable income, it is the level of investment which appears as the determinant of the overall level of activity in the economy. And if we look beyond the 1930's depression to the longer-term development of the capitalist economies and try to give the model a dynamic element, it is the fluctuations in investment which once again appear as the crucial factor. So the greatly increased interest in and understanding of macroeconomic questions, which Keynes's ideas stimulated, brought with it a new appreciation of the significance of investment. This meant that any theory which wanted to argue that there was a difficulty in finding a demand for the surplus product had to be able to explain why investment could not fill the gap that was left by consumption.

A question which might arise at this point is: if

underconsumption theories nowadays have to include a thorough discussion of the role of investment, do they still qualify as under*consumption* theories? In my opinion they do, but I shall leave a detailed discussion of this issue until after the examination of the theories themselves.

In the post-Second World War world, there was not just a new theoretical atmosphere in the universities of the advanced capitalist countries, but also a radically changed political and economic situation. As time progressed, it became increasingly clear that the end of the war was not going to result in a return to a 1930's-type depression, and indeed the whole capitalist world experienced a sustained boom with unprecedentedly high employment levels and growth rates, and with recessions which were only minor compared with those of earlier periods. For those who had argued that stagnation was the long-term tendency of capitalism and that the 1930's experience was prime evidence of it, this obviously represented a serious challenge. Had capitalism succeeded in rescuing itself? Either it had, and the argument had to be abandoned, or an explanation had to be found.

The most common theory, and one which has been influential in left-wing circles throughout the post-war period, is that colossal military expenditure has sustained aggregate demand which would otherwise have been deficient. Modern underconsumption theorists have tended to suggest that, although there may well be political motives behind this expenditure associated with the Cold War, the arms race has had more than just a political dimension for the capitalist countries; it has been an economic necessity without which the recent economic performance of these countries would have been very much poorer. Military expenditure has in fact been the major explanation of the difference between the 1930's and the 1950's. In an essay which first appeared in *Monthly Review* in 1959, Paul Sweezy, one of the most prominent of modern underconsumptionists, wrote that the vastly increased size of the arms budget is the only really new feature of post-Second World War capitalism — all other government spending has remained at about the same percentage of the Gross National Product as in 1929. He concludes that it is mere wishful thinking to believe that if the arms budget were to be reduced to 1930's proportions the economy would not return to the conditions of that time.[4]

Whether this type of theory is acceptable as an explanation of the last thirty years of history can only be decided after a detailed examination of post-war underconsumption theories.

Probably the earliest post-war example of an underconsumptionist type of analysis of military expenditure is to be found in Joan Robinson's 1951 introduction to the English translation of Rosa Luxemburg's *Accumulation of Capital.* In discussing Luxemburg's treatment of militarism, Robinson disagrees with her emphasis on taxation of workers as the main source of finance for militarism and argues that its economic significance lies in the degree to which it provides an outlet for the investment "which, unlike other kinds of investment, creates no further problem by increasing productive capacity".[5] She also hints that she would regard this as a correct diagnosis of the problems of a modern capitalist economy. The idea that there is a problem of absorption of the surplus which is produced over and above what is consumed by workers is a familiar characteristic of a Sismondian type of underconsumption theory, and this type of underconsumption theory would agree with Joan Robinson in thinking that military expenditure could not help to solve the problem if workers were forced to finance it. But Robinson does not discuss the question any further on this occasion.

Joan Robinson's own study of growth in a capitalist economy, also called *The Accumulation of Capital,* appeared in 1956. The book is written on a high level of theoretical abstraction, and does not directly discuss any aspect of economic history; but the impression given by the many references to the possibility of stagnation in a capitalist economy and the severe conditions necessary for sustaining a "Golden Age" suggest that the author regards the threat of collapse into stagnation as a serious one. The short note at the end of the book on the impact of the concentration of capital on the rate of innovation reinforces this impression, and her argument on this point is quoted with approval by Baran and Sweezy. But one cannot find here an explicit statement of underconsumption theory; there is only general support for a stagnationist view of twentieth-century capitalism.

BARAN AND SWEEZY

It is indeed a severe problem, in writing about modern

underconsumption theories, that their influence seems to have far exceeded the extent of their theoretical exposition. In part this must be a tribute to the one book which stands out on its own in this category: Baran and Sweezy's *Monopoly Capital* (1966). But it is striking that Baran and Sweezy, who are well acquainted with the literature, can find only two modern writers whom they feel to have made a real contribution to their line of argument — Joseph Steindl and Michal Kalecki — and both of these are significant for questioning the inherently dynamic nature of capitalism rather than for specifically underconsumptionist qualities.* So if this chapter appears to be focussed very much on Baran and Sweezy, this is just a reflection of the uniqueness of their book as a modern statement of underconsumptionism.

Baran and Sweezy identify themselves with the Marxist tradition, and they see their work as an attempt to provide the theory — up to now absent — of the monopoly stage of capitalism. Marx's work, and most subsequent Marxist analysis, they say, has been based on the assumptions of competitive capitalism, and although Lenin had some powerful insights into the characteristics of the new monopoly stage, he did not go back and thoroughly re-examine the fundamentals of theory in the light of the latest developments. This work, therefore, remains to be done.[6]

In order to accomplish this task, the authors make use of a new concept: the economic surplus.

> The economic surplus, in the briefest possible definition, is the difference between what a society produces and the costs of producing it.[7]

The meaning of this depends entirely upon the interpretation given to the term 'costs of production'. For Baran and Sweezy costs of production comprise only the absolutely necessary costs involved in the production of a good of a type which properly corresponds to human needs. The surplus, therefore, includes all the elements of the Marxist concept of surplus value, but it also includes all costs which can be attributed to the wasteful and irrational nature of monopoly capitalist society: armaments expenditure, advertising, research that is related to selling

*For a further discussion of these writers see below.

rather than to production, etc. All these costs would be unnecessary in a rationally organised society and so should be counted as part of the surplus, according to Baran and Sweezy. This concept is in fact closely related to a similar one of the same name used by Baran in his earlier work *The Political Economy of Growth*, discussed in Chapter Seven. In both cases the standard of measurement is a hypothetical rationally organised society, and the concept is one which is not restricted to monopoly capitalism or to capitalism in general but can be applied to any economy. Baran and Sweezy refine the concept further by making a distinction between the actual surplus — that which is actually produced — and the potential surplus — that which is produced plus what could be produced with the resources which are always lying dormant in a capitalist society: unused capacity and unemployed labour. Naturally the authors are most interested in the potential surplus as the true measure of the extent of the waste in monopoly capitalist society, but the degree to which the actual surplus falls short of the potential they would regard as partly a reflection of the absorption problem which they analyse.

This concept of surplus is the kernel of Baran and Sweezy's argument. It is a characteristic of monopoly capitalism, they say, that there is a persistent tendency for the surplus to rise as a proportion of total output, and this creates more and more acute problems of absorbing it.[8] They base this tendency on an analysis of the market situation of the modern firm and its implications for pricing behaviour. The appropriate price theory for modern capitalism, they argue, is traditional monopoly theory, in which one seller dominates the market. The typical situation is that an industry is dominated by three or four sellers, but in this case the price will tend towards that which would be most profitable for a monopolist. The prices set by each oligopolist will stand in close relation to one another, for each of them will be afraid to cut prices for fear of precipitating a price war, and none can have a significantly higher price than the rest without losing customers. The firms will therefore gradually feel their way towards the price which is most profitable for themselves collectively, which is the monopoly price. The one difference from a monopoly situation, however, the authors argue, is that downwards price movements are extremely difficult to accomplish, because a price reduction is liable to be interpreted as an aggressive move by competitors, and therefore any reduction in costs will tend to appear as extra profits (or at least extra surplus) rather than as lower prices.[9] At the same time, any increase in money wages gained by workers will, the authors say, be passed on as price rises, so unions are not really able to eat into the surplus to any significant extent. The crux of the tendency of the surplus to rise, then, lies in oligopolistic price theory.

Surplus can be consumed, invested or wasted. Baran and Sweezy argue that both consumption and investment are likely to account for a smaller proportion of the surplus as capitalism develops. The argument on consumption is based on empirical studies of how dividend pay-outs respond to changes in profits. In the long run, the evidence shows that approximately half of profits are distributed to shareholders; but there are considerable lags in the adjustment process, so that if, as Baran and Sweezy argue, the surplus is tending to rise, these lags will result in a lower proportion of profits being distributed. So, the authors say,

> A continuous rise in earnings would be accompanied by an equally continuous decline in the pay-out rate.[10]

The argument on investment is based on the relationship of oligopolistic competition to technical innovation. The concentration of industry has led to an emphasis on non-price competition and therefore has tended to stimulate research into technical progress and has probably increased its rate of development; but, argue Baran and Sweezy, it restricts the volume of investment outlets in which these innovations would be embodied. In a fully competitive situation a new technique must be immediately employed in the production process because if it is not the firm will quickly be undercut by competitors. But in an oligopolistic situation old plant is still profitable, and so investment in new techniques is only worthwhile if the extra profit is greater than what can be got by some alternative investment.

> We conclude that from the monopolist's point of view, the introduction of new techniques in a manner which involves addition to productive capacity (demand being assumed unchanged) will normally be avoided.[11]

The authors' general conclusion is that technical progress determines the form which investment takes at any given time rather than its amount.[12]

Baran and Sweezy have argued that the surplus has a tendency to rise as a proportion of national income, while consumption accounts for a smaller and smaller proportion of that surplus. So if the gap is going to be filled by investment, then investment must account for a steadily increasing proportion of national income, which would imply a faster and faster rate of growth. Either that, or investment is not sufficient to achieve this and industry runs at a lower level of capacity, at which profits represent a lower proportion of output, and the surplus is kept down to a manageable level at which a kind of 'equilibrium' is established.[13] The latter solution is identified by the authors as the normal situation, and they give figures of capacity utilisation in the U.S. economy in the 1920's and 1930's as an illustration of their argument.[14]

They also allow for the possibility of what they call epoch-making innovations. By epoch-making innovations they mean innovations which lead to the creation of a vast new field of investment outlets, and they suggest that there have so far been only three such innovations in the history of capitalism: the steam engine, the railway and the automobile. Baran and Sweezy argue that but for the stimulating effect of these innovations and of wars, which have been particularly important in the twentieth century,

> The United States economy would have entered a period of stagnation long before the end of the nineteenth century, and it is unlikely that capitalism could have survived into the second half of the twentieth century.[15]

The authors identify three major means of absorbing the surplus in the form of waste: the sales effort (advertising, product differentiation, etc.), militarism and civilian government spending. The arguments on the first two are straightforward and need no elaboration. One aspect of their treatment of civilian government spending is important, however. They recognise that by and large government spending has not been deficit spending but has been financed by taxation, but they point out that even in this case there is a net addition of demand to the economy: in Keynesian terms there is a multiplier of one.

They therefore argue that government spending, however financed, helps to absorb the surplus; and their collaborator J.D.Phillips in a Statistical Appendix treats the whole of government expenditure as part of the surplus. This is significant because although Phillips's figures show the total surplus to have risen from 46.9 per cent of GNP in 1929 to 56.1 per cent in 1963, the government component of surplus — Phillips estimates the surplus via its means of absorption — has risen from slightly over 20 per cent to slightly over 50 per cent of the total in the same time. This means that non-government surplus absorption has fallen as a percentage of GNP from 37 per cent in 1929 to 27 per cent in 1963.[16] The argument about government expenditure is therefore crucial to the statistical demonstration of the tendency of the surplus to rise. If it were not total government expenditure but only some fraction of it that could be treated as part of the surplus, then the surplus could actually have fallen as a percentage of GNP, following Phillips's estimates.

The first question to discuss is the one which was raised briefly earlier, namely: is Baran and Sweezy's theory an underconsumption theory? In my view it is, according to the definition adopted at the beginning of this book. Although a considerable amount of space is devoted to a discussion of investment and government expenditure, the central argument is that the consuming power of the population, primarily of the working class but also of the rentiers who receive only a certain share of the profits, is limited, and therefore these other forms of expenditure have to be brought in to fill the gap. Baran and Sweezy make an advance over many of their predecessors in recognising that a government pound note, or an investor's pound note, is just as good as a consumer's, but their analysis is based around a perceived tendency for consumption to re-present a constantly decreasing proportion of output, and it is only after this has been demonstrated that the role of other forms of expenditure is examined. Therefore, because primacy still rests with the behaviour of consumption demand, the term 'underconsumption theory' remains appropriate.

Baran and Sweezy's work is in many ways extremely impressive. Every step in the argument is carefully thought out and presented, the writing is lucid and simple, and some sections, especially the chapter which discusses the theory of the firm and profit maximisation, are brilliant. But there are one or two weaknesses which, if the criticisms presented here are correct, would tend to undermine the empirical contentions upon which their theory is based. If, in fact, it is not so certain as it appears from their exposition that the surplus has risen as a proportion of GNP over the past half-century, then their thesis becomes somewhat dubious.

The first criticism relates to their discussion of government expenditure. Following a Keynesian type of analysis, they argue that since government expenditure financed by taxation yields a multiplier of one, it absorbs a portion of the surplus, whether the taxes are paid by workers or by big corporations. However this argument seems to be definitely based on a mistake. It is true that if we accept all the usual conditions about the stability and equality of the marginal propensity to consume, one could expect an increase in the government budget financed by taxation to translate itself into a similar increase in GNP, and some extra employment will be generated. But what does this increase consist of? It consists of the additional output of goods and services directly created by the extra government spending. Suppose this is financed by taxation on workers. If the extra money has been spent on employing more administrators and research workers, i.e. if it has gone mainly on labour costs, this should have no discernible effect on demand or on capacity utilisation in manufacturing industry, and effectively this represents a simple transfer of income within the working class. The only surplus which is being absorbed here is the reserve army of unemployed. The question is more complicated if the money is spent on armaments produced by capitalists, since in this case the sectors involved in the supply of military equipment will receive a boost; but this proviso is not made by Baran and Sweezy.*

Let us look a bit more closely at military expenditure, since this is what Baran and Sweezy tend to emphasise. Suppose that it is effectively financed by taxation on workers. We can divide this expenditure into payment of wages and salaries of military personnel, plus purchasing of equipment and supplies from

---

*Kalecki argues that the question of how government expenditure is financed is crucial even if the government buys armaments from capitalists (1971, pp.153–4).

capitalist industry. That part which is devoted to wages and salaries plays the same role as any other such expenditure, namely, it simply represents a transfer of income from formerly employed to formerly unemployed workers. Purchase of equipment and supplies creates demand in the capitalist sector. It will therefore absorb some of the excess capacity utilisation as well as some of the reserve army of unemployed. But note: only a part of military expenditure achieves this. That part — probably a significant slice — which goes on wages and salaries does not increase capacity utilisation in the capitalist sector. Furthermore, none of this expenditure has a direct impact on profits. Profits are determined by capitalists' consumption and investment, and since it is the workers rather than the capitalists who are being forced to maintain the army, these remain unchanged. Capitalists in the consumption goods sector experience no increase in demand, while those involved in arms supply experience an increase only as a direct result of government orders. If, therefore, there exists a tendency for capitalists' consumption and investment to fall short of the profits which would be obtained at high levels of capacity utilisation, then there is no reason for either consumption or investment to be stimulated so as to resolve this problem. This is why Kalecki and Joan Robinson (in her introduction to Rosa Luxemburg) stress the importance of the source of finance of such government expenditure: it is only if the money is being stolen (or borrowed) out of the capitalists' pockets that it can help to absorb the surplus.

Baran and Sweezy, on the other hand, identify the creation of effective demand with surplus absorption. They write:

> It has been through changes in the overall total of spending that government has exercised its greatest influence on the magnitude of effective demand and hence on the process of surplus absorption.[17]

and

> The massive absorption of surplus in military preparations has been the key fact of post-war American economic history.[18]

Baran and Sweezy do not believe that deficit financing has been of great significance in the post-war world, and since the bulk of taxes are paid by workers, they are effectively arguing that this can help to absorb the surplus. It may be that it can, if the increase in capacity utilisation in the arms supply industry could be shown to stimulate investment above and beyond immediate government requirements. This might occur either because increased government orders stimulate expectations of future requirements, and therefore lead to new capacity being installed in anticipation, or because firms do not distinguish between government and other orders, and so expect demand to continue to rise as if there was a general upturn in the economy. The second of these hypotheses, at least, seems rather implausible, while the significance of the first is difficult to judge. But whatever the truth, in view of the fact that these are only indirect effects of government expenditure, and further-more only of that part of it which does not go on wages and salaries, Baran and Sweezy's easy addition of the whole of the state budget into the process of surplus absorption seems unjustified. And without it, their attempt to demonstrate with statistics the rise of the surplus as a proportion of GNP from 1929 to 1963 is jeopardised.

The second point of weakness of Baran and Sweezy's theory is at the point of generation of the surplus. As we have seen, they base the tendency of the surplus to rise on oligopolistic price theory, which can be summed up, following their analysis, as monopoly pricing with stickiness in a downward direction. In the typical modern industry a few sellers dominate the market, and Baran and Sweezy argue that prices will approximate to what a monopolist would have charged, which is the level which maximises the collective profits of the oligopolists. The tendency for the surplus to rise arises out of a differential response to cost reductions as compared with cost increases. Since major cost movements tend to be common to the whole industry, the forces of competition do not produce the same kind of downward pressure on prices that they would in a less restricted situation. Therefore, Baran and Sweezy argue, cost increases will tend to be passed on to the consumer, and this will be particularly true of wage increases, which, if they are similar to those occurring in the rest of the economy, will allow the level of consumer demand to be maintained even if prices are raised. The authors reject the notion that trade unions are strong enough to prevent this, saying:

The workers in more strongly organised industries generally do better for themselves than workers in less strongly organised branches of the economy. This does not mean, however, that the working class as a whole is in a position to encroach on surplus or even to capture increments of surplus, which, if realised, would benefit the capitalist class relative to the working class. The reason is that under monopoly capitalism employers can and do pass on higher labour costs in the form of higher prices. They are, in other words, able to protect their profit margins in the face of higher wages.[19]

Cost reductions, however, do not lead to price reductions because of the fear of triggering off a debilitating price war, so that the corporations appropriate the lion's share of the fruits of increasing productivity directly in the form of higher profits.[20]

It is striking that this analysis of response to cost changes, which is crucial to the argument, is not backed up by the same array of factual material as most of the other chapters of the book. In fact, it remains as little more than a plausible assertion. But one could set up an equally plausible counter-argument along the following lines: wage increases and cost reductions due to investment in technical innovations are occurring simultaneously. The overall movement of prime costs is therefore a combination of the effects of these two forces. There are definite costs associated with a price change and firms cannot be absolutely certain that competitors will introduce similar changes. Prices will therefore not be increased lightly, and in general only when increases in prime costs make a change necessary to maintain profit margins. So, on the whole, workers get their share of the gains from increasing productivity since wages increase faster than prices in proportion to the rate of increase of productivity.

If this counter-argument were true, there would be no tendency for the surplus to rise. Suppose that a company habitually raises its prices in the wake of the annual round of wage negotiations. Suppose further that it is agreed to raise wages by 5 per cent, while output per worker is expected to increase by 3 per cent. The crucial question, which Baran and Sweezy do not discuss at all, is: *by how much* does the company raise its prices in this situation? If it raises them by 5 per cent, then Baran and Sweezy's argument is correct; but if it only raises them by 2 per cent, as the counter-argument would suggest, then it is utterly incorrect. So in fact a detailed analysis of the process of inflation is necessary before Baran and Sweezy could say that the existence of the tendency of surplus to rise had been in any sense proved, and it is a grave weakness of the book that it avoids this problem altogether. My own inclination is to believe that the counter-argument is much closer to the truth on this question.

So a probing of the weaker points of Baran and Sweezy's analysis casts grave doubts on it, and not least on the question of whether there is a tendency for the surplus to rise at all. To a definite degree, it evinces a strong belief in the ultimate weakness of the working class in the economic struggle. The surplus rises, as much as anything, because workers are unable to prevent it from doing so. This pessimism has its political counterpart. The authors argue that the organised core of North American workers has been so integrated into capitalist culture as "consumers and ideologically conditioned members of society" that it is no longer in a position to take its place at the head of the revolutionary movement. The workers are no longer the system's "special victims"[21], and the new "special victims" — the unemployed, the aged, the drop-outs — are too heterogeneous and disorganised to be a revolutionary force. The prospects for monopoly capitalism would therefore be simply a progressive degeneration into social and moral decay, were it not for the decisive impact of the national liberation movements of the underdeveloped world.

> If we confine our attention to the inner dynamics of advanced monopoly capitalism, it is hard to avoid the conclusion that the prospect of effective revolutionary action to overthrow the system is slim.[22]

This Third-Worldism has a strong tinge of Marcuse about it, and now that another decade of history has passed, Sweezy would no doubt feel somewhat differently. In fact he has already said as much.[23]

It would be grossly unfair to judge anyone's economic ideas by their political views, and that is not the intention here. I mention Baran and Sweezy's political comments simply to point out that there is probably a connection between their pessimism about the potentially revolutionary role of the working class and the pessimism about their capabilities in the economic struggle which is implicit in any Sismondian type of underconsumption theory.

Other modern underconsumptionists do not match up to Baran and Sweezy in either sophistication or depth of argument. In Britain the one left-wing political organisation which has consistently maintained that a high level of arms expenditure is a necessity for modern capitalism is the 'International Socialists' (I.S.) group, but when expressed in theoretical terms this has not always been argued in an underconsumptionist fashion. Michael Kidron, for instance, in his book *Western Capitalism Since The War*, presents quite a different theory. Tony Cliff, a leading I.S. ideologue, sets "the poverty and restricted consumption of the masses" alongside the tendency of the rate of profit to fall as one of the two main causes of capitalist crises.[24] He quotes the underconsumptionist passages in Marx, and says that in the final analysis the cause of crises is the appropriation by capitalists of a greater and greater part of the income of society, and the direction of more and more of it to buying means of production rather than means of consumption, which, in time, must lead to overproduction. This is not an elaboration but just a restatement of the central idea of underconsumptionism. Other left-wing economists, of other political tendencies, have from time to time stated their belief in the necessity of arms expenditure to the maintenance of effective demand, but the theory is left implicit, and is to be found explicitly stated, really, only in *Monopoly Capital*.

A GENERAL ASSESSMENT OF UNDERCONSUMPTION THEORIES

The criticisms made here of Baran and Sweezy are not the same as those made of earlier underconsumptionist writings. The objections are, as much as anything, practical: that their argument for the existence of a long-term underconsumptionist tendency is not convincing. In pre-Keynesian underconsumption theories, there was always found to be a fundamental theoretical error which undermined the attempt to demonstrate the existence of overproduction. If such an error is to be found in *Monopoly Capital*, it is in the relationship of government expenditure to surplus absorption, but the implications are not so serious. They impinge only on the statistical demonstration of the tendency of surplus to rise and the degree to which the existence of such a tendency seems likely. Baran and Sweezy could accept these criticisms, and modify their argument accordingly, and still maintain the central themes of their book. What would be lost would be some of the elementary attractiveness of their theory, since only part of government expenditure could now be claimed to be surplus-absorbing.

This implies that underconsumption theories can be constructed free of elementary mistakes, and therefore the whole tradition of thought cannot be rejected on these grounds alone. In skeletal form they can be presented as follows: the consumption of the working class always falls substantially short of the total productive capacity of the community, while capitalists will always only absorb a limited portion of the surplus value in personal consumption. On average, there is a tendency for capitalists not to plan to invest sufficiently to fill this gap between production and consumption, so that the economy is constantly being pressed down towards stagnation because of inadequate effective demand. This is identified as the dominating fact of capitalist economic life. Counteracting tendencies may come into play for significant periods of time and mask the effects of the underconsumptionist tendency, but they cannot liquidate it, and ultimately there must come a moment when they are no longer strong enough to prevent a major, and possibly permanent, economic crisis. It is in the nature of the analysis of the underconsumption tendency as the dominating force in the economy that there is no guarantee of eventual escape from a severe depression.

This theory can acquire either revolutionary or reformist political overtones, according to the inclinations of the theorist. It can either be argued that this is a necessary and inevitable result of the class antagonisms inherent in capitalist society, or that it only occurs because of the existence of a particular institutional structure which could be modified. Many socialists have suggested that the problem is likely to become increasingly severe as capitalism develops. This is natural enough for those who believe in the ultimate apocalyptic economic collapse of capitalism. For if it has not yet occurred, this can only be explained by postulating the existence of accomodating factors whose influence must wane in the future.

This theory cannot be refuted simply on the basis of internal logical mistakes, as could all pre-Keynesian underconsumption theories. One cannot point, for instance, as one can in Malthus, to an assumption that all desired savings are automatically invested, which then removes the possibility of the very overproduction whose existence the theory is trying to prove. What the theory is saying is that, as a matter of observation, workers only receive a certain share of the total product in capitalist society, and capitalists tend to consume only a certain proportion of their share, while the incentive to invest tends not to be strong enough to fill the gap which is left. Given the complexity of the factors which must enter into any investment decision and the still inadequate understanding of their operation, it would be rash indeed to dismiss this idea out of hand. The important point is that one cannot say *a priori* that the theory is wrong; one can only argue that in fact the world works differently. Therefore, only a study of the major characteristics of modern capitalism can now decide whether it is in fact dominated by an underconsumptionist tendency or not.

In a historical study of economic thought it is not possible to launch into an independent investigation of the adequacy of underconsumption theories; one can only summarise the results of the researches of others. It is probably fair to say that in fact left-wing theoreticians are by no means agreed on the issue. If we take as an index of opinions the problem of the economic significance of military expenditure, then we find disagreement across the whole political spectrum of the left. Only the I.S. group has officially adopted the 'permanent arms economy' thesis, but there are many other economists, including such prominent individuals as Joan Robinson, Sweezy and Kalecki, who have intimated their belief that military expenditure has been important to the maintenance of effective demand. Similarly, there is a large body of people (including myself) who would challenge this, and there have been dissenting opinions even within the I.S. group at various times. It is true that there is not an exact coincidence between positions on the question of military expenditure and attitudes to underconsumptionism, but the association is generally acknowledged, and it is a convenient index to take. Attitudes to underconsumptionism may be quite complex and difficult to discern, but beliefs about military expenditure have often been stated (but not, of course, theoretically justified) in a couple of sentences in a variety of contexts.

The lack of significant political differentiation between the two sides of the debate is a symptom of its underdevelopment. Because the issues have not been probed sufficiently to bring out the theoretical implications for politics, the debate has not yet taken on political overtones. As it develops, the correlation between theoretical and political positions will probably increase.

At the moment the debate is still at a relatively low level. Since it concerns issues of such fundamental importance to an understanding of the economic functioning of capitalism, this is perhaps surprising, and is probably a result of the dominance of mechanistic interpretations of Marxism over a long period, inhibiting fruitful discussion. *Monopoly Capital* is undoubtedly the major work in the debate, on either side. Its lucidity and the consistency and neatness of its reinterpretation of capitalist economic history in the light of its theory have justly given it a wide readership. But as we have seen, it has weaknesses, which have hardly been probed by the opposition. There is no published work which springs to mind as an answer to *Monopoly Capital.* There is a lot of opposition to it and disquiet about it which has remained without proper theoretical expression.

In debate the factual evidence marshalled in support of theoretical argument too often does not get beyond figures of military expenditure as a proportion of GNP. On the one hand, it is said that this proportion is far higher than at any earlier time in history, while on the other it is stated that it has in fact been falling ever since the early 1950's. These statistics obviously have some significance: at the very least they require an explanation, be it political or economic. But it is possible to delve far more deeply. Baran and Sweezy's theory is such that all government expenditure is counted as surplus-absorbing, but others, such as Joan Robinson and Kalecki, who regard military expenditure as a necessary stimulant to aggregate demand, are aware that this is a mistake. So one obvious line of investigation is to examine the sources of government finance in the major capitalist countries in the post-war period. Has it been financed by borrowing, by taxation on capitalists or by taxation on workers? Of course it will never be possible to know how military expenditure in particular has been financed, since budget decisions are not taken on that basis; nor is it possible to know what source of finance would have been cut back had military expenditure been substantially less than it is. But at least such an investigation would give us more information which might yield some useful pointers.

Another possible area of research is the discussions which have taken place amongst the ruling class about military expenditure decisions, particularly at the beginning of the Cold War, which was, after all, instigated by the capitalist countries. Of course such research would be severely restricted by the secrecy surrounding official documents, but something could be gleaned from newspaper articles and other published writings of the time, although interpretation of these items is inevitably complicated by the intrusion of the additional factor of the need to secure popular acceptance of ruling-class policies. But research of this kind is entirely absent.

Since the issue of military expenditure plays such a significant role in the debate nowadays, it seems worthwhile to outline the various possible positions on it. Firstly, it can be argued that it is necessary for the maintenance of full employment and economic growth, since otherwise the surplus could not be absorbed, and that the State has consciously embarked on a programme of armaments build-up in order to sustain the economy. This position is the most satisfactory underconsumptionist one. It implies that the State, as the executive committee of the bourgeoisie, has recognised the existence of an underconsumptionist tendency and has taken the measures necessary to counteract it. Secondly, it can be argued that military expenditure is necessary to sustain the economy, but has in fact come about for some entirely different reason, a political one for instance. This position is a sort of second line of defence for the underconsumptionists. It entails an acceptance of the reasons for the growth of military expenditure put forward by their opponents, and implies that high State officials do not in fact understand the workings of their own economy, and have hit upon the right policy for some completely extraneous reason. In fact writers such as Sweezy do not usually specify whether in their opinion the ruling class grasps the existence of an underconsumptionist tendency or not, although they tend to imply that they do. The third possible position is that similar rates of growth and employment levels could have been attained in the advanced capitalist countries in the 1950's and 1960's without the vast growth in military expenditure. The explanation most commonly put forward for the armaments boom by supporters of this position is a political one: that it was part of a campaign of sabre-rattling or, if political conditions permitted it, direct military intervention to roll back socialism in Eastern Europe and Asia. This explanation implies that military expansion had definite economic drawbacks, through absorbing funds which could otherwise have been used either for investment or for increasing working-class conusmption, with the consequent political dividends for the ruling class.

These opposed positions reflect theoretical conceptions which imply very divergent interpretations of capitalist economic history. Underconsumptionists see the economy as dominated by a tendency which is always dragging it down into stagnation, and the 'cycle' of alternating boom and slump represents the alternation of periods in which this tendency is masked by the action of some countervailing force with periods in which it operates unrestricted. This is not a genuine business cycle but a struggle of opposing tendencies, in which sometimes one gains the upper hand, sometimes the other. But underconsumptionists clearly see the countervailing tendencies as *ad hoc* responses to a continuous and ever more threatening problem: Baran and Sweezy's invocation of a number of unconnected 'epoch-making innovations' and subsequently military expenditure to explain the maintenance of effective demand is a case in point. In this conception it is natural, when examining the growth of state intervention in the economy, to consider first the hypothesis that it is a response to the action of the underconsumptionist tendency and an attempt to stave it off.

The opposing conception sees a capitalist economy as relatively dynamic but unstable. A prolonged depression is obviously possible — the 1930's are evidence of this — but it does not represent the action of some long-term tendency to stagnation but a specific conjunction of circumstances combining to keep effective demand low. In any depression the appearance of some new factor is always conceivable which would suffice to stimulate a new boom. Therefore, one cannot look forward to some ultimate apocalyptic economic crisis of capitalism. Indeed the post-Second World War period has been characterised by unprecedentedly high growth rates and employment levels and economic fluctuations of a relatively small amplitude. One possibly important factor in this has been the discovery of how to use the State apparatus to influence the level of aggregate demand, and to boost it if necessary. The knowledge that the State would intervene to stimulate demand should the growthrate flag has encouraged capitalists to invest on the assumption of a maintenance of that growthrate, and their confidence has in fact rendered massive State budget deficits unnecessary. This is a plausible explanation of the recent period which makes no reference to military expenditure.* The implication of this conception is that, while the tendency to fluctuation is an important feature of a capitalist economy, this economy continues to be a fundamentally dynamic one in spite of its instability.

The question of the correctness or otherwise of underconsumption theories is therefore a crucial one for a scientific analysis of capitalist economies. My own inclination is definitely to believe that underconsumption theories are wrong. So much of the support for them, historically, seems to have been based either on ideological conceptions of the economic role of consumer demand, or on a rather mechanistic interpretation of the transition from capitalism to socialism which feels a necessity to prove that capitalism must break down due to its own economic contradictions. Baran and Sweezy's stated belief that but for the impact of certain epoch-making innovations the stagnation of the economy would have stimulated socialist revolutions in the advanced capitalist countries before the middle of the twentieth century is an example of this. The association of underconsumptionism with these types of ideas should itself generate suspicions. Up till now, no underconsumption theory has appeared which is really convincing. *Monopoly Capital* is the best attempt, and does present some statistics to back up the argument, but the criticisms of it which have been set out above undermine the statistical demonstration of the existence of the tendency, and this demonstration is crucial to the plausibility of the whole thesis.

Furthermore, underconsumption theories necessarily bear an

*Obviously this is by no means a complete explanation, however.

air of pessimism about the potential achievements of working-class organisation. The rate of surplus value rises because workers are not strong enough to make sure that they get their share of the proceeds of increased productivity. This entails a number of possible consequences none of which is entirely satisfactory. One must believe either (a) that increased political consciousness and militancy on the part of the working class, by forcing capitalists to make concessions on the wages front to defuse the movement, in fact help to overcome the main economic contradiction of capitalism; or (b) that capitalists cannot be forced to make economic concessions in this way, and that there is no connection at all between political and economic militancy; or (c) that an effective revolutionary movement will only come about as a result of the stagnation produced by the underconsumptionist tendency, as the crisis makes workers aware of the inevitable consequences of capitalism. The first of these positions is obviously theoretically somewhat paradoxical, while the last two do not correspond with historically observed facts.

But, as emphasised above, the debate is far from closed. Far too little serious practical research has been carried out, and until now, the necessary theoretical preparations in establishing a concept of underconsumptionism and studying its various implications have not been carried out either. Hopefully this book will have made a contribution in the latter regard at least.

OTHER MODERN STAGNATION THEORIES

Two points remain to be made. Both of them are a tribute to the influence of underconsumptionism generally.

The first is that underconsumptionism is probably the most significant theory used to justify the thesis that modern capitalism is dominated by a tendency towards stagnation. Apart from Baran and Sweezy, Steindl and Kalecki are the two most prominent modern writers who have attempted to justify this thesis theoretically, and although it would be wrong to classify either of them as underconsumptionist, both have obviously been influenced by underconsumptionist ideas.

The main idea of Steindl's book, *Maturity and Stagnation in American Capitalism* (1952), is that the concentration of capital has weakened the incentive to invest, and so mature capitalism

must therefore also be stagnant capitalism. A crucial assumption
is that technical innovations do not affect the level but only the
form which investment takes, and that the level of investment is
determined by what Steindl calls "endogenous" (i.e. strictly
economic) factors.[25] He picks out the rate of "internal accumulation" of businesses (retention of profits as savings), the degree of
capacity utilisation, the gearing ratio and the rate of profit as the
main factors; and all of these are themselves influenced by the
rate of investment which is going on.[26] Suppose there is a
primary decline in investment, so that demand is reduced.
Steindl says that in a competitive industry, the brunt of the
impact will be on profit margins: prices will fall relative to wages
and real output will be substantially maintained. In an oligopolistic industry, however, profit margins are unlikely to fall and
instead capacity utilisation will decrease, with unfavourable
effects on investment plans.

> The changes introduced into the economic system by the
> spread of oligopoly thus make it liable to react (in the absence
> of counteracting forces) to a *primary* decline of capital
> accumulation by a further retardation of growth.[27]

The implicit assumption here is that the effect on investment of
a fall in capacity utilisation in an oligopolistic situation is more
catastrophic than the effect of a fall in profits in a competitive
one.

More important, however, is his long-run argument, which is
based on the effect of an *increase* in the concentration of capital.
The growth of monopoly, he writes, should lead to an increase
in profit margins, and hence a fall in capacity utilisation as the
same volume of expenditure is spread over fewer units of
output. This will have an adverse effect on investment and the
rate of growth will decline. A second possibility is that since
greater concentration increases the barriers to new entry in the
industry, the need to maintain excess capacity as a discourage-
ment to new entry will decrease, and this factor too will depress
investment. Therefore a continuing increase in the concentration of capital will exert a constant downward pressure on the
trend rate of growth in the economy, and Steindl suggests that
there has in fact been a steady reduction in the growth rate of
the U.S. economy from the 1890's to the 1930's. In his view, the

zero average growth of the 1930's is a symptom of the economic maturity of capitalism in North America.[28]

This argument is not necessarily based on an assumption of a long-run decline in the share of wages in the total product. The second thesis, concerning the direct effects on capacity utilisation, assumes nothing about the distribution of the product, and the first could be argued simply on the basis of the effects of the redistribution of profits within the capitalist class as the monopolists take a more than proportionate share, without assuming an increasing rate of surplus value.* Therefore, one could not say that Steindl's theory is necessarily an underconsumptionist one. But in his final chapter on Karl Marx, he comes down heavily in support of Sweezy's interpretation that Marx was moving towards an underconsumptionist theory of capitalist development. He puts forward the hypothesis that each rise in the concentration of capital has created more excess capacity in the economy due to the inability to realise all of the surplus value which could be produced, until nowadays the wasted resources represent a very significant proportion of the economy. Steindl's own theory, then, can in his own view be treated as an organic development of Marx's own underconsumption approach.[29]

Steindl's support for underconsumptionism is a tribute to its influence, and it reflects the force which it lends to his own theory. A theory of the progressive weakening of the incentive to invest becomes very much stronger if it can be married to a suggestion that consumption also has a tendency to fall as a share of potential output. It is therefore convenient for Steindl to believe that a rise in oligopoly increases the rate of exploitation. The weight of personal consumption in total expenditure is such that any theory of deficient effective demand must pay considerable attention to it. This simple practical truth is bound to make an underconsumptionist tendency an important feature of most stagnationist theories.

Unlike Steindl and Baran and Sweezy, Kalecki does not present an elaborate thesis to show the existence of stagnationist tendencies; his work constitutes a theoretical analysis of the impact of various factors on the dynamics of a capitalist economy, and it is only in a few asides that he indicates his opinion about the long-term movements of these variables.

*Steindl does in fact argue that increasing maldistribution of profits would tend to depress investment (ibid, pp.126–7).

Thus, for instance, in the essay on Tugan-Baranowski and Rosa Luxemburg already quoted, although he criticises the idea that all government military expenditure, independent of the source of finance, can absorb the surplus, he still writes that:

> The 'external markets' in the broad sense of Rosa Luxemburg in the form of armaments orders and ancillary expenditure — in so far as they are financed by loans and taxation of capitalists — play today a leading role in the functioning of modern capitalism.[30]

But he does not elaborate, or attempt to demonstrate this statistically. A crucial idea which Kalecki takes over from Rosa Luxemburg is that in the absence of 'development factors' the natural rate of growth of a capitalist economy is zero. External stimuli are required to escape from simple reproduction. The development factor stressed by Kalecki is technical innovation, which in his view, unlike that of Steindl, pushes investment to a level above what it would otherwise have reached. He also mentions the markets of the non-capitalist sector of the globe, provided that there is a surplus of exports to over imports from them, and state expenditure, subject to the conditions of finance already discussed, as potentially stimulating influences. In 1954 he had this to say about innovations:

> The slowing down in the growth of capitalist economies in the later stages of their development is probably accounted for, at least partly, by the decline in the intensity of innovations. Three broad reasons may be given for such a tendency. The most obvious is the diminishing importance of opening up new sources of raw materials, etc. Another is the hampering of application of new inventions which results from the increasingly monopolistic character of capitalism. Finally, 'assembly industries', such as those manufacturing automobiles, wireless, and other durable mass consumption goods, are gaining in importance and in such industries technological progress is largely concentrated on a 'scientific organisation' of the assembly process which does not involve heavy investment.[31]

The slowing down of growth rates is here taken to be an empirical fact. Twenty years on, with the experience of the post-war boom behind us, we would probably not make this assumption. The plausibility of it at that time, however, is obviously a factor to be taken into account when reading both Steindl and Kalecki.

An important aspect of Kalecki's thought is the concept of 'the degree of monopoly'. This concept represents simply the ratio of the value of total output of a firm to its prime costs (wages + raw materials costs), and the underlying theory is that prices of finished goods in a capitalist economy are set by the application of a certain mark-up factor to prime costs per unit. Kalecki terms this mark-up the degree of monopoly because he believes that increasing concentration of capital leads to an increase in the mark-up. He also suggests three other factors which might affect the degree of monopoly: the development of sales promotion through advertising, selling agents, etc; changes in the level of overheads relative to prime costs; and the power of the trade union movement. The first two of these factors create direct pressure to increase the degree of monopoly, if they have a tendency to rise in the long run (note that Kalecki's theory of the relation between selling costs and prices is the reverse of Baran and Sweezy's, since they assume that selling costs help to absorb the surplus, whereas his idea implies that the surplus is raised specifically in order to pay for selling costs). The stronger the trade union movement, however, the more likely that it will be able to keep the degree of monopoly down.[32] The reasoning here is straightforward enough.

The impression given is that as a result of the combined effects of all these factors, there has been a long-run rise in the degree of monopoly. The share of wages in the distribution of income, however, does not depend exclusively on the degree of monopoly: it also depends on the relative movements of unit wage and raw materials costs. Obviously, if raw materials costs fall relative to unit wage costs with the degree of monopoly remaining the same, the total of overheads plus profits will also fall relative to wages. Kalecki tentatively suggests that the approximate constancy of the relative share of wages in the U.S. over the period 1881 to 1924 was a result of the accidental balancing of the two influences of the rising degree of monopoly and falling relative costs of raw materials.[33]

Kalecki's theory of effective demand, stated baldly, is as follows: profits are determined by investment and capitalists' consumption. The total wage bill of the economy is related to profits by the degree of monopoly and the ratio of unit labour to raw materials costs. Given these factors, the level of profits determines the total wage bill, which equals total workers' consumption, if we assume that workers do not save. Two important consequences flow from this. Firstly, if trade unions are able to reduce the degree of monopoly, this must stimulate demand, since the same level of profits (determined by investment and capitalists' consumption) will be associated with a larger wage bill. The theory therefore justifies working-class struggle over wages. But conversely, if the tendency for the degree of monopoly to rise does operate, then consumption out of wages will not rise as fast as investment and profits, and total output will also grow more slowly than investment and profits (we are omitting the complications of overheads and changes in capital intensity here). Kalecki seems to believe that this is what has happened historically. A decreasing share of wages in total output therefore becomes an explanation for a slowing down in the rate of economic growth.

The above summary of the theories of Kalecki and Steindl has been extremely brief, but it is sufficient to make the point: even where writers have not relied mainly on underconsumption theories, the influence of these theories as a basis for the existence of a long-term tendency to stagnation in capitalism has been significant.

UNDERCONSUMPTIONISM AND MARXISM

The second point is that underconsumption theories have had considerable influence amongst Marxists. The passages from Marx which might appear to support an underconsumptionist interpretation were extensively discussed in Chapter Six, and it was indicated at the end of Chapter Eight that similar influences could be detected in Hilferding and Lenin. The argument throughout has been that these passages represented a slipping-back into modes of thought prevalent elsewhere in the working-class movement from a theoretical position which was essentially anti-underconsumptionist. In the case of Marx, they appear in the unpublished volumes of *Capital* which were obviously destined for substantial reworking before publication, and do not constitute a central part of the analysis being developed in the surrounding pages. In the case of Lenin, who

had written many exhaustive criticisms of the mistakes of the
Narodniks in his youth, they occur in a popular pamphlet whose
detailed theoretical argument he never had time to elaborate.
Nevertheless, since these writers have set the tone for the work
of all subsequent Marxists, it would be surprising if, given the
existence of these passages and the widespread influence of
underconsumptionism in the working-class movement, underconsumptionist influences could not be discerned in much
Marxist economic writing, even though the strictures of Marx
against underconsumptionism have generally been taken to
heart.

The main vehicle of the influence of underconsumptionism
on Marxism has been the theory of the relative impoverishment
of the proletariat. This theory is really an elementary statement
of the basic idea of underconsumptionism, although it has not
always been recognised as such. It has been expressed by one
Marxist writer as follows:

> The older capitalism gets, the deeper the cleft between
> productive and consuming power. The differences between
> the growth in producing and consuming power, increasing
> with technical progress, multiply. The gap between them
> widens unceasingly. And the bigger this gap, the more must
> labour productivity be held back. This is however no longer
> possible to the required extent.
>
> And it is this which first creates the danger of a permanent
> crisis. The threat of a long-term crisis does loom, but only in
> late capitalism.
>
> With the increasing age of capitalism the booms get shorter
> and the depressions longer. . . .
>
> It is clear then that the immiserisation theory, which is the
> core of Marxist theory, explains not only cycles but changing
> phases of capitalism, not only the periodic crises of high
> capitalism but also the structural (long-term) crisis of late
> capitalism. This is the decline of capitalism.[34]

This particular writer differentiates herself from underconsumptionists on the grounds that they believe that the insufficiency of mass consumption will lead not to worsening periodic
crises but to one permanent crisis, out of which capitalism will
never escape.[35] On the basis of what we have seen so far this
seems a needlessly restrictive definition of underconsum-

ptionism, but it is probably indicative of a widespread feeling amongst Marxists that it is bad to be classified as an undercons-umptionist, however similar one's views might be and in spite of the fact that the most common Marxist definition of the causes of crises sets underconsumption alongside disproportionality as the two main types of crisis.

The best indicators of the influence of underconsumptionism amongst Marxists are probably the textbooks and writings of prominent economists of the world Communist movement. In the early days of the Communist International, it was generally believed that any sort of economic crisis was liable to set off a decisive revolutionary uprising in the main centres of world capitalism, so that theorising about long-term tendencies seemed somewhat superfluous. It is really only with the proclamation in the late twenties of the 'temporary stabilisation' of capitalism that these issues began to receive more serious attention; and at this time the theme of the impoverishment of the working class was commonly invoked as proof that the stabilisation could not be permanent. All of the inter-war works of E.Varga, for instance, stress the continuous relative im-poverishment of the workers under capitalism, which develops into absolute impoverishment at periods of crisis.[36] Varga attributes the impending general crisis of capitalism to the contradictions which stem from this:

> The relative diminution of consuming power of society poses the problem of markets in an ever acuter form, making it ever more difficult to dispose of commodities. For in the final analysis, as Lenin says, all means of production serve for the production of means of consumption. ... This is the economic basis for the general crisis of capitalism, for the chronic idleness of a large part of the productive apparatus, for chronic mass unemployment.[37]

This idea continued to be propagated after the Second World War, although as time went on the obvious increase in real wages in the West was bound at least to induce some modifications of it. Nowadays, it would be difficult to say that there is any particular theory of this kind which is generally accepted within the world Communist movement; what does seem fairly clear, however, is that when Communists came closest to having an 'official' theory, the impoverishment of the working class was a prominent aspect of it.

The purpose of these remarks has been simply to indicate that the theory of relative impoverishment is basically a form of underconsumptionism (this has not always been recognised), and also to point out that with this theory as a vehicle underconsumptionism has at times become quite influential amongst Marxists. It was suggested in Chapter One that this was one of the reasons why Marxism had not yet produced a thorough analysis of underconsumption theories. Without a clear concept of underconsumptionism, it is difficult to identify the points at which Marxists have been influenced by it, but without eradicating these influences, it is difficult to arrive at a clear characterisation of it. So the influence of underconsumption theories amongst Marxists has certainly acted as a barrier to a deeper understanding both of their faults and of their relationship to other theoretical systems.

It has also acted as a barrier to a more profound analysis of modern capitalism. It is easy, and politically attractive, to attribute the economic problems of capitalism to the relative poverty of the workers, and to imply that they can only get worse with time — so the only answer can be socialism. Such reliance on inexorable laws of capitalist development has always appealed to mechanistic or economist versions of Marxism. But revolutions arise out of political developments and not in any automatic way out of economic crises. These crises will undoubtedly recur — but do we have to believe in an ultimate economic collapse of capitalism? I feel it is definitely wrong to do so, but some Marxist writing is still predicated on precisely this assumption. Our analysis of contemporary developments is very much dependent on the answers given to questions of this kind. Until these issues are resolved, and until simplistic conceptions are decisively rejected, Marxist economics will not escape out of dogmatic declarations from on high and domonstrate its true explanatory power.

NOTES

1 J.M.Keynes, *Essays in Biography*, p.121.
2 ibid, p.103.

3 ibid, p.117.

4 P.M.Sweezy, *Modern Capitalism and Other Essays*, p.77.

5 R.Luxemburg, *The Accumulation of Capital*, pp.27–8.

6 P.Baran & P.M.Sweezy, *Monopoly Capital*, pp.17–20.

7 ibid, p.23.

8 ibid, Ch 3.

9 ibid, p.76.

10 ibid, p.88.

11 ibid, p.101.

12 ibid, p.103.

13 ibid, pp.90–5.

14 ibid, Ch 8.

15 ibid, p.216.

16 ibid, p.374.

17 ibid, p.148.

18 ibid, p.155.

19 ibid, p.85.

20 ibid, p.80.

21 ibid, p.349.

22 ibid, p.350.

23 Sweezy, *Modern Capitalism and Other Essays*, Foreword.

24 T.Cliff, *Russia: a Marxist Analysis*, pp.162–3.

25 J.Steindl, *Maturity and Stagnation in American Capitalism*, p.133.

26 ibid, p.112.

27 ibid, p.123 (emphasis in original).

28 ibid, pp.223–6.

29 ibid, p.246.

30 M.Kalecki, *Selected Essays in the Dynamics of a Capitalist Economy*, p.155.

31 M.Kalecki, *The Theory of Economic Dynamics*, p.159.

32 ibid, Ch 1.

33 ibid, p.34.

34 N.Moszkowska, *zur Kritik modernen Krisentheorien*, pp.101–2.

35 ibid, p.90.

36 *The Decline of Capitalism* (English translation 1928), *The Great Crisis and its Political Consequences* (1935), *Two Systems* (1939). Varga is chosen here not for any personal reasons but as a representative of the general atmosphere of the time. If anything, he was in fact less given than most to sweeping generalisations and forecasts.

37 E.Varga, *The Great Crisis . . .*, pp.19–20.

BIBLIOGRAPHY

ANONYMOUS WORKS

An Inquiry into those Principles, respecting the Nature of Demand and the Necessity of Consumption, lately advocated by Mr. Malthus; London; 1821.
Considerations on the Accumulation of Capital; London; 1822.

ALPHABETICAL LIST OF AUTHORS

Althusser, L.
— *For Marx*; London; 1969.
— (with Balibar, E.) *Reading Capital*; London; 1970.
— *Lenin and Philosophy and Other Essays*; London; 1971.

Baran, P.A.
— (with Sweezy, P.M.) *Monopoly Capital*; London; Penguin; 1966.
— *The Longer View*; New York & London; 1969.
— *The Political Economy of Growth*; London; 1973.

Blaug, M.
— *Ricardian Economics*; New Haven; 1958.

Brailsford, H.N.
— *The Life-work of J.A.Hobson*; London; 1948.

Chalmers, T.
— *On Political Economy*; London; 1832.

Cliff, T.
— *Russia: a Marxist Analysis*, 3rd edition; London; 1970.

Dobb, M.H.
— *Theories of Value and Distribution since Adam Smith*; Cambridge; 1973.

Docker, F.J.
— *Douglas Delusions*; Sydney; 1933.

Douglas, C.H.
— *The New and the Old Economics*; n.d.

Durbin, E.F.M.
— *Purchasing Power and Trade Depression*; London; 1934.

Fetter, F.A.
— *Lauderdale's Oversaving Theory*; American Economic
Review Vol. XXXV No.3; 1945.

Foster, W.T. & Catchings, W.
— *Profits*; London; 1926.

Furniss, E.S.
— *The Position of the Labourer in a System of Economic
Nationalism*; Boston; 1920.

Gottschalk, H.
— *Die Kaufkraftlehre*; Jena; 1932.

Gray, J.
— *Essential Principles of the Wealth of Nations*; London;
1797.

Haberler, G.
— *Prosperity and Depression*; London; 1958.

Heckscher, E.F.
— *Mercantilism*; London; 2 Vols; 1935.

Hilferding, R.
— *Das Finanzkapital*; Berlin; 1909.

Hobson, J.A.
— (with Mummery, A.F.) *The Physiology of Industry*;
London; 1889.
— *The Economics of Distribution*; London; 1900.
— *Imperialism*; London; 1902.
— *The Problem of the Unemployed*; London; 1908.
— *The Industrial System*; London; 1910.
— *The Evolution of Modern Capitalism*; London; 1926.
— *The Economics of Unemployment*; London; 1931.
— *Confessions of an Economic Heretic*; London; 1938.

Institut National d'Etudes Démographiques
— *Pierre de Boisguilbert*; Paris; 2 Vols; 1966.

Kalecki, M.
— *Theory of Economic Dynamics*; London; 1954.
— *Selected Essays in the Dynamics of a Capitalist Economy*;
Cambridge; 1971.

Karataev, N. (ed.)
— *Narodnicheskaya Ekonomicheskaya Literatura*; Moscow;
1958.

Keynes, J.M.
— *Essays in Biography*, 2nd edition; London; 1951.
— *The General Theory of Employment, Interest and Money*;
London; Macmillan; 1967.

Kidron, M.
— *Western Capitalism since the War*; London; Penguin;
1968.

Lange, O.
— *The Rate of Interest and the Optimum Propensity to
Consume*; Economica Vol. V No. 17; 1938.

Lauderdale, Lord
— *An Inquiry into the Nature and Origin of Public Wealth*;
London; 1804.

Lenin, V.I.
— *Imperialism, the Highest Stage of Capitalism*; London;
Lawrence & Wishart; 1934.
— *The Development of Capitalism in Russia*, 2nd edition;
Moscow; Progress; 1967.
— *Collected Works* Vols 1, 2, 3; Moscow; Progress; 1960.

Luxemburg, R.
— *Die Akkumulation des Kapitals, oder was die Epigonen aus
der Marxschen Theorie gemacht haben*; Leipzig; 1921.
Translated in Tarbuck, 1972.
— *The Accumulation of Capital*; London. With an
Introduction by Joan Robinson; 1951.

M—, C.G.
— *The Nation's Credit*; London; 1932.

McCulloch, J.R.
— *Mr. Owen's Plans for Relieving the National Distress*;
Edinburgh Review Vol. XXXII No. 54 Art. XI; 1819.

Macfie, A.L.
— *The Theory of the Trade Cycle*; London; 1934.

Malthus, T.R.
— *Observations on the Effects of the Corn Laws*; London;
1814.
— *An Inquiry into the Nature and Progress of Rent*; London;
1815.
— *Principles of Political Economy considered with a view to
their practical application*; London; 1820.
— *Principles. . .*, 2nd edition; London; 1836.

Mandel, E.
— *Marxist Economic Theory*; London; 1968.
Mandeville, B.
— *The Fable of the Bees*; London; 1714.
Marshall, A.
— *Principles of Economics*; London; 1890.
— *Money, Credit and Commerce*; London; 1923.
Marx, K.
— *Capital* Vol. I; London; Lawrence & Wishart; 1970.
— *Capital* Vol. II; Chicago; Kerr; 1919.
— *Capital*, Vol. III; London; Lawrence & Wishart; 1971.
— *Theories of Surplus Value* Part I; London; Lawrence & Wishart; 1963.
— *Theories . . .* Part II; London; Lawrence & Wishart; 1968
— *Theories . . .* Part III; London; Lawrence & Wishart; 1972.
— (with Engels, F.) *Selected Works in One Volume*; London; Lawrence & Wishart; 1968.
Meek, R.L.
— *Economics of Physiocracy*; London; 1962.
— *The Rise and Fall of the Concept of the Economic Machine*; Leicester; 1965.
— *Economics and Ideology and other Essays*; London; 1967.
Mill, James
— *Spence and Mill on Commerce*; London; n.d.
Mill, J.S.
— *Principles of Political Economy*; London; 2 Vols; 1848.
Moszkowska, N.
— *Zur Kritik modernen Krisentheorien*; Prague; 1935.
Nagels, J.
— *Genèse, contenu et prolongements de la notion de reproduction du capital selon Karl Marx, Boisguillebert, Quesnay, Leontiev*; Brussels; 1970.
Nemmers, E.E.
— *Hobson and Underconsumption*; Amsterdam; 1956.
Nicolas-on
— *Histoire du Développement de la Russie depuis l'affranchissement des serfs*; Paris; 1902.
Owen, E.R.J. & Sutcliffe, R.B. (eds)
— *Studies in the Theory of Imperialism*; London; 1972.

Paglin, M.
— *Malthus and Lauderdale (the anti-Ricardian tradition)*;
New York; 1961.

Plekhanov, G.V.
— *Selected Philosophical Works* Vol. I; Moscow; 1960.

Plough, P.
— *Letters on the Rudiments of a Science*; London; 1842.

Quesnay, F.
— (ed. Oncken, W.) *Oeuvres Economiques et Philosophiques*;
Frankfurt-am-Main & Paris; 1888.
— *Tableau Economique* 3rd edition; translated as Kuc-
zynski, M. & Meek, R.L., *Quesnay's Tableau Economique*;
London; 1972.

Ricardo, D.
— (ed. Sraffa) *The Works and Correspondence of David
Ricardo*; Cambridge; 10 Vols; 1951–73.
— (edited with an Introduction by Hartwell, R.M.) *On
The Principles of Political Economy and Taxation*;
London; Penguin; 1971.

Robinson, J.
— *The Accumulation of Capital*, 3rd edition; London;
1969.

von Rodbertus-Jagetzow, K.
— (edited with an Introduction by Clark, J.B.)
Overproduction and Crises; London; 1898.

Roll, E.
— *History of Economic Thought*; London; 1938.

Say, J.B.
— *A Treatise on Political Economy*; London; 1821.

Schumpeter, J.
— *A History of Economic Analysis*; London; 1954.

Simonde de Sismondi, J.C.L.
— *De la Richesse Commerciale*; Geneva; 2 Vols; 1803.
— *Political Economy*; in Sir D. Brewster's *Edinburgh
Encyclopaedia* Vol. XVII pp.37–78; 1815.
— *Nouveaux Principes d'Economie Politique*; Paris; 2 Vols;
1819.
— ditto, 2nd edition (contains 2 additional articles); Paris;
2 Vols; 1827.
— ditto, abridged, ed. Weiller, J.; Paris; 1971.

Skinner, A.
— *Of Malthus, Lauderdale and Say's Law*; Scottish Journal
  of Political Economy Vol. XVI p.177; 1969.
See also Smith, A. 1970.
Smith, A.
— *An Inquiry into the Nature and Causes of the Wealth of
  Nations*; London; 2 Vols; 1776.
— ditto, edited with an Introduction by Skinner, A.;
  London; Books I–III only; 1970.
Smith, V.E.
— *The Classicists' Use of "Demand"*; Journal of Political
  Economy Vol. LIX No.3; 1951.
Spence, W.
— *Spence and Mill on Commerce*; London; n.d.
— *Tracts on Political Economy*; London; 1822.
Steindl, J.
— *Maturity and Stagnation in American Capitalism*;
  Oxford; 1952.
Sweezy, P.M.
— (with Baran, P.A.) *Monopoly Capital*; London; 1966.
— *The Theory of Capitalist Development*; New York &
  London; 1968.
— *Modern Capitalism and Other Essays*; New York &
  London; 1972.
Tarbuck, K. (ed.)
— *R.Luxemburg and N.Bukharin: Imperialism and the
  Accumulation of Capital*; London; 1972.
Turgot, A.
— *Reflections on the formation and distribution of Wealth*;
  London; 1793.
Varga, E.
— *The Decline of Capitalism*; London; Communist Party of
  Great Britain; 1928.
— *The Great Crisis and its Political Consequences*; London;
  1935.
— *Two Systems*; New York; 1939.
Venturi, F.
— *Roots of Revolution*; London; 1960.
Walicki, A.
— *The Controversy over Capitalism*; Oxford; 1969.
Weulerrse, G.
— *Les Physiocrates*; Paris; 1931.

INDEX

260